Advances in Contemporary Educational Thought Series

Jonas F. Soltis, Editor

FAITH, HYPE, AND CLARITY

Teaching About Religion in American Schools and Colleges

ROBERT J. NASH

Teachers College, Columbia University
New York and London

To Madelyn, my spiritual soulmate;
and to Jonas F. Soltis

Published by Teachers College Press, 1234 Amsterdam Avenue, New York, NY 10027

Library of Congress Cataloging-in-Publication Data

Nash, Robert J.
    Faith, hype, and clarity : teaching about religion in American schools and colleges / Robert J. Nash.
       p.   cm. — (Advances in contemporary educational thought series ; v. 22)
    Includes bibliographical references and index.
    ISBN 0-8077-3806-9 (cloth : alk. paper). — ISBN 0-8077-3805-0 (pbk. : alk. paper)
    1. Religion in the public schools—United States.   I. Title.
II. Series.
LC111.N25   1998
379.2'8'0973—dc21   98-42228

ISBN 0-8077-3805-0 (paper)
ISBN 0-8077-3806-9 (cloth)

Printed on acid-free paper
Manufactured in the United States of America

06 05 04 03 02 01 00 99   8 7 6 5 4 3 2 1

Contents

Foreword

Religion has always been a moving force in human history and in individual lives. In the West, from the Medieval battles of the crusaders and the European exploitation and colonization of the world to the more recent Holocaust and various wars of ethnic/religious "cleansing," we see in our past and present the evils religion can give rise to. However, we also can see the good that it can do. Not only has religion inspired many people to live moral and giving lives, but it also has provided justification for nonviolence, peace, and equality, and has offered charitable assistance to the world's needy and neglected. Moreover, as individuals, we are born in a certain time and place into a particular family and culture, which sets the stage for defining our religious beliefs. In a pluralistic world, however, we come to know that there are others who hold different beliefs and belong to different religions.

This pervasiveness of the religious dimension in our individual lives and in the history of human societies underwrites the claim of some contemporary educators that a study of religion and the acquisition of religious literacy should be a part of a truly liberal education and, indeed, an important part of every citizen's education in a pluralistic democracy. Given the doctrine of separation of church and state, the delicacy of talking about religion, and the presumption of neutrality and tolerance regarding religion in our public schools and colleges, how can religion be taught if we are to take these liberal education and democratic citizenship arguments seriously? Robert Nash takes on this weighty task in this book. It is a superb piece of writing on a difficult topic that ought to be part of every teacher's education. With so much current concern for navigating the shoals of multicultural education, it cannot be long before educators also must face straight on the religious diversity students bring with them into our public schools and colleges. Nash provides a rich, sound, accessible framework for fairly examining and thinking about the major forms religiosity takes in our pluralistic society today and how to teach about them.

He puts 30 years of teaching experience to good use as he weaves his personal pedagogical narrative in and out of a very readable scholarly examination of fundamentalist, prophetic, alternative spiritualities, and post-theist religious positions. He helps educators see what religious literacy and dialogue can do and how they can help achieve the legitimate educational goal of providing "pluralistic perspective in religious belief in a democratic society." He outlines a pedagogy and curriculum of religious education worthy of being instituted in all our schools and colleges.

In this book, Nash deftly uses the device of narrative/story to display religious belief systems, thereby avoiding the propositional and declaratory stance that might put off readers of different persuasions. This also allows him to point out positive aspects as well as potential dangers inherent in each of the four religious positions he describes. His fourfold category structure—fundamentalist, prophetic, alternative spiritualities, and post-theist—is all encompassing and keeps the vast content of diverse religions manageable, orderly, and in focus. He writes in a personal voice that is tentative when called for, but firm and solid in calling for intelligent inquiry and open-mindedness. He also integrates a rich set of relevant readings into the text rather than hiding them in footnotes or in an extended bibliographic essay end piece.

This is an amazingly up-to-date, far-reaching, informative, and thought-provoking volume. To my knowledge, there is nothing like it on religion and education for teachers and policymakers today. It will be an excellent source book and pedagogical tool for teachers who want to deal intelligently and responsibly with religion in the public schools.

It is indeed a very important advance in contemporary educational thought.

Jonas F. Soltis
Series Editor

Acknowledgments

Someone once said that religion is always an unsatisfying attempt to express what is essentially inexpressible. Whether one refers to it as spirituality or religion, this ever-present force represents the hunger of the human soul for understanding the impossible, for reaching the unattainable, and for imagining the inconceivable. For me, a restless, and often reluctant, religious seeker, religion is, of necessity, the language of the heart, the language that friends, lovers, children, and parents speak best. In writing this book, I have found it to be the language of people who have been helpful to me in both my personal and professional life.

I want to thank my wife, Madelyn, for helping me to understand that it is, indeed, possible to live the religious life in the most authentic and consistent way.

I hope that the book's dedication to Jonas Soltis, William Heard Kilpatrick Professor Emeritus, Teachers College, Columbia University, and editor of the *Advances in Contemporary Educational Thought Series*, adequately expresses my gratitude for the enthusiasm and support he has shown for my work over the last two decades.

I am thankful once again to Susan Liddicoat, Acquisitions Editor, who, with continuing discernment and skill, and at times with a disarming honesty, has good-naturedly edited my three books for Teachers College Press.

I am deeply indebted to a brilliant reviewer, David J. Blacker, a philosopher of education currently teaching at the University of Delaware, for his invaluable critical comments on this book, and on my earlier *Answering the "Virtuecrats."* Professor Blacker rarely makes an observation that has not significantly improved my manuscripts in some way. For the current project, I also wish to thank Susan B. Varenne, a teacher in an alternative public school in New York City. Both as a practitioner and, I suspect, as a believer, Dr. Varenne helped me to moderate the overall tone I use to frame and express my arguments throughout the book.

Others who have been directly helpful to me in my thinking through many of the ideas here are: my colleague Robert Griffin, for many 1970s conversations on Eastern religion; my friend Anu Ailawadhi, for her assistance on the correct usage of Sanskrit in the prophetic chapters; my graduate students in "Religion, Spirituality, and Education," Spring 1998, for their inspiration and forbearance; my oldest daughter, Mika, for her very useful observations on the neo-Gnostic narrative; Professor Constance Krosney for materials on the alternative spiritualities chapters; and all those unsuspecting students and colleagues at the University of Vermont whom I was able to entrap in a religious dialogue during the writing of this book, sometimes against their better judgment. It should go without saying, of course, that I alone take full responsibility for the way I might have misunderstood and misapplied all the insights of those I name above.

CHAPTER 1

Transcendental Narratives and Education

Several years ago, Paul Kurtz (1986) wrote a very controversial book, *The Transcendental Temptation: A Critique of Religion and the Paranormal*. Kurtz, the well-known author of *Humanist Manifesto II*, founder of the major publishing house Prometheus Press, and perhaps the leading secular humanist philosopher in the United States, took direct aim at what for him had become a lifelong project: debunking the claims of the major monotheistic religions—Christianity, Judaism, and Islam—along with such paranormal belief systems as parapsychology, spiritualism, channeling, and UFOlogy. Among his concerns, Kurtz was deeply troubled by those people who turn their backs on science and rationality and instead "seek to escape to an imagined [religious] universe based upon faith and credulity" (p. xi), especially during those times when they were likely to find their lives overwhelmed by the inexplicable catastrophes of modern living.

What most chagrined Kurtz about *homo religiosus* was people's lingering tendency to succumb to what he considered to be a compelling, recurring human weakness—a "transcendental temptation," in spite of all the evidence to the contrary of God's presumed existence. For Kurtz, this took the odious form of professing belief in the "incredible myths" promised by

> Moses on Mt. Sinai delivering the Ten Commandments to God's "chosen people," Christ crucified beckoning man to salvation, Mohammed the true prophet of Allah so appointed by Gabriel, Buddha the Light, Joseph Smith and the New Zion of the Mormons, or the Chariots of the Gods transporting extraterrestial beings from outer space to observe humankind. (p. xiii)

In a highly polemical style, and echoing John Dewey's (1929/1960) attack on philosophers' 2000-year "quest for certainty," Kurtz, a self-acknowledged atheist, called for educators at all levels to teach skepticism and the scientific method in schools and colleges everywhere. According to Kurtz, skepticism involved three elements—evidence, logical validity, and practicality—and these qualities comprised a "critical intelligence" that students would need to combat "gullibility, ignorance, cowardice, and fear," the source of so "much nonsense in religion, ideology, morality, and politics" (p. 62). Kurtz, a rigorous scientific rationalist, advocated an education from grade school to the university that challenged the "extravagant claims of the supernatural, miraculous, mysterious, noumenal, or paranormal realm" (p. 23). Like Dewey (1934) and Bertrand Russell (1957) before him, Kurtz went on to spend a lengthy career attacking the notion of conventional religious faith as a justification for any kind of belief (e.g., see Kurtz, 1997), and in *The Transcendental Temptation* (1986), he devoted over 500 pages attempting to demonstrate that religious faith was nothing more than one long argument posited by the ignorant. Thus, for Kurtz, any human conviction not grounded in a sound evidential base, consistent with the scientific rules of rationality, logic, and common sense, was educationally inadmissable.

EDUCATORS, RELIGION, AND THE CLASSROOM

Although I think educators can learn something valuable from many of Kurtz's criticisms of religion, I reject outright his blanket dismissal of so powerful a force in people's lives. Where I believe Kurtz goes awry is in his dogged refusal to acknowledge any good whatsoever in religion. The truth I think Kurtz completely misses in his anti-religious diatribe is that even though the existence of God cannot be scientifically or logically demonstrated, millions of people still choose to live their lives as though it can be, and life is often made better for them, and others, as a result. While deploring his overstatements, however, I still contend that today, well over a decade after the publication of his critique, Kurtz's outcry warning educators about the dangers of religious extremism seems particularly prescient, and might even be helpful to them in some way. Although Kurtz has spent close to a half-century critiquing what he calls the "magical thinking" characteristic of belief in religion and the paranormal, at the present time, in my opinion, the "transcendental temptation"—*especially in the form of its many extremist offspring*—appears to have become even more seductive, and more dangerous. Educators, I suggest, need to take notice.

My book title, *Faith, Hype, and Clarity: Teaching About Religion in American Schools and Colleges*, indicates the general direction I think educators ought to take in introducing students to the study of religion. What Kurtz totally fails to understand about the transcendental experience is the powerful and beneficial role that a humble *faith* often plays in the lives of believers. Faith—the theological virtue I would define as a confident and trusting belief in a benevolent supreme being, even though such a belief is empirically undemonstrable—is the heart and soul of human spirituality. I would make the simple point here that students need opportunities to examine and to talk with each other about the centrality (or absence) of faith in their own lives, as well as in the lives of people throughout the world who may express their deepest, unprovable beliefs quite differently.

Unfortunately, however, while religious faith has been a ubiquitous and often benign force through the ages, it has also been an agent of *hype*, as Kurtz so convincingly demonstrates; the harsh truth is that too many religious claims throughout history have turned out to be flamboyant and dishonest, producing nothing better than what appears to be a shameful confidence game. This too students must know.

And, finally, *clarity* in teaching about religion has to do with discernment, with helping students to distinguish the good from the bad, the authentic from the bogus, in religious matters. If faith is the heart and soul of human spirituality, then I contend that discernment is the irreducible core of the educational experience, particularly when it comes to teaching about religion. At the present time, sadly, there is so much that is fraudulent in religion, in our own culture as well as in others, that I would argue educators have a moral responsibility to expose what is counterfeit even as they affirm what is bona-fide.

As I write, books and television series on angels, miracles, spontaneous religious conversions and testimonials, and the paranormal dominate the popular media. There is today a tremendous growth in religious fundamentalism, pentecostalism, evangelicalism, and "New Age" belief systems of all types, as well as various cults and sects. In the last decade alone, for example, Christian and Islamic fundamentalist movements have become serious, destabilizing worldwide phenomena. And during the last two decades, Jonestown in Guyana, the Branch Davidians in Waco, and Heaven's Gate in California have become immediately recognizable, albeit terrifying, names and places for anyone even remotely in touch with electronic and print media.

Finally, contemporary fascination with extrasensory perception, clairvoyance, psychokinesis, mental telepathy, out-of-body experiences, reincarnation, sun-sign astrology, horoscopes, UFOlogy, extraterrestrial life, space-alien abductions, and tales of out-of-control, demonic computer technology finds an apparently inexhaustible outlet in film, television dramas (e.g., *The X-Files*), magazines, and the daily newspaper. I suspect that if Tertullian (ca. 160–220), a North African Christian theologian, were alive today, he would be able to declare that, indeed, his assertion, *Credo quia absurdum est* ("I believe because it is absurd"), is as relevant in late-20th-century America as it was in the early Christian church.

And just as the general interest in religion has intensified throughout the United States during the last several years, so too the number of scholars has grown (two of the very earliest are Pannoch & Barr, 1968) who are arguing strenuously that the formal study of religion must now become a required part of the curriculum in America's public and private schools and colleges. (For example, see Barna, 1992; Carter, 1993; Gaddy, Hall, & Marzano, 1996; Haynes, 1994; Marsden, 1997; Moran, 1989; Neuhaus, 1987; Noddings, 1993; Sears & Carper, 1998; and Simonds, 1994.) I find the reasons they give highly convincing. Briefly, their argument usually emphasizes the following main points, among others:

- Many schools and colleges have historically shown a veiled, if not outright, hostility toward the formal study of religion, viewing religion to be merely faith-driven, largely anti-intellectual, and therefore peripheral to any formal academic experience. However, because these perceptions are demonstrably false, educators have a moral and intellectual responsibility to correct this misimpression of religion as being antagonistic to reason and, hence, undeserving of an official place in the curriculum.

- Whether covertly or overtly, the secular worldview predominates in the humanities, social sciences, and sciences, and it drives out all other alternatives. Educators tend to promote a secular humanist (i.e., ultimate values reside exclusively in worldly human beings and possess no supernatural origins) account of the disciplines, and they end up marginalizing the religious perspective while favoring the nonreligious. This one-sidedness is a violation of the establishment clause in the First Amendment, which stipulates the need for fairness and neutrality in religious matters.

- Religion is such a fundamental part of human existence that students simply cannot understand the history or politics of most societies, including the United States, without a serious examination of religion's central role in producing both good and evil throughout the world during the last several millennia.

- A genuine liberal education requires an in-depth study of religious influences on the history, anthropology, science, literature, philosophy, art, music, theatre, and ethics of any culture. The exclusion of religion from school and college curricula, whether deliberate or not, results in an illiberal education, because students get only half the story. Thus secular, intellectual standpoints get privileged, while important religious perspectives are ignored, denied, or trivialized. Some type of religious study ought to be required of all students at all levels of schooling for the same reasons that other subject matter is seen as necessary for a liberal education: Not only is there undeniable functional utility in becoming a liberally educated, religiously informed citizen in a pluralistic world, but religion is also a subject worthy of study for its own sake.

- Moral education at any level of schooling is ultimately empty unless students have the opportunity to gain a serious understanding of religion's contribution to ethics, morality, and the formation of character. Despite claims to the contrary, certain traditional religious virtues (e.g., faith, hope, love, piety, forgiveness, obedience, self-respect) still have considerable value in secular pluralist societies. And for many people, a purely secularized morality seems foundationless, and hence relativistic.
- All students, but especially those who come from strong religious backgrounds, have a civil right to explore in schools and colleges how they can resolve the tensions that exist in their private and public lives between "tradition and modernity, community and individualism, consensus and pluralism, faith and reason, and religion and secularity" (Nord, 1995, p. 380). Schools and colleges must be very careful to consider the intellectual needs and rights of *all* students, both secular and religious.

One central figure in this movement to incorporate the study of religion into the formal curriculum at all levels of schooling, Warren A. Nord (1995), director of the Program in the Humanities and Human Values at the University of North Carolina at Chapel Hill, believes that it is possible for educators to be "obstinately agnostic" (p. 5) when teaching about religion; many politicians, lawyers, textbook publishers, and theologians are inclined to agree with him, as the glowing blurbs on the back of his book jacket attest. While it will soon become apparent that with certain refinements I support this growing movement to require the formal study of religion in schools and colleges in the United States, in the chapters to come, I intend to take Nord's and others' work one major step forward. I will discuss in concrete, personal terms how one university teacher educator, myself, actually goes about dealing with the topic of religion in his own courses, with pedagogical implications for schools and colleges everywhere. My intention in this book is *not* to provide a rationale for the teaching of religion in secular schools and colleges. Nord (1995) and other scholars I have cited above have already done this quite well, in my opinion.

Thus far in the public dialogue, what these scholars have *not* talked about are the *what* and the *how* of dealing with religion in the actual classroom; they prefer, understandably, to concentrate on the *why*, along with the more controversial policy issues. In the pages that follow, I will attempt to fill this gap. As my students are mainly undergraduate and graduate students in the human service professions, particularly public school teachers and instructors in colleges and universities, they register for my elective courses in philosophy of education, applied ethics, and religion and education because they are genuinely interested in articulating, clarifying, and deepening the underlying philosophical and ethical beliefs that drive their practices. It does not take long, however, for most of my students to realize that their background beliefs also include powerful religious assumptions, a few of which they can articulate, but the majority of which, if they have not been discarded as irrelevant, lie essentially dormant and half-formed.

Throughout the book, in addition to discussing pedagogy, I will examine critically at least four ways of thinking about religion, what I will call the four *narratives*, for reasons I discuss throughout the text. I refer to these religious orientations as narratives because in my teaching I treat each as a coherent story/worldview, an imaginative myth in the most edifying sense—what Andrew M. Greeley (1990) calls "spiritual poetry"—that believers have created in order to make sense of what is inescapably ineffable in human experience (Postman, 1996; Smart, 1983). It is not my intention to use the term *narrative* in a demeaning or dismissive sense. The genius in all religions, I believe, apart from their doctrinal, ethical, ritual, or revelational claims, resides in their narrative power to help us discover and create meaning. For me, the ultimate "truth" of a religious narrative is not scientifically or logically provable; instead, it is pragmatic and aesthetic. I ask the questions any narrativist might ask— Does it work? Does it tell a convincing story, move people, provide a sense of purpose, foster community, inspire moral action, and explain the unknown (Postman, 1996)?

In the chapters to come, I critically examine each narrative at some length, and at times I will be just as likely to use aesthetic and pragmatic, as well as educational, theological, and philosophical, criteria to determine how cogent a particular religious account of reality might be. Each of these narratives has gathered surprising strength throughout society over the last several years, and even now, in the early stages of their educational integration into some classrooms, their presence has been the subject of considerable controversy in communities around the United States (see Gaddy, Hall, & Marzano, 1996; Simonds, 1994).

I call these four religious narratives, respectively:

1. The Fundamentalist narrative
2. The Prophetic narrative
3. The Alternative spiritualities (neo-gnostic) narrative
4. The Post-theistic narrative

I have chosen these particular narratives because they represent the four types of religious belief and nonbelief that students most frequently profess in my courses each year. The particular applications of these labels are my own. And, as I will show later, each of the narratives presents a more or less coherent response to what adherents believe are the deficiencies of modernism, secularism, and liberalism in American society.

Probably because I teach in the Northeastern section of the United States, I have only a few Christian *fundamentalist* students register for my courses, although I have been told by colleagues in other parts of the country that, increasingly, fundamentalist students, along with pentecostals, charismatics, and evangelicals, are constituting a quorum in their teacher-preparation seminars. I consider the fundamentalist narrative (in its Jewish, Christian, and Islamic incarnations) a significant religious movement in this country and throughout the world, and so I devote two chapters to it, as I do the other narratives.

The *prophetic* narrative is a politically progressive variation on liberal, mainstream religion in this country, and it too is attracting a number of followers, many of them young, idealistic, politically inclined, and disenchanted with the accommodations they think the mainline churches have made with the power elites in America. Each semester, I have a number of educators in my seminars, mostly Christians and Jews, who have chosen to remain in the churches and temples of their youth, but who seek an alternate religious experience much more devoted to issues of social justice than they have previously experienced. These students believe they have found a salient way to politicize their religious beliefs, and therefore I include a unit of study in my courses I call the prophetic narrative.

The *alternative spiritualities* narrative is, perhaps, the most popular of the religious choices among my younger students, and it appears to be gaining adherents among many older students as well. This narrative—the most eclectic, and in some ways the most secular—is very difficult to pin down as a strictly *religious* orientation. Genuinely postmodern and individualistic, it counts among its enthusiasts a number of garden-variety New Agers, environmentalists, holistic health advocates, serious devotees to Eastern mysticism, and other alternative religions. Students who identify with this orientation prefer to call themselves "spiritual" rather than religious, and those who are educators tend to incorporate some of their spiritual beliefs and practices into their curricula, at all levels of school-ing. I refer to these students as neo-Gnostics, a designation I explain in Chapter 7.

Finally, the *post-theist* narrative includes a growing number of agnos-tics, atheists, pagans, and postmoderns who search for genuine alterna-tives to religion and spirituality. Suspicious of metaphysics as a worth-while, philosophical course of study; critical of any God-centered system of belief; and skeptical about the truth claims theological authorities make, post-theists constitute an emerging, highly vocal minority in my courses. In my opinion, post-theism is the wave of the future among religiously disenchanted youth (see Altemeyer & Hunsberger, 1997), all the religious opinion polls in America to the contrary, and therefore I include this unit in my courses for educators to examine.

While it is true that Kurtz's (1986) highly skeptical, indeed dismissive, take on religion is a far cry from Nord's (1995) "obstinately agnostic" approach to religious education, my own approach to *teaching* is not "agnostic" at all. A part of Kurtz's critique does manage to capture some of my own discomfort regarding the all-too-frequent evidence of religious excess throughout the world. In some senses, I tend to agree with Karen Armstrong (1993) that in the United States, the mainline God of churchly doctrines appears to be dying (too dogmatic, legalistic, and demanding), as does the cosmological God of the natural philosophers (too abstract). But unlike Armstrong, I maintain that at least among my students, the God of the social reformers, as well as the God of the mystics, is alive and well; the spirit that has animated these two conceptualizations still manages to attract a growing, highly committed cadre of enthusiasts, as I will try to show in the chapters to come.

Also, I am far more willing than Kurtz (1986) and Armstrong (1993) to acknowledge that many human beings will probably always look to some transcendental source to explain the confounding mystery of their finitude—the paradoxical presence of soaring love and ecstasy in life that is frequently offset by intolerable human failure, accident, pain, poverty, anxiety, dread, injustice, suffering, and death. I agree wholeheartedly with Russell Pregeant (1988) that life always "points inexorably to some mystery that encompasses it, some foundation that upholds it, some source of warmth and love and joy and meaning that dwells within it" (p. 12). Yet it is also true that when things are going well, in the ebullience of their successes, people throughout history have been a lot less likely to look toward the heavens for a sense of ultimate meaning and purpose.

What mainly disturbs me about the continuing lure of some transcen-dental narratives, though, are the frequent bursts of anti-intellectualism, self-indulgence, superstition, apocalypticism, evangelicalism, dogmatic sense of certainty, and violence they tend to spawn in different ways in different eras. Twentieth-century analysts as dissimilar as Harold Bloom (1993), Richard Hofstadter (1964), James A. Haught (1990), Bruce B. Lawrence (1989), and Regina Schwartz (1997) have chronicled the extraordinary lengths to which individuals will go to escape the emptiness and desolation of their lives. They have shown how many people are willing to give themselves over to what Sigmund Freud (1927/1964) called a persistent "illusion"—the perfervid hope that someone, somewhere, will deliver them from the catastrophic (or torpid) events that disrupt (or numb) their lives.

And, as Mark W. Muesse (1997) has argued, the suicides of 39 members of the Heaven's Gate religious sect in Rancho Santa Fe, California, in April 1997 dramatically symbolizes, in the extreme, all that is wrong whenever individuals unquestioningly surrender their autonomy to some higher, transcendent cause or leader (whether religious, political, or philosophical). The tragic results throughout history have been intellectual impoverishment; violence against supposed heretics, miscreants, infidels, and nonbelievers; martyrdom; mass suicides; self-immolation; and other forms of self-sacrifice. What Muesse (1997) contends is that there may only be a difference *in degree* between "cultists" who engage in "ritualized death experiences, castrations, and expectations of rescue operations by alien beings in spacecraft" (p. B7), and those more traditional religionists who believe in the virtue of crusades, martyrdom, celibacy, and resurrection, and who seek eternal salvation (or nirvana) in some distant heaven (or afterlife).

Where I, and most Americans, depart markedly from Kurtz's and, to some extent, Muesse's polemics against religion, however, is that I refuse to dismiss *all* religious belief as mere superstition and, therefore, as an unalloyed evil. Obviously, no aspect of human culture—whether technology or law, government or education—is entirely immune to violence or nonsensical beliefs. In fact, for starters, I have far less faith in the redemptive potential of science to save us from the more notorious excesses of religion, and human folly, than Kurtz (1986) does. Certainly, from my view, a case can be made that an uncritical worship of science represents a danger to the world (and to education) that is every bit as dogmatic, close-minded, and lethal as religion at its worst. (For one horrific example, see Robert J. Lifton's study of scientific/medical killing, *The Nazi Doctors*, 1986.)

Also, unlike Kurtz and other similarly minded analysts, I believe that religion has been, at worst and on balance, a mixed force in the world, representing much that is both beneficial and harmful. Among its benefits, according to one agnostic scholar, Guenter Lewy (1996), is the deep spiritual comfort religion provides for people who have been overwhelmed by life's cruel vicissitudes, as well as religion's generally high regard for human life. Christians, Jews, and Muslims, in particular, have cared deeply for the oppressed, the poor, the impoverished, the sick, the aged, and the enslaved. And religions throughout the world—including Confucianism, Buddhism, and Hinduism—have made moral teaching one of their primary functions, stressing at various times and places self-control, self-discipline, love, peace, conscience, and reconciliation. Among its more glaring liabilities, both in the United States and elsewhere, according to Nord (1995), has been religion's excessive bloodthirstiness in advancing "God's" cause; zealotry; sexual, intellectual, and political repression; charlatanism; superstition; and social divisiveness and dislocation on a massive, worldwide scale.

Notwithstanding my differences, however, where I am in strong *educational* agreement with Kurtz (1986) is that I, too, believe skepticism can be a healthy antidote today to the excesses and deficiencies of the various religious narratives that work their way into the schools and colleges. I will argue in the chapters ahead that in addition to helping students understand the worldviews (the hermeneutical prisms) and the more obvious strengths and weaknesses of the various religious narratives facing them, educators must also help them, at times, to "transcend the transcendental temptation" (Kurtz, 1986, p. 477) itself by offering alternative, immanent ways of making sense of reality and mystery, joy, and suffering. Sometimes reason, logic, and the scientific method will help in this regard; but so too, I suggest, will an appeal to postmodern hermeneutics, narrative, myth, aesthetics, language, and even politics. And *how* we talk about religion with each other in the classroom will be important to me as well.

Furthermore, unlike Kurtz, I believe religion need not necessarily breed self-righteousness, ignorance, fanaticism, or violence. If history is an accurate judge, whatever it is that causes people to cultivate faith in a variety of transcendental forces will not disappear, although it is more than likely that new forms of transcendence and meaning-making will appear as life's existential dilemmas grow more ominous, complex, and unpredictable. I will speak to these issues in greater detail in the pages to follow.

Finally, in the chapters to come, I will attempt to abstain from making dramatic personal judgments about the overall worth of religion when these might be distracting to the reader, although I will, at times, express my own views on the truth claims of particular religious and secular views of reality as I do in my classroom. I come out of a distinct perspective on religion—what I call the "post-theistic" view—and so I do take sides. As I try in my teaching, I hope to do this in my writing with prudence, intelligence, balance, and compassion. But I am human, and I feel deeply and passionately about many things, especially religion. I regret that at times my reach for perspective and fairness on this controversial subject will probably exceed my grasp, and for this I apologize to the reader beforehand.

Moreover, I will not be spending time examining such topics as textbooks, evolution and economics, and vouchers. While I hold that these subjects are extremely beneficial to the general reader, I will gladly defer this project to the aforementioned Warren Nord, who has ably covered this material in his widely acclaimed book *Religion and American Education* (1995). I actually spend very little time on these issues in my teaching, as I find that my students are less interested in legal and policy questions in relation to religion than in the deeper philosophical, theological, and pedagogical questions that continue to absorb them. In some instances, however, my intellectual interests will overlap with Nord's, as both of us are concerned with particular philosophies of education and world-views that underlie the various initiatives he discusses.

DEFINITIONS OF TRANSCENDENCE, RELIGION, AND SPIRITUALITY

What do I mean when I use such ambiguous terms as *transcendence*, *religion*, and *spirituality* throughout this study? For definitional purposes, I will use *transcendence* somewhat neutrally to refer to any belief that describes a realm of being surpassing creaturely existence and under-standing, a realm of being that presupposes a divine power allegedly exceeding the capacity of any natural reality (see O'Meara in McBrien, 1995). This definition presupposes, then, a supreme being (a supernatural reality or a transcendental force, impersonal or personal in nature) who is always above and beyond human existence and superior to it. In *The Idea of the Holy*, Rudolf Otto (1923) depicted transcendence as a "terrible and fascinating mystery" ("*mysterium terribile et fascinans*")—terrible be-cause it is so shockingly disorienting to earthly creatures, and fascinating because it constantly tempts us to give ourselves over so totally to it. For Kurtz (1986), of course, there can be no transcendent realm of being beyond this world, because science is incapable of conclusively proving its existence. And because this "terrible and fascinating mystery" is simply poor epistemology, Kurtz questions the intelligence of people who will-ingly surrender their destinies to those authority figures who claim to be in sole possession of such a "nonordinary" reality; that is, a transcendent set of Truths.

I use the terms *religion* and *spirituality* as roughly analogous, although today it seems to be intellectually fashionable to draw a distinct line between the two. Many of my students judge the latter to be superior to the former, because they consider spirituality to be less "dogmatic," less "churchy," less "patriarchal" and "hierarchical" than organized religion (Roof, 1993). I prefer the definition of religion in the *HarperCollins Dictionary of Religion* (Smith, 1995), as "a system of beliefs and practices that are relative to superhuman beings" (p. 893). I would add to this definition the observation that throughout history, people have constructed a number of illuminating religious narratives, complete with appropriate symbols, doctrines, rituals, and moral precepts, in order to "mobilize the feelings and wills of human beings" (Smart, 1983, pp. 1, 7, 8). In my estimation, this amplified definition of religion has the advantage of being somewhat more specific than such vague, indeterminate definitions as "ultimate concern," "higher power," or even the etymological (L., *religare*) "binding together" of worshippers in a "faith community," terms that themselves require further definitions (Smith, 1995, p. 893). This definition manages to put a little less emphasis on the institutional dimension of religion, even while it calls attention to the fact that religions are mostly discrete systems characterized by certain types of beliefs and practices, myths and rituals. It is also a more politically sensitive designation in that it is inclusive of beliefs in polytheism, process theology (Whitehead, 1929/1978), and feminine deities.

I use the term *spirituality* in a technical sense, in what theologians (see Elizabeth Dreyer, in McBrien, 1995, pp. 1216–1220) call its *kataphatic* (Gr., that which can be spoken about and shared) usage: By definition, this is a "positive spirituality," because believers claim to find God primarily in created things, in immanent reality. As we shall see in the following chapters, generally those thinkers who believe in, and practice, what I am calling the "alternative spiritualities" tend to be kataphatic in their orientation to religious life. These scholars tend to speak of God as an inner spirit, or a friend, or a sense of oneness, or love, and they experience God less as a vertical force than as a horizontal presence, dwelling in human relationships, nature, and even in personal tragedies and successes. And they urge teachers to be kataphatic in the way they approach the topic of religion with their students.

In contrast, the *apophatic* (Gr., that which is detached and unspeakable) use of the term denotes a "negative spirituality," in the sense that God is clearly considered to be a transcendent otherness, a vertical being, an omniscient, omnipotent force absolutely separate from creaturely existence and superior to it. Notwithstanding this radical disjunction between God and creature, though, believers can come to know the apophatic God through some type of authoritative revelation, and through doctrine, as well as through prayer, meditation, contemplation, and other forms of supplication. Those believers who embrace what I am calling the "fundamentalist" narrative are more likely to be apophatic in their understanding of religious reality, and they attempt to teach in this way.

Regarding these two understandings of spirituality, I wish to issue one important caveat, however: As I suggested earlier, such sharp distinctions between religion and spirituality, kataphatic and apophatic, action and contemplation, are often untenable, because I agree with Dryer (in McBrien, 1995) that the notion of transcendence often includes both kinds of experience, the positive *and* the negative, the personal *and* the institutional, the active *and* the contemplative. As much as I am able, I hope to avoid setting up irreconcilable dualisms—what philosophers call "false binaries"—in the chapters to come. My intention throughout the analysis will be to avoid giving in to the enticement of oversimplifying complex religious and educational ideas in order to fit conflicting data to my preconceived argument. But, alas, once again, I am only human.

WHAT DOES THE FIRST AMENDMENT SAY?

This question always comes up in my classes: "Doesn't the First Amendment of the United States Constitution require a strict separation [what Thomas Jefferson called a "wall"] between church and state that forbids the study of religion in state-subsidized schools and colleges?" Because I do not intend to write a book on the First Amendment and its implications for teaching religion in public schools and colleges, I can only reiterate, in brief, what Supreme Court Justice Thomas Clark, writing in the majority opinion, declared in the famous *Abington School District v. Schempp* decision in 1963. According to Clark, "Nothing we have said here indicates that such study of the Bible or religion, when presented objectively as part of a secular program of education, may not be effected consistently with the First Amendment" (quoted in Nord, 1995, p. 117). That is to say, the schools may *study* religion, but they must not *practice* or *promote* religion by way of official prayers or devotional Bible readings. Neither, though, can the schools denigrate religion or teach, either by omission or commission, that alternatives such as secular humanism are "superior" (i.e., more reasonable) substitutes for religion. The schools and colleges, like the state, must always practice a rigorous neutrality, neither favoring nor discriminating against religion.

Obviously, however, the legal issues are far more complex and challenging than I have simply alluded to here, and it will always be left to the courts to determine the limits and the possibilities of the free exercise and establishment clauses in the First Amendment whenever difficult cases arise in the educational arena. For those readers who are interested in a fuller treatment of the technical constitutional/legal issues as they relate to education, I highly recommend Nord's (1995) aforementioned text, especially Chapter 3, as well as Stephen Bates's *Battleground* (1993), a book-length account of the famous *Mozert v. Hawkins County Board of Education* case (1986), brought by a group of fundamentalist Christians against the Hawkins County public schools in Tennessee. It will be my position throughout the book that religion must find an educationally appropriate voice in the schools and colleges; not one that promotes, proselytizes, or practices, but rather a voice that teachers and students can explore for its intellectual (narrative) strengths and weaknesses, just as they would any other kind of "voice" in the curriculum.

WHAT DO THE POLLS SAY ABOUT RELIGION IN AMERICA?

Once again, my students often ask: "Isn't America a Christian nation after all? Don't the polls annually show that most Americans believe in a god? How many nonbelievers or believers would teachers actually offend if they taught about religion? Wouldn't the vast majority of Americans approve of the teaching of religion, especially the Christian religion?" In fact, a number of national polls, including the prestigious Gallup Poll (1988/1991/1994), have reported that 9 out of 10 Americans believe in a god, 7 out of 10 believe in an afterlife, and 8 out of 10 want religious training for their children. According to the Gallup Poll (1988), a whopping 84% believe that Jesus is God. In the Gallup Polls of 1991 and 1994, Christians comprise 82% of the adult population, and 70% of adults report that they attend a church or synagogue (data cited in Reeves, 1996). In contrast, only 7.5% of the adult population claim to be agnostics, atheists, or humanists (data cited in Lewy, 1996). It would certainly appear that if self-reports are any indication, Americans are believers, and most are active, religious practitioners.

Upon closer look, however, the polling data on religious faith in America are notoriously inconsistent, sometimes even contradictory, and always problematic. Polls tend to show that increased education often correlates with a radical diminution of religious belief and observance, especially among youth, professional scientists, and academicians (see Lewy, pp. 77–80; also E. J. Larson, 1997). The polls also report that 64%

of Americans do *not* believe in moral absolutes, 44% believe that people can be religious totally independent of churches or synagogues, and 54% have little or no confidence in the clergy. And a recent sociological study (1993) reports that actual church attendance during the course of a year, in spite of claims to the contrary, is only 26.7% (the data are reported in Reeves, 1996).

The conclusion Reeves (1996) draws from these statistics is that at best, formal religious belief in America is superficial, highly individualistic, ambivalent, and materialistic. Believers appear to "consume" their religion in the same way they make other consumer choices, out of self-interest and a penchant for material comfort and convenience. In Reeves's (1996) words, "Pious rhetoric is not necessarily an indication of a deep-seated, life-changing commitment. . . . We . . . go about our lives pretty much the same as those who have no faith at all" (pp. 20–21). Thus, while religious belief is still very much alive and, in some sectors, thriving in the United States, it is clear from the data that America at this time is not a thoroughly religious society, and probably never will be.

MY APPROACH TO THE TOPIC

Although I am not a professional theologian, I do have a graduate degree in theological studies, and I have read widely in the areas of religion and education for a period of over 30 years. As a teacher-educator, I have also directly examined religious and educational issues in my work with thousands of teachers over the same period of time, in such courses as philosophy of education, applied ethics, moral education, and, very recently, religion and education. As a trained philosopher of education, and as someone who is vitally interested in the intersection of religion, modern culture, educational policy, teaching, and the classroom, I intend to cover the *educational* dimensions of the topic at hand, particularly philosophical, curricular, and instructional issues—as these apply to my own teaching. But, frequently and whenever appropriate, I will also be examining the pertinent *theological* elements of the subject as well, as much as my expertise in this area will allow. Finally, I have tried to write a book relatively free of technical jargon—from the perspective of a philosopher of education who is looking at the discipline of religious studies from the *outside in*, rather than from the *inside out*. I have intentionally adopted a writing style that, I hope, will speak engagingly to readers who are unlikely to have studied religion (or philosophy) in any formal, systematic way.

Please note that I am not arguing that henceforth teacher-educators must become religious studies scholars. Rather, I am urging educational philosophers, and any others who are interested and qualified, to offer at least one semester-long course that helps teachers, students, and parents to become religiously literate; moreover, I am recommending that we think seriously about incorporating a brief unit on religion into *all* our professional courses, just as we try to do with the topic of multiculturalism. Obviously, it is not our job, or our expertise, to train educators to be religious studies scholars, but it is in our best interest, and theirs, to know enough about religion to be able to discuss it intelligently in the classroom, with students of all ages.

Either directly or indirectly, I will be exploring throughout the book the following types of interrelated questions:

- How can we teach religion in both public and private settings in a way that does not offend a number of differing, sometimes contentious, constituencies? Or is this offensiveness inevitable, given the nature of the subject matter? In this regard, is a narrative approach *ipso facto* too controversial to achieve the desired educational objective—informed religious literacy?
- Will a narrative/worldview (Smart, 1983) approach to the teaching of religion "de-divinize" the subject matter enough so that students can genuinely appreciate the cultural, aesthetic, literary, philosophical, and political components of the religious experience?
- Whose religions do we teach, and how do we teach them? And does this include the study of agnosticism and atheism as well? Should we try to countermand, reinforce, or take a neutral stance regarding the religious upbringing some students might receive in their particular faith communities (Christian, Islamic, Hindu, Jewish, Sikh, Buddhist)? Are these "at-home" religious teachings untouchable, or are they, too, up for grabs? Or is it naive to assume that the majority of young people receive any substantive religious training at all in their own communities?
- Is religious education, by definition, indoctrination, and thus an oxymoron for teachers in public schools and colleges? Is there a useful distinction to be made between religious *studies* and religious *education*, the former suggesting the acquisition of knowledge (teaching *about*) and the latter a type of training (teaching *for*)? How can educators remain impartial when teaching such controversial, heart- and soul-felt subject matter? Is it possible, or even desirable, to remain *value-free* when teaching such *value-loaded* subject matter? What if we genuinely believe that religion has been a major source

of evil or good in the world? Why should we suppress our deepest convictions about such a powerful force?

- What specific religious subject matter should we teach—doctrines? existential questions? comparative religions? natural religion? metaphysics? history of religion? particular religious themes (e.g., good and evil, salvation, redemption, sin)? Should our main intention in teaching content be a dual one—to help teachers become religiously literate *and* pedagogically skilled, so that perhaps one day they might be able to teach about religion in their own classrooms?

- Regardless of the specific subject matter, how can teachers realistically separate the *cognitive* subject matter of religion as a field deserving of academic study for its own sake from the *emotional* experience of students who might also happen to be believers or seekers? After all, what might be merely a "worldview" or a "story" or a "field of study" for some is likely to be a "revealed, eternal Truth" to others.

- Should the study of religion have as its main objective a profound commitment to Transcendental Truths rather than a mere intellectual self-understanding, or even an "appreciation" and "tolerance" in the name of a politically correct, watery religious pluralism? Is it true that a "thick" religious education is subversive of democracy with its "thin" rules of respect for diversity, consensus, impartiality, fairness, and individual liberty?

- What religious narratives make the most valid truth claims, or is it even right to ask this kind of question in secular, pluralist educational establishments that, in the past, have emphatically ruled this type of inquiry out of order? How should teachers handle the delicate, potentially volatile questions that students themselves raise about the "truth" of particular religious claims, some of which appear to be in direct conflict with each other?

- Do public school teachers have the same kind of academic freedom that their university counterparts do? Or are there limits on academic freedom when it comes to teaching religion, even in the university? Is it possible that academic limits are actually self-imposed, and that a prudent pedagogical style and intellectual mastery are enough to overcome any controversy?

- What kind of professional training will teachers need in order to teach religion most effectively? Do teachers need to be "religious" themselves in order to do the subject justice? What will teachers need to know by way of specific disciplines? Should subject matter be mostly grounded in the humanities? social sciences? natural sciences? Should religion be taught in discrete courses or across the curriculum?

- Does the religious worldview, with its objective truths, supernatural realities, and authoritative doctrines and rituals, clash irreconcilably with postmodernism's tendencies toward agnosticism, relativism, secularism, and skepticism?

My way of attempting to respond to many of these questions will be to approach them *laterally*, through a discussion of what (and how) I actually teach college students. I hope to find a balance in this discussion between a systematic and a somewhat freewheeling analysis. In Chapters 2, 4, 6, and 8, respectively, I present a sympathetic analysis of each narrative. And in Chapters 3, 5, 7, and 9, respectively, I will discuss in more critical, albeit respectful, ways what I believe to be some serious failures of each of the narratives. Throughout the book, I will speculate, philosophize, and discuss specific pedagogical strategies, intentions, and goals, and I will tell stories about my teaching, myself, and my students. In a more technical way, I will also be talking about "hermeneutical perspectives/prisms," textual analysis, postmodern conversational techniques, countertexts, religious languages, and narratives, among other topics.

CONCLUSIONS

Before I close this chapter, I want to spell out a little more clearly my own personal perspective on religion as a kind of truth-in-packaging for readers. What follows is a brief statement I include in a syllabus I distribute to students whenever I teach a graduate course in philosophy of education, applied ethics, or religion and education. The sentiments I express here will underlie much of what the reader will experience in the chapters to come.

At this time early in the semester, I want you to understand the *personal* background I bring to the issues we will be covering for the next several weeks. Obviously, to some extent, this context will color whatever I say and do this term on the topic of religion and education.

Culturally, I am an Irish Catholic, having attended parochial schools for the first eight years of my life, and later, as a mid-life adult, having gone on to earn two graduate degrees from Catholic universities, one in theology, the other in applied ethics and liberal studies. I spent my early, formative years living in ethnically Catholic neighborhoods in a predominantly Catholic city in the Northeast. At the time, I could not wait to escape what I thought was a suffocatingly anti-intellectual, working-class world; although now I look back on those years with much fondness and gratitude, and I never stop being surprised at how constitutive those experiences were in terms of who I am, and what I believe, today.

Theologically, I am an existential agnostic, a "seeker," who has yet to foreclose on the major religious questions that continue to intrigue me to this day. I have been greatly influenced by the work of such existential theologians as Karl Jaspers (1990), John Macquarrie (1977), Gabriel Marcel (1980), Karl Rahner (1978), and Paul Tillich (1952) who feature religious analyses of such themes as freedom, phenomenology, anxiety, finitude, choice, nonexistence, authenticity, responsibility, absurdity, and courage (Nash, 1985). At this time, however, I remain unconvinced that their peculiar "transcendental" solutions to the existential problems they so powerfully define are able to touch my own life in any meaningful way. I do respect the depth of their analyses, and admire their intellectual courage, however, and I will probably be referring to them in our conversations together this term.

Philosophically, and largely the result of having earned two graduate degrees (including a doctorate in philosophy of education) from major, secular universities, as well as teaching in another one for 30 years, I have become a postmodern skeptic on most matters, including the religious; although, paradoxically, I have strong, virtually insatiable, metaphysical curiosities. I do not believe there can ever be a final or definitive religious meaning for everyone, never a "master [religious] narrative" binding on each of us, because reality is endlessly interpretable and always a product of our unique historical and cultural conditionings. Whatever reality's divine or secular origins, I believe our religious views must always be mediated by our particular vocabularies, beliefs, and intentions. While I respect, and even at times I will admire, some of your own particular religious, political, or moral axioms, please do not expect me, or the course, to confirm for you, once and for all, the truth of what is so dear to you. Deep down, as metaphysically attractive or convincing as I might believe your religious view to be, I am still convinced that you and I believe the way we do mainly because of the way we were raised, and not because we have access to any superior moral or religious revelation. Some contemporary philosophers with a postmodern twist who have influenced me in this kind of thinking are Jacques Derrida (1976), Stanley Fish (1994), Hans G. Gadamer (1993), Jurgen Habermas (1988), Jean-François Lyotard (1984), and Richard Rorty (1989).

At the present time, though, I must confess that I worry about the political authoritarianisms, and the moral and epistemological nihilism, that seem to accompany so much postmodern thinking today, especially when epigones evoke the work of such thinkers as Jean Baudrillard (1983), Seyla Benhabib (1992), Judith Butler (1990), and Michel Foucault (1965/1988). And because few current postmodern philosophers have taken the trouble to address the questions about God's mysterious "disappearance" that someone like Friedrich Nietzsche raises, or about the terrible evil and suffering that someone like Elie Wiesel describes in reference to the Holocaust, then, I fear, they will remain largely beside the point as ordinary people continue to search for the vital religious "reference points" they need to make sense of their lives.

Where then does this leave me in the here-and-now, with regard to the religious and philosophical content of this course? I find I am in strong agreement with Thomas Sheehan (1986), the postmodern philosopher and theologian, who said:

> What makes us human is our inexorable finitude, which condemns us to being acts of indirection and mediation. . . . All of us . . . are inevitably and forever a question to which there is no [final] answer. (p. 226)

Like each one of you, I am a fallible interpreter whose life is an ongoing, lived interpretation, and whose "ultimate" direction is unsure. And like all the great religious figures throughout history, and the billions of believers who were influenced by them, I struggle to understand my world from the vantage point of my unique cultural and historical context. My religious and philosophical beliefs, like yours, and like the major teachers' and prophets' beliefs that have moved you, are but reinterpretations of all those who preceded them, and so on *ad infinitum.* You see, we are all equal here this semester, because we are all hermeneutes—mediators— asking our questions and forging our provisional answers. It is in this spirit that I hope to spend the next several weeks with you.

CHAPTER 2

The Fundamentalist Narrative

At the beginning of our conversations on fundamentalism, many of my students can barely conceal their deep-seated hostility toward this orientation. There is rarely balance or nuance in their intemperate attacks on fundamentalism. Of all the narratives we cover during the semester, I find that my mainly liberal, northeastern students bring the most negative prejudgments to this particular religious worldview. Frequently, in response to my opening gambit regarding who or what, if anything, students might actually know of this religious movement, they sneeringly shout out such names as Phyllis Schlafly, Pat Robertson, Oral Roberts, Jim Bakker, Mel and Norma Gabler, Jerry Falwell, and even Billy Graham, and then they proceed to add the descriptors: "born-again Christians," "taking the Bible literally," "hustling money on TV," "anti-abortion, anti-gay, anti-choice, and anti-environment," "Republicans," "Moral Majority," and "Christian Coalition." For good measure, some students also add the epithets "conservatives," "reactionaries," "hypocrites," "dumb rednecks," and occasionally "sexually repressed." It soon becomes obvious to me, and to them, that what they actually know about fundamentalism is negligible, simply a series of prejudicial clichés they parrot from the media; and these stereotypes almost always are one-sided, patronizing, politically loaded, and harshly critical. Intriguingly, in light of my students' near-dogmatic reluctance to make judgments of any kind about people's moral, sexual, or religious beliefs, for fear of being seen as "judgmental" and "imposing values," they are surprisingly quick to put down fundamentalism.

WHAT IS FUNDAMENTALISM?

In America, fundamentalism is largely a Christian movement most closely identified with various forms of Protestantism, and thus, it is this fundamentalism I will be examining in this chapter. Actually, fundamentalism is a worldwide phenomenon, including religious groups as diverse as

Hasidic Jews, Sunni and Shi'i Muslims, evangelical Catholics, and Protestant Christian fundamentalists, located in such places as Canada, England, Asia, and South America. What unifies all of these groups, though, in spite of their specific religious, cultural, and political differences, is their opposition to one common enemy: *modernism* (Lawrence, 1989). Briefly stated, fundamentalists everywhere are against modernism because they think it embraces the following: a homogeneous world community; a leadership of liberal elites; an ethic grounded in individual autonomy, relativism, and secular humanism; a hedonistic lifestyle that denigrates family values and absolute moral standards; a devaluation of local traditions, communities, and churches; and an economic philosophy that enthrones a consumer-driven capitalism and technological progress.

Religious fundamentalists in the United States, through the sophisticated use of communications media, attempt to present a powerful "countertext" to modernism. They want to challenge, and destroy, its key premises. On television and in the churches, as well as in their neighborhoods, businesses, and Christian schools and colleges, religious fundamentalists stress one special set of assumptions:

> There is only one God in the universe who has given us one law via one scripture, and it is the duty of Christians everywhere both to learn this law and to live its moral imperatives in certain, prescribed ways. (Lawrence, 1989, p. 18)

A BRIEF HISTORY

Fundamentalism was a word first coined by C. L. Laws, a journalist, in 1920. In 1895, in Niagara, New York, at a Bible conference, a group of very conservative Protestants declared "five fundamentals" to be the bedrock for Christian believers: inerrant scripture; Jesus's divinity; the Virgin birth; Jesus's death and sacrifice; and Jesus's resurrection. Later, a collection of writings, *The Fundamentals*, attacked a number of key fundamentalist targets: Roman Catholic dogma, Christian Science, Mormon teachings, evolution, modernism, and historical-critical study of the Bible.

Throughout fundamentalism's development, internecine warfare often raged between factions I will call the *political militants* and the *separatists*, concerning the most effective way to deal with the increasing numbers of liberal, "neo-orthodox" believers who had broken from the fundamentalist communion. Eventually, in the 1980s and 1990s, the ultraconservative separatists retreated into their own organizations and communities, while the proselytizers and militants developed a "right-wing" political agenda. Despite their significant differences over what they consider the appropriate degree of societal involvement, however, what all Christian fundamentalists have in common is their unwavering belief that the Bible is absolutely errorless; the world will end in total disaster; Christ will return to Earth to issue a "final dispensation"; and all those who repudiate fundamentalist teaching will be among the "damned" when the final dispensation (the "end time") of history has occurred (J. Z. Smith, 1995; L. J. Averill, 1989).

Fundamentalist educators abhor the permissiveness, relativism, and intellectual skepticism of modernist schools and colleges. Believing themselves to be in sole possession of absolute biblical truths, fundamentalist educators choose to indoctrinate students with those divine religious imperatives which, when followed to the letter, will deliver students to eternal salvation. In some parts of the country, fundamentalists lobby openly for prayer and Bible reading in the public schools and colleges, as well as for the teaching of creationism as a Christian antidote to the "theory" of evolution, a theory currently dominating science curricula everywhere. Whether separatist, proselytical, or militant, fundamentalist educators struggle to provide a genuine Christian alternative to the "religion" of secular humanism, a belief system they are convinced permeates every public school in contemporary America.

Christian *evangelicalism*, while not strictly defined as fundamentalism, receives its inspiration from St. John the Evangelist, one of the 12 apostles and author of the Fourth Gospel. John accompanied Peter to preach in the Temple (Acts 3–4), and traveled to Samaria to win new converts there (Acts 8:14–25). Evangelicals believe in supernatural truth, a divinely inspired Bible, conversion, forgiveness, eternal life, prayer, and preaching. Today, because of a series of revivals in Europe, Africa, and America, there are evangelical wings within a number of Protestant denominations, Roman Catholicism, and Pentecostalism. Evangelicalism as an actual religious movement began during the Protestant Reformation in the 16th century, inspired by Martin Luther's emphasis on a personal, experienced faith in Jesus Christ as all that one needs to achieve salvation, along with the authority of the Scriptures and the priesthood of all believers. In 18th-century America, a major "spiritual awakening" sparked hundreds of religious revival meetings; and in the 19th century, American evangelicalism was actually the mainline religion, easily the most popular form of Christianity, until Catholic Americans became more numerous. Even today, some experts estimate that up to one-fourth of all adults in the United States count themselves as evangelicals (M. S. Hamilton, in McBrien, 1995).

Pentecostalism is a related Christian movement, dating back in the

United States to 1900, when Charles F. Parham, a Methodist minister, laid hands on a member of his church and she responded by speaking in "tongues." The Book of Acts records that 50 days after the Resurrection Jesus's disciples were filled with the Holy Spirit and started speaking in languages nobody understood (Gr., "glossolalia" [tongue]—incomprehensible speech while in the throes of religious ecstasy). Pentecostals are charismatics, people who are given certain gifts (prophecy, healing, glossolalia) by the Holy Spirit, and today there are charismatic groups in a number of Protestant congregations, including the Holy Rollers (an African-American group), and even in some conservative Roman Catholic communities. At the present time, there is a major charismatic renewal movement among religious Americans of every race and ethnicity (Bawer, 1997).

I believe that Christian evangelicalism and Pentecostalism have a great deal in common with fundamentalism, because over the years distinctions have blurred (Bawer, 1997; Cox, 1995; Lawrence, 1989): All three are highly conservative in that they look to biblical authority as the final word. Also, all three steadfastly resist the sinfulness of the secular world, particularly in matters of sexual morality. However, the majority of evangelicals and Pentecostals reject fundamentalism's strict emphasis on biblical inerrancy and affirm, instead, biblical "infallibility"—the belief that biblical truth is ultimately reliable, but not inerrant, given all the internal ambiguities, contradictions, and multiple secular interpretations of specific passages.

Moreover, evangelicals and Pentecostals adopt an irenic style in contrast to fundamentalist rhetorical excess. Both are more likely to acknowledge incompleteness in their own beliefs and, in some cases, partial truth in theological views opposing their own (Averill, 1989). And Pentecostals tend to be far more expressive in their worship than fundamentalists. Some African-American evangelicals (and Pentecostals), while resolutely orthodox, appear to be more joyous in their worship, less inclined to stress a doctrinal Christianity, and far less likely to charge others with heresy. African-American evangelicalism and Pentecostalism, as some scholars (Skillen, 1990) have pointed out, have been uniquely shaped as adaptive responses to the terrible conditions of slavery—disenfranchisement, oppression, and suffering—that American blacks have experienced during their history in America. (See the African-American Peter J. Gomes, 1996, for a very evangelical, yet liberal, rendering of Christian teachings on race, anti-Semitism, women, and homosexuality; also see *The African-American Devotional Bible*, King James Version, 1997.)

Evangelical and Pentecostal educators stress two kinds of teaching: conversion and confession. Conversionist educators aim for complete personal conversion—the acceptance of Jesus—in students' lives. The goal is always *metanoia* (Gr., change of heart), a conversion from sin to God. And confessional educators, in addition to actively changing hearts and minds to accept Jesus, also seek to "interpret, systematize, and formulate Christian meaning" (Smith, 1995, p. 350). Thus, confessional educators take a more intellectual stance toward conversion and preaching. Whatever their educational and stylistic differences, though, I treat evangelicalism, Pentecostalism, and fundamentalism as very similar narratives and worldviews, as do many scholars (e.g., Averill, 1989; Bawer, 1997; R. Wuthnow, 1988).

THE FUNDAMENTALIST WORLDVIEW

As a teacher, I work very hard, especially at the outset, to get my students to understand this religious narrative from the "inside out." I contend that before we can explore the *dark side* of this particular orientation, we must first do our best to actually live inside the head and heart of fundamentalists, if only for a little while, in order to discern the *bright side*. We need to suspend our cynical disbelief, get beyond the media-generated oversimplifications, and read the fundamentalist "countertext" to modernity as honestly as we can, *on its own terms*, as far as this is possible. I find the fundamentalist worldview to be rooted in a specific set of philosophical-religious beliefs so diametrically opposed to the American modernist/postmodern ethos that most of my students unquestioningly embrace that teaching this story with integrity seems, at times, to be intellectually and pedagogically impossible.

I know that both sides on this religious perspective stand to lose if the unit is not done, at least in the beginning, with some evenhandedness: If I allow the spirit of modernism (or postmodernism) to control the analysis, then we fail to capture accurately the genuine religious fervor; the doctrinal consistency; the beauty of such characteristic Christian virtues as faith, hope, love, compassion, and forgiveness; and the profound respect for revealed biblical truth and tradition that fundamentalists cherish. (See an important book on the positive role of women within the movement by Linda Kintz, 1997, *Between Jesus and the Market*.) If I favor the spirit of fundamentalism, then we risk compromising two key modernist principles: a commitment to the value of an emancipatory intellectual skepticism—an expectation that all beliefs should be equally up for grabs in a college classroom; and a realization that because we live in a secular, pluralistic democracy, we must never allow religion to become a divisive, intolerant force, an influence that reinforces, rather than ameliorates, exploitation, oppression, and injustice. The balancing act, I find, can often be excruciatingly difficult and delicate, particularly in a secular university that justifies its existence on the grounds that instructors and students must be free to debunk and demystify any type of authoritarian claim to an exclusive truth.

FUNDAMENTALIST TEXTS AND CLASSROOM VISITORS

And so, in order to understand the fundamentalist mindset from the inside out, and after introducing the class to the brief, factual overview of fundamentalism I have included above, I, and they, embark on careful readings of a few key texts that explicate this religious perspective. In the past, I have successfully used such texts as Stephen Bates's *Battleground: One Mother's Crusade, the Religious Right, and the Struggle for Our Schools* (1994); Harvey Cox's *Fire from Heaven: The Rise of Pentecostal Spirituality and the Reshaping of Religion in the Twenty-First Century* (1995); Stanley Hauerwas and John H. Westerhoff's *Schooling Christians: "Holy Experiments" in American Education* (1992); Arthur F. Holmes's *The Idea of a Christian College* (1975); George M. Marsden and Bradley J. Longfield's *The Secularization of the Academy* (1992); Mark A. Noll's *The Scandal of the Evangelical Mind* (1994); and Alan Peshkin's *God's Choice* (1988), among others. What all these texts have in common, despite their authors' different academic backgrounds and religious commitments, is an overriding intention to present fundamentalism in a sympathetic and engaging manner. All of the authors, with the exception of Alan Peshkin, a Jewish educational anthropologist, and Stephen Bates, a "lapsed Episcopalian" and a lawyer/journalist, are theologians, and, excluding these two and Cox (1995), they are also practicing fundamentalists/evangelicals.

In the event there are no fundamentalist students enrolled in the seminar who are able and willing to present their views to us, we then follow up these readings by inviting some very vocal and articulate fundamentalist Christians to the seminar for a few meetings. The latter experience always proves to be enlightening, and challenging, because our visitors inevitably turn out to be more than merely entertaining guests. They are often smart, devout, and passionate, full of dogmatic certainty. They end up being formidable defenders of a religious worldview that my modernist/postmodernist students find both intellectually incomprehensible and intolerably anti-democratic and judgmental. Most important, though, the visitors give a very human shape to the relatively abstract religious ideas we analyze in our readings.

In his well-received study of a fundamentalist school, *God's Choice*,

Alan Peshkin (1988) introduces his readers to a Pastor William Muller, who prides himself on giving a "sermon" to his Bethany Christian Academy pupils on "extremism." In his message, Muller states: "We are extreme in our belief. In essence, we negate all the other religions of the world. . . . They're wrong. There is no getting into heaven except through Jesus Christ" (p. 6). His musings typify the presentations of most of our fundamentalist guests. Pastor Muller is proudly "extremist" in his dogged certainty that all other religions are simply wrong, unless they put Jesus Christ at the center of their teachings. After all, for Muller, it is irrefutable that Jesus is God, that he was conceived without the participation of a human father, that he is coming again to Earth to judge the wicked and make things right, and that all those who have declared their faith in Jesus and witnessed to others will be among the chosen ones. But Pastor Muller is no fool; he knows full well the fate that befalls those Christians who choose to go public with such indisputable religious convictions. The relativists, skeptics, and agnostics in the media, and in secular schools and colleges, often ridicule and dismiss fundamentalists as irrational, self-righteous zealots.

I remember vividly an "extremist" Christian educator, a member of Citizens for Excellence in Education (R. L. Simonds, 1994), who came to my class once, armed to do battle against the "secular humanist" teachers who had registered for my course in philosophy of education. (For dramatic effect, here, as throughout the book, at times I present the composite voices of several students and visitors to my classes in a number of different courses as if they are individuals in the same course.) After the initial polite introductions, her presentation, and the resultant interchange with my students, grew increasingly menacing and vituperative. Her presentation went something like the following:

> I am a conservative Christian parent who is frequently outraged at what goes on in my children's public school classrooms. Whenever I express my concerns to school officials over what I see as teaching that is too secular, affective, and atheistic, they try to humor me or talk down to me or pull professional rank on me. All I know is that my children are getting very little cognitive learning in their elementary schools; the curriculum is so watered down to the lowest common denominator, so politically correct, and anti-Christian, it is a mess. Faith in the Christian God is ignored or subtly belittled, while Native American spirituality, New Age religions, relaxation and imaging exercises, and environmentalism serve as voguish substitutes. My children, in the space of just a few short months, have already learned about condoms, birth con-

trol pills, AIDS, homosexuality, self-esteem, multiculturalism, global education, and evolution, but they do not know any history, English, science, or math. Neither, by the way, do the teachers seem to know much about these academic subjects, if the truth be told.

I am here to tell you that *we* parents own our children; *you* do not! We are taxpayers who subsidize the schools. You are accountable to *us*, not the other way around. We want you to do *real* character education, in a way that respects the teachings of the Ten Commandments and the Christianity of our Founding Fathers. If you cannot do this, then leave character education to us, where it rightfully belongs, and get out of our Bibles, our churches, and our families. Furthermore, we demand that you teach what you are paid to teach: core subject matter along with some healthy doses of respect for authority, patriotism, and personal responsibility. You are not social workers, or politicians, or therapists. Stop the social experimentation with our children, or you will face a number of lawsuits. And stop trying to intimidate us by calling us names. Many of the parents in my community have more college degrees than you do, more political influence, and we are far more organized than you. Some of us will be running for school boards and for other public offices. The day of reckoning is at hand.

With the battle lines now clearly drawn, my students and the fundamentalist visitor quickly moved in for the kill. In the rancorous exchange that followed, the visitor saw herself as a staunch defender of God, moral standards, and family and church values, and my students saw themselves as enlightened defenders of pluralism, academic freedom, secularism, and nonjudgmental humanism. From our visitor's perspective, public school teachers expounded a godless philosophy of secular humanism, moral relativism, values clarification over genuine moral discernment, godlessness, and rampant self-esteem. From my students' perspective, fundamentalist parents and educators represented the worst type of biblical dogmatism: moral absolutism, a narrow, judgmental religiosity, and blind obedience to external authority.

On that particular day in class, sadly, neither side was able to bridge the ideological chasm that loomed between them, because neither side was willing to shift perspectives, to understand the opposing worldview from the *inside out* of the other. Both sides were stuck in the *outside in* exchange of true believers, stone deaf to differing points of view. Our visitor all but shouted: "*My* truth is God's truth! I will not compromise! I will not give in to the lure of your worldly certainties. I will strive to convert you, and if I can't, I will surely pray for you." My students all but shrieked back: "*Our* truth is the most reasonable truth. We are pluralists, not absolutists. We will try to be open to compromise, of course, but we refuse to give in to your religious certainties! Don't you see? At the very least, we must agree to disagree with each other, to find some common ground."

ABSOLUTE TRUTH VS. MODERNISM

It is my experience that the discovery of common ground is rare whenever we study religious fundamentalism. Fundamentalists are pre-Enlightenment absolutists who believe they alone possess Divine Truth as unerringly revealed by God in the Bible. In contrast, my students are relativists and subjectivists, most modernists, others postmodernists, who believe they alone construct truth; what is more, for them, their truth, far from unerring, is at best reason-based, amenable to scientific verification or refutation, contingent, uncertain, and always incomplete. Frequently in class, both groups confront each other across a vast epistemological divide, speaking two unfathomably contrasting languages, emanating from two strikingly dissimilar narratives. Sometimes, because they lack mutually comprehensible words, they end up spouting rhetoric and shouting angry names at each other.

Philosophically, the "vast epistemological divide" I refer to above began to take shape during the Enlightenment (17th and 18th centuries). Although, in my mind, Richard Tarnas (1991) tends to overestimate the dialectical *interdependence* of the early Christian (pre-Enlightenment) and modernist (post-Enlightenment) outlooks, generally, I believe, he makes many insightful observations regarding the substantive *differences* that exist between the two worldviews. According to Tarnas (1991), these differences are as follows:

1. Before the Enlightenment, a personal God, omniscient and omnipotent, both created and watched lovingly over the Christian cosmos. After the Enlightenment, the cosmos stood on its own, less in need of a personal God, and now it is understandable by modernists mainly in scientific and mathematical terms.
2. Before the Enlightenment, Christians emphasized the "supremacy of the spiritual and transcendent" (p. 285); after the Enlightenment, modernists engineered a radical inversion—now the "material and concrete" became supreme.
3. Before the Enlightenment, the Christian revelation (scripture) as "pre-

eminent intellectual authority" (p. 286) dominated the scene; after the Enlightenment, modernist faith in human reason, scientific knowledge, and secular humanism ruled the day.

4. Before the Enlightenment, the Christian worldview emphasized emotion, personal ephiphany, conversion experiences, imagination, and the aesthetic; after the Enlightenment, a modernist preference for logic, scientific rationality, and material progress gained ascendancy. Now, in the postmodern age, neither the universe nor God is said to possess intelligence or purpose; only human beings do.

5. Before the Enlightenment, an anthropocentric (person-centered) and geocentric (Earth-centered) view of the universe was the reigning scientific doctrine; after the Enlightenment, a galactocentric (galaxy-centered) and multiverse (multiple universes) cosmology evolved. Now the Earth is said to exhibit no anthropomorphic qualities, and many modernist cosmologists (e.g., Smolin, 1997) dismiss the notion of a divine or supernatural presence in the universe as "primitive superstition and wishful thinking" (Tarnas, p. 288).

6. Before the Enlightenment, Christians stressed a belief in the "Bible's purposeful creation"; after the Enlightenment, there emerged a theory of evolution that explained human progress by an "amoral, random, and brutal struggle for natural survival" (p. 289). Rejected now as scientifically and evolutionarily implausible are such Christian beliefs as Miraculous Intervention, the Incarnation (God's enfleshment as Jesus), the second Adam, the Virgin Birth, the Resurrection, and the Second Coming (p. 289).

7. Before the Enlightenment, people depended on God for a sense of human worth and eternal salvation; after the Enlightenment, modernists constructed a philosophy of "natural rights, existential autonomy, and individual expression" (p. 289). Gone now is a belief in Original Sin, the Fall, and "collective human guilt." What remains is a sense of human freedom, independence, the autonomous human intellect, and the social construction of reality.

In dramatic contrast to this post-Enlightenment (modernist) view of the world, I believe that Kolakowski (1990/1997) poignantly captures the essence of the absolutist Christian worldview, as I understand it. Such modernists as Friedrich Wilhelm Nietzsche (1844–1900) and Jean Paul Sartre (1905–1980), according to Kolakowski, lead us astray whenever they claim that we are self-created, liberated, traditionless, fully self-reliant agents in the world. For Kolakowski, in contrast, there is a Creator God; we are His creatures; we must study His Word; and we must come to love, and obediently live out, this God's sacred, absolute truth—as revealed in the Bible and in church teachings. For those modernists who believe that human beings are basically alone in a Godless universe, reacting exclusively to their own "arbitrary whims" and struggling mightily to define themselves in a world where no truth perdures, their ultimate, tragic fate will be to lose themselves forever in the void. This modernist outlook, Kolakowski believes, is the surest path to cynicism, anxiety, despair, and endless darkness.

Kolakowski's (1990/1997) reaction to those modernists who would question God's existence in the face of wars, natural disasters, fatal accidents and illnesses, and death camp horrors is to assert that in fact it is only in the face of such atrocities that the existence of God makes any sense. Without a God to turn to in the wake of unimaginable human wickedness and natural catastrophe, life has no meaning. What Kolakowski, a conservative Polish Catholic philosopher, is saying, in a far more refined and elegant language (but no less absolutist and transcendent) than our fundamentalist visitor's words, is that the modernist worldview is ultimately empty because it possesses no truth that is independent of worldly realities, able to rise above a specific time, location, or event. Or in Berman's (1982) graphic description of modernism: "To be modern is to ... find one's world and oneself in perpetual disintegration and renewal ... to be part of a universe in which all that is solid melts into air" (p. 345).

The antidote to nihilism and despair, at least for Kolakowski, is a very conservative Christianity. In Kolakowski's (1990/1997) memorable words:

> There are reasons why we need Christianity, but not just any kind of Christianity. We do not need a Christianity that makes political revolution, that rushes to cooperate with so-called sexual liberation, that approves our concupiscence [sexual desire] or praises our violence. There are enough forces in the world to do all these things without the aid of Christianity. We need a Christianity that will help us to move beyond the immediate pressures of life, that gives us insight into the basic limits of the human condition and the capacity to accept them, a Christianity that teaches us the simple truth that there is not only a tomorrow but a day after tomorrow as well. (pp. 84–85)

Kolakowski's Christianity is grounded in an uncompromising belief in original sin, the possibility of divine redemption and human salvation, and the gift of grace. The truth of Christianity, for Kolakowski, is precious and enduring precisely because it is "one-sided," because it recognizes the fractured and partial quality of all other claims to truth, and because it alone has access to an unconditional set of moral absolutes. Both in the short span of human life and from the perspective of eternity, Christian truth, for Kolakowski, for a Pastor Muller, and for our fundamentalist Christian visitor, is the one "solid" element that will manage to survive an ambiguous and disintegrating universe.

To much of this, most of my students can only respond: What "nihilism and despair"? What set of "unconditional moral absolutes"? Who says so? And why is Christianity the answer and not the problem? What is the real story here?

THE FUNDAMENTALIST NARRATIVE VS.
THE MODERNIST NARRATIVE

Just what is the real *story* here? If I can convince students to respond to each of the religious orientations we cover in class as "stories," then I find many are usually more open to looking for the strengths, rather than ferreting out the weaknesses, of a particular religious narrative. And their questions become far less cynical and defensive. Stories, in my experience, help students to shift perspective more easily, to assume the vantage point of the other. The Greek word for stories or narratives is *mythoi*, the root of "myths." For religious scholars, narratives, like myths, are neither true nor false; instead, they function more neutrally to remind us that people construct religious stories to explain the nature of life, and to provide a sense of cosmic purpose, personal identity, and morality (Hauerwas, 1977; McFague, 1987; Smart, 1983).

A good religious narrative, therefore, helps believers to make metaphysical sense of their lives, because it gives them a satisfying account of where they came from, why they are here, and where they might be going. In Neil Postman's (1996) words, a cogent religious narrative is one that "tells of origins and envisions a future, a story that constructs ideals, prescribes rules of conduct, provides a source of authority, and, above all, gives a sense of continuity and purpose" (pp. 5–6). Some of the most comprehensive religious narratives, in Postman's sense, can be found in such texts as the Hebrew Bible, the New Testament, the Qur'an, the Tao Te Ching, the Analects, and the Upanishads.

Instructionally, I make the point to students that even though we will be reading little or no fiction during the semester, I believe that each of the religious texts we will be studying is actually telling a story: It has a set of distinctive characters, a plot, a climax, a lesson to teach, lots of description, and a unique setting. Sometimes a religious text tries to inspire, other times to persuade, or defend, or criticize, or laud, or regale. We read our religious texts as stories, and we listen to the presentations

our visitors make as stories, because I believe it is often more fruitful to
concentrate on whether the texts are imaginative, provocative, powerful,
and compelling, *at the level of narrative*, than on whether they are true or
false, *at the level of propositions*. I prefer to ask: Does the story touch our
lives in some ways? Does it hold together? Does it accomplish what its
author might have set out to do? Does the story transport, or entertain,
or excite, or edify us? Does it help us to see the "real world" in a more
imaginative way? Is the lesson in the story clearly rendered? defensible?
plausible? realistic? useful? What do you think of the author's use of
religious language?

For at least one fundamentalist, the Christian story begins with what
he perceives to be the *crisis* of modernism:

> We may indeed be approaching midnight. But if there is any hope, it is to
> be found in a renewed and repentant people possessed of a moral vision
> informed by Scripture, respecting of tradition, and committed to the recovery
> of character. We must be a people of conviction, prepared to offer the world
> a story filled with courage, duty, commitment, and heroic effort—that will
> inflame the moral imagination of the West. (Colson, 1989, pp. 181–182)

These are the words of Charles Colson, a former White House operative during Richard Nixon's presidency, a self-described political "hatchet
man," a convicted felon, and, at one time, a "complete secularist and
confirmed conservative . . . [even] a social utopian" (Colson, 1989, p. 11).
But then, while serving a jail sentence as a result of his criminal involvement in the Watergate controversy, something strange happened to
Charles Colson: He became a Christian, and he suddenly realized that
"the crisis of our culture that could topple our monuments and destroy
our very foundations, is *within* us . . . That is why Christians are the only
ones who can offer viable answers" (pp. 10–11). Colson, an engaging
storyteller, had indeed found his "story," one he hoped would "inflame
the moral imagination of the West" (p. 182).

In many ways, Charles Colson (1989) artfully captures the drama of
the typical fundamentalist narrative. Neither separatist nor militant (in
fact, at times moderately evangelical in tone, at other times passionately
fundamentalist), Colson, an enormously popular religious speaker and
bestselling author, rejects "pallid attempts at ecumenism" and seeks instead to establish "common ground on the fundamental, orthodox tenets
of our faith" (p. 12). What follows is essentially the story he tells in every
book he writes, and in every speech he makes, with only minor dramatic
variations:

America is in precipitous moral decline, as the "new barbarians" besiege us from within. Enlightenment liberals, radical individualists, relativists, hedonists, homosexuals, anti-family feminists, postmodern, permissive educators, immoral, unprincipled politicians, and New Age clergy, who have rejected "Christian absolutes," have produced a "crumbling culture," a new "dark age" that threatens to engulf us all. No mere political or educational structure can cure what ails us. Only the "true church" can save us, the church that "cleaves to the absolute standards of Scripture," and insists that Christians be "committed to biblical obedience." (pp. 134, 136)

If we are to be Christians . . . we must take on [God's] whole Word wholeheartedly. That means reading the Bible, studying it, committing it to memory, allowing his words to dwell richly in our minds. (p. 150)

Through Biblical repentance and living a holy life, Christians can overcome original sin. This entails renouncing a radical individualism, affirming the inherent dignity of human life, and recovering respect for revelation, tradition, and history. (pp. 178–179)

This is the one "story filled with courage, duty, commitment, and heroic effort—that will inflame the moral imagination of the West." (p. 182)

Colson's account of his own *metanoia* (Gr., "conversion") contains all the elements of a moving and inspiring Christian story, and thousands of people throughout the country continue to line up to buy his books and listen to his lectures. His narratives always include the following features: personal, candid confessions about his wrongdoing, major ethical conflicts, memorable characters (heroes and villains, mentors and evil influences), religiously defining events, critical interpersonal incidents, biblical enlightenment, moral and political transformation, present and future obstacles yet to be overcome, public testimony, forgiveness, reconciliation, and the expectation of ultimate redemption. Colson's language is simple yet compelling, and because it is so profoundly sincere and confessional, his readers and listeners believe in him and follow his teachings.

Colson's narrative reaches its epiphany during his darkest personal moment while in prison, where he underwent an extraordinary religious conversion. He "miraculously" found God, thanks to prison prayer meetings, where he discovered God's inspired, absolute Word in Holy Scripture. Subsequently, he repented of his personal and political misdeeds. Later, as he looked at the world around him, for the first time he saw clearly the omnipresent "barbarians" who had plunged civilization into the "new dark ages." These barbarians had turned their back on God's laws, publicly denied His existence, chosen instead to deify skepticism, relativism, and hedonism, and, in the process, created a culture of death. The story ends with a warning: While it is not too late for people to repent—after all, Colson himself did—we must hurry, because civilization as we know it is entering the final stages of darkness. Christians everywhere must stand "against the night" and, like Charles Colson, offer the "good news" to the "barbarians."

Whenever students "read" fundamentalist visitors, and authors like Charles Colson, as storytellers, with deeply felt worldviews to share, principles to delineate, ideals to exemplify, and convictions they would be willing to die for, they stop responding to cardboard characters. While it is true that no students ever undergo any startling religious *metanoia* of their own in my classes, most manage to get beyond the stereotypes of fundamentalists as bombthrowers, anti-abortion picketers, censors, and mindless Bible-thumpers. Frequently, students will even develop a begrudging respect for some of the more outspoken fundamentalists who visit our classroom, because these steadfast believers actually manage to hold their own, with considerable integrity, when confronting a group of doctrinaire skeptics like my students.

Another consequence of a classroom encounter with fundamentalists is that often students become a little clearer about the hidden content, and impact, of their own modernist/postmodern educational narrative. Stephen Bates (1994) has argued that most schools and colleges actually operate from a "no-ultimate-or-absolute-truths" narrative that is the direct antithesis to the fundamentalist story. The dominant *educational* story in America today is a complex, somewhat inconsistent combination of secularism, humanism, modernism, and postmodernism. And this story advantages Piagetian constructivism over behavioral psychology, pluralism over individualism, the new over the old, relativism over absolutism, egalitarianism over merit, immanence over transcendence, democracy over hierarchy, process over product, tolerance over faith, uncertainty over certainty, and self-esteem over religious well-being (Hirsch, Jr., 1996; Postman, 1996). Most of my students come to realize that these antinomies, whether the schools intend them or not, frequently create an unbridgeable fissure between the secular curriculum and religious belief.

Many of the fundamentalist visitors to our classroom, as well as the authors we read, have already reached this conclusion, of course, and in direct defiance of the modernist/postmodern worldview, they declare their belief in absolute Christian truths. As Bates points out (1994), fundamentalists want educators to respect their religious beliefs, if for no other reason than to promote a genuine diversity of viewpoints in the schools. In fact, fundamentalists want educators to be *radically* tolerant, that is, to "tolerate intolerance," the same way that the Constitution tolerates, but does not condone, flag burning, Nazi marches, and Jehovah's Witnesses distributing anti-Catholic pamphlets.

And when schools and colleges deny the rights of fundamentalist parents to object to textbooks, teaching methods, and curricula that they feel demean, distort, or ignore the Christian narrative in favor of the ruling secularist story, then fundamentalists grow angry. Some choose to leave the public schools and colleges forever. In my own view, whenever this happens, the ultimate victim is diversity. Teachers and students lose contact with an important religious countertext that, for better or worse, is the only serious challenger left to the hegemony of modernism and postmodernism in our nation's schools and colleges.

CONCLUSIONS

When I recently distributed the following comments by a man named Mojtaba, a fundamentalist Islamic Iranian, on his acerbic view of the depraved state of American life, many of my modernist students were at a complete loss as to how to respond:

> We are rigid, to be sure, but we don't murder a million babies a year through abortion; we don't have tens of thousands of unmarried teen-age mothers; we don't have shelters for battered women, because there are no battered women in my country. We don't have a drug problem; we don't have homo- sexual marriages; we don't have abused children or unsafe schools; we don't have an AIDS epidemic; we don't have any of the social problems that are destroying your society. Think about that please, and tell me if your right to dance and drink alcohol or look at women half-naked or read political commentary in a press that is as self-censored and self-limiting as any in the world compensates for the sicknesses that are killing your country. (Policano, 1998, p. 10)

Because I believe there is discomforting truth in the fundamentalist narrative, including even Mojtaba's harsh version, I continually caution students to resist dismissing fundamentalism as merely an authoritarian, religious anachronism whose time has long since passed. In my mind, fundamentalism has actually become a viable, albeit somewhat danger- ous, "alternative discourse" in the modern world. Religious scholars such as Harvey Cox (1995), along with Martin E. Marty and Scott Appleby (1991), are quick to point out that around the globe, millions of fundamen- talist believers (as well as many of their opponents) see themselves as a powerful avant-garde. Whether Hindu, Buddhist, Jewish, Muslim, or Christian, zealous fundamentalists everywhere, armed with a set of unshakeable religious truths, set themselves up as soldiers marching into battle (some literally) against those modernist forces who, they are convinced, have caused massive personal, social, and cultural disruptions.

From the fundamentalist perspective, these social upheavals include the worldwide ascendancy of such secular values as individualism, liberalism, religious skepticism, and consumer hedonism; the breakdown of traditional communities, family structures, and sex roles; the erosion of absolute moral standards; the crisis of political authority; the loss of respect for the dignity of human life; and the supercession of technology, science, and bureaucratic rationality—over religion—as the only reasonable way to understand, and organize, the confounding realities of everyday life. (Mojtaba, quoted above, would love the social activism of two fundamentalist organizations in the United States—James Dobson's "Focus on the Family" and Bill McCartney's "Promise Keepers." See Bawer, 1997, pp. 247–265.) In fact, as early as 1864, Pope Pius IX's *Syllabus of Errors*, and in 1907, Pope Pius X's encyclical, *Pascendi Dominici Gregis* (*Feeding the Lord's Flock*), condemned similar kinds of evils, among them, pantheism, naturalism, political liberalism, and scientific rationalism (McBrien, 1995, p. 1233). In the opinion of many Catholic fundamentalists in this country still loyal to Rome, both popes proved to be clairvoyant prophets.

Against these modernist "heresies," and the widespread alienation and despair that often accompany them, contemporary fundamentalists attempt to make their case. Shorn of the inflammatory and unyielding religious rhetoric, their claims are compelling to millions; and when my students are ready to listen, some are surprised to find themselves a little less judgmental, and a little more receptive to the possibility of finding even a modicum of truth in what they heatedly oppose. For millions of followers throughout the world who may once have been disenchanted, rootless, and unstable, the fundamentalist story provides both a coherent religious tradition and a dedicated community of believers. Moreover, the biblical narrative contains a set of consoling truths that fortify believers against the personal uncertainties of human finitude that plague all of us: chronic unhappiness and dissatisfaction, catastrophic accidents and illnesses, disheartening personal failure in work, love, and learning, lingering anxiety, and the crushing finality of death.

Educationally, for fundamentalists, biblical moral principles offer a more permanent foundation to moral education than does secular humanism, because they are rooted in God's eternal law and are unchanging. Furthermore, Gaddy, Hall, and Marzano (1996) cite surprising empirical research demonstrating that orthodox Christian students tend to be healthier and happier, less stressed, able to get along better with others, and less psychologically troubled than their non-Christian counterparts in schools and colleges around the country (pp. 169–170). And statistics from the U.S. Department of Education, as well as a number of academic studies, prove that on average, fundamentalist students from Christian schools and academies score up to two grades higher than public school students on standardized tests; and a much larger percentage enter college than do public school graduates (data reported in Diego Ribadeneira, 1997, p. 30).

Finally, fundamentalists remind us that democracy itself is in an extremely precarious position, unless Americans can agree on traditional Christian principles to shore up its foundations. For example, the Christian axiom that all human beings are sacred, made in the image and likeness of their God, provides government leaders with an unimpeachable rationale for treating citizens equally, justly, and humanely, and for listening to their political views, no matter how diverse or unorthodox.

"Does fundamentalism really have a future in America?" students will often ask. "Why should we take this religious narrative seriously? What does all of this have to do with education?" After spending some time carefully studying the fundamentalist narrative, my students and I both agree that like it or not, liberal/modernist Christianity and fundamentalist Christianity are dialectically linked. As liberal/modernist churches become increasingly secular in mission and outlook—offering 12-step therapy programs; advancing peace-and-justice political agendas; celebrating watered-down, quasi-secular liturgies; challenging or, in some cases, even denying conservative biblical teachings on such moral issues as homosexuality—then fundamentalist communities will continue to expand exponentially. Disenchanted churchgoers in record numbers will seek out those conservative religious communities that proudly proclaim the traditional, unchanging biblical truths. After all, many of the faithful will wonder, who, if not the fundamentalist churches, will act as the "saving remnant" of the true Christian faith?

Robert Wuthnow (1993) warns liberal Christians to avoid dismissing fundamentalists as ignorant, insecure, and fearful people who are no match for well-educated, religious modernists. In reality, fundamentalists are selective and resourceful modernists themselves. For example, they are not above using the media in some very sophisticated ways to get what they want. And fundamentalists understand only too well the overwhelming need many faithful have for a sense of religious comfort and security. All of us long at times for a community that offers some kind of spiritual substance as a hedge against all those occasions we spend in the secular world making one moral compromise after another.

Finally, I contend that teachers have a great deal to learn about their own practices from analyzing fundamentalist strengths. Fundamentalists know how to provide that safe religious space, and what is more, they know how to retain the people who retreat to it in droves. They preach well. They know their Bible. They respond to genuine human concerns. They make people feel wanted and valued. They know how to raise money in order to enlarge their membership. And many Christian fundamentalists have learned brilliantly how to work the political system, both locally and nationally, to recruit and to evangelize, and to advance a number of important political causes. At the very least, I would argue that it behooves educators to understand the continuing lure such a robust religious narrative has on the lives of its adherents, many of whom are students and parents who live in communities that educators serve all over the United States.

In the next chapter, despite its many successes, I intend to analyze the downside of what I am calling the fundamentalist narrative. It is my contention that well-informed educators need to know something about the intellectual, theological, and political excesses of fundamentalism if they are to acknowledge its strengths and address its deficiencies with balance and discernment in the classroom.

CHAPTER 3

The Failure of the Fundamentalist Narrative

Notwithstanding the positive construction I have put on my reading of fundamentalism, I believe that the fundamentalist orientation, as either a religious, political, or intellectual *style*, is deeply and seriously mistaken. In Rauch's (1993) words, fundamentalism "is the strong disinclination to take seriously the notion that you might be wrong" (p. 89). Fundamentalism fails as *religious narrative*, I submit, because, essentially, it tells an unconvincing, indeed unbelievable, story for a democratic, pluralistic world ever to embrace. And it tends to demonize all counternarratives. It also fails *intellectually*, I contend, because it is much too certain that it alone has made *the* airtight case for the existence of a superior religious truth—in the face of compelling religious and postmodern challenges to the contrary. My students are quick to realize that fundamentalism as narrative leads inevitably to an authoritarian politics that is socially repressive and democratically erosive. And, likewise, students see that fundamentalism as a hermetically sealed belief system leads unavoidably to a narrow anti-intellectualism. This usually takes the form of ignoring, or repudiating, the inevitability of hermeneutics in translating, interpreting, understanding, and applying the meaning of canonical religious texts such as the Bible for the current age.

Other related criticisms that frequently come up in class are directed at the fundamentalist tendency to rehash the same old apocalyptic visions, which many of my students see as a transparent scare tactic in order to "win souls for Jesus." (This "tribulationist," apocalyptic agenda has to do with God's penitential time of testing us with natural and human catastrophes just before the millennium.) Students also continue to balk at the fundamentalists' inclination to insist on their own absolute, arrogant, and very narrow interpretation of scripture and history as ultimately authoritative and normative for all, bar none. And they always express grave misgivings whenever fundamentalists attempt to insinuate a veiled bigotry against certain minority groups (e.g., Jews and homosexuals) into their "Armageddon theology," under the cover of a millenarian prophecy (Christ's return to Earth for a thousand years to redeem the world's misery).

THE DANGER OF ALL-ENCOMPASSING NARRATIVES

At the level of narrative, listen to the following words by a major fundamentalist religious leader: "Islam contains everything . . . Islam includes everything. Islam is everything," says the Ayatollah Ruhollah Khomeini (cited in Rauch, 1993, p. 99). Unfortunately, in my opinion, what makes the fundamentalist narrative so seductive in the modern world—its unwavering conviction that it alone is in possession of the sure thing—is also what makes it extremely dangerous. Like Rauch, I and my students are put off by Khomeini's grand (Islamic) narrative, because Khomeini was actually speaking "literally" and not figuratively about his faith. This literality, this "obsession with fixed beliefs" (Rauch, 1993, p. 99), this demand for all-inclusive truths, feeds a fundamentalist mentality that requires absolute certitude at all times. In order to belong to the fold, one must ask no questions, provoke no disagreements, express no doubts, and entertain no alternatives. Khomeini's "story" is so sure of itself that its "readers" are strictly forbidden, even under the sentence of death, to consider the plausibility of any alternative narratives.

Religious fundamentalists like Khomeini, Pastor Muller, Charles Colson, and Pat Robertson, as well as many of the guests who come to my class, judge those of us who refuse to yield to the presumed certainties of the fundamentalist narrative to be lost souls, miscreants who choose, either out of ignorance or arrogance, to live beyond the Truth. If there is to be any hope for us, they warn, we must undergo a major *metanoia*. We must realize that because exclusive Truth resides only *inside* the fundamentalist narrative, and because all opposing religious stories exist *outside* the text, then just two choices are possible for us: Either we must deny the outside text and achieve salvation, or we must accept the outside text and live a life of self-deception, loss, and ultimate damnation. Only the fundamentalist orientation guarantees us the final positive outcome. The fundamentalist narrative alone tells us the one true religious story worth hearing.

Reverend Bailey Smith, president of the Southern Baptist Convention in 1980, in an address to the membership, captured the self-certain, totalizing spirit of the fundamentalist narrative frighteningly well:

> God Almighty does not hear the prayer of a Jew. . . . because no one can pray unless he prays through the name of Jesus Christ. It is not Jesus among many. It is Jesus, and Jesus only. It is Christ only. There is no competition for Jesus Christ. (quoted in Gomes, 1996, p. 105)

Even in the midst of the huge controversy that Smith's perceived anti-Semitic comments stirred up, he held fast to the superiority of his fundamentalist story by quoting over and over again the following biblical proof-texts (Gomes, 1996, p. 106): "For there is but one God, and one mediator between God and men, the man Christ Jesus" (I Timothy 2:5); and "Neither is there salvation in any other: For there is none other name under heaven given among men, whereby we must be saved" (Acts 4: 12). For Smith, God has spoken: Unless one prays as a Christian, believes as a Christian, and reads the Bible as a Christian, then God turns a deaf ear to any and all entreaties in His name.

The unwavering confidence that there is "only salvation in Christ Jesus's name" (Gomes, 1996, p. 105) was brought home to my class one day with shocking suddenness. One of our graduate students, an extremely pleasant, hitherto quiet man and a principal of a very orthodox Christian school, made the following comment in class:

> I agree with the principle of pluralism when it refers to race and ethnicity, but *not* when it includes religion. Religious pluralism, as an ideal, is bankrupt, a sham, because it assumes that religious differences are merely a matter of opinion and taste, and not a matter of absolute truth. This is unacceptable to me as a conservative Christian. I believe that those people who profess to be Christians, but who are willing to privatize their faith and their life, are religious cowards. They are living an existence absolutely antithetical to the teachings of the Bible. As a Christian, I am called to proclaim my commitment to the one truth that alone will set me free. When I fail to do this, I have betrayed the principles of my Christian faith, and I am lost. Religious pluralism is a recipe for spiritual disaster, because it courts error in the name of political correctness.

What this educator believed, as a matter of uncompromising conviction, was that Christian schools must take seriously the necessity of indoctrination in everything they do. He noted that 90% of the time any child spends in school (Christian or public) is actually spent on indoctrination, via the hidden curriculum, and the other 10% is spent on instruction. For him, the major purpose of Christian education is to teach the absolute truth, as revealed in the Bible, and this can be accomplished only through *catechesis*: oral religious training using rote questions and answers, example, and instruction.

The other students in my class—confirmed secular pluralists all—found the disclosure highly upsetting because, after many hours of subsequent conversation, both in and out of class, they were unable to shake a colleague's conviction that the Christian story alone is the one story worth teaching in a democracy, to the deliberate exclusion of all others. Although not as overtly bigoted as Reverend Bailey Smith, the suspected anti-Semite, the fundamentalist principal's convictions were just as discomfiting to my students because for them his assertions led in only one direction: His students must learn to accept a single truth unquestioningly, and to suppress all other alternative views. They worried rightly that the lesson many of his Christian students would bring home with them would be emphatically anti-democratic: Religious dissidence is repugnant, and religious totalitarianism, in the service of biblical truth, is always and everywhere desirable.

One other alarming example of how an all-encompassing religious narrative tries to drive out, stigmatize, or demonize opposing texts comes readily to mind. I recently brought to class an expensive-looking publication I received from a group calling itself the Citizens Commission on Human Rights International (CCHRI). The booklet, *Creating Evil: Psychiatry Destroying Religion in the Name of Salvation* (1997), published by the United States International Association of Scientologists Members' Trust, was sent to me gratis, as well as to every one of my colleagues at the university where I work, and was accompanied by a personal letter from a Shelly Uscinski. Uscinski, a "Christian mother" of three children, and a local school board member, tells us unequivocally how horrified she is because the public schools are "foisting" sex education and "self-esteem" training on children as young as age 6. Uscinski comes to the dire conclusion that the villain is "not teachers, but psychiatry and psychology." She is convinced that the mental health profession has usurped the church's role in improving humanity, not only by blaming organized religion for setting the stage for two world wars, the threat of nuclear destruction, and natural disasters, but by infiltrating the churches themselves with "humanistic," and psychotherapeutic, methods of problem-solving.

The glossy booklet features short, exposé-like articles with such titles as "Religion Under Attack," "Psychology: Eradicating Souls," "Psychology Destroys Pastoral Counseling," "Rogerian Therapy Destroys Religious Orders," "Psychiatry Desecrates Jesus and the Christian Church," and "Psychiatry Eradicates Morals." The accompanying photographs are deliberately meant to shock: On the booklet's cover is a snake wrapped menacingly around the Christian cross (various snakes in all their fearsome ugliness appear frequently throughout the booklet). Inside is a picture of a starkly empty church; graphs that purport to show the extent of various crises caused by psychology's ascendancy (dwindling church membership and growing rates of suicide, drug addiction, violent crime, and teen pregnancy); and photographs of a rat in a cage; gruesome scenes of Holocaust victims; an array of self-help books; group therapy sessions; a terrifying surgical operation on the frontal lobe; an involuntary commitment scene; a Holy Bible in a trash basket; a helpless, very young, pregnant teenager obviously in her final trimester; and a cartoon showing the "grim reaper" chopping down Jesus on the cross while declaring, "Your kind are no longer needed." All of these highly disturbing images, presented as the inevitable byproducts of a "godless" mental health profession, are at times juxtaposed with scenes depicting the peace and blessedness of Christian life, from churches full of devout worshippers, to prayerful nuns, to a nuclear family humbly saying grace before dinner in a 1950s-style home.

When my students closely examine the booklet, though, they become angry and cynical. The text is far from compelling for them, because the story it tells is so simplistic, overwrought, and reductive. The Commission author (never identified) draws too sharp a line between good (conservative Christianity) and evil (psychiatry and psychology), and ends up creating a mishmash of outrageous stereotypes and caricatures. No honest attempt is ever made to distinguish between good and bad social science; rather, it is all unredeemably sinister and harmful. The language in the booklet's story is so one-dimensional and polarized, so utterly devoid of imagination or subtlety, that students tend to disregard, rather than to challenge or learn from, its extremist declarations.

While most of my students, including counselors and psychiatric social workers, accept the reality that psychologists and psychiatrists have a professional responsibility to respond to a careful critique of their abuses and excesses (we have at various times read, for example, Foucault, 1965/1988; Rieff, 1966/1987; and Szasz, 1974), they reasonably refuse to make these disciplines the ultimate culprits in causing all the world's ills. In the words of the CCHRI writer (1997), psychiatry and psychology are responsible for the creation of "war and conflict," and for "destroy[ing] peace and harmony." They have also produced the following: "millions enslaved by nerve-damaging drugs and barbaric treatments, a drugged and illiterate society deprived of spirituality and religious guidance" (pp. 62–63). And when the author finally gets around to presenting a Christian wish list of "solutions" (pp. 64–65)—including, of course, the obligatory advice that "churches must rid schools of atheistic psychological and psychiatric curriculums," and that clerics and parishioners must "insist only on *scriptural*, moral approaches to address inevitable problems in life"—then my students recoil with incredulity. How, they wonder publicly, can they ever acquiesce to such a one-sided, oversimplified account of complex human problems? Thus, in this case, the fundamentalist narrative fails because the story it tells is unconvincing to many of my students who must live their lives, and practice their professions, in a less than certain, shades-of-gray world.

THE FUNDAMENTALIST NARRATIVE AND POLITICS

In his ringing critique of fundamentalism, Rauch (1993) identifies the foremost "fundamentalist social principle" he finds particularly terrifying: "Those who know the truth should decide who is right" (p. 100). Dissent is unacceptable. Thus, in 1989, the Ayatollah Khomeini decreed that the writer Salman Rushdie must die, because he dared to blaspheme against the Islamic understanding of absolute religious truth. Many fundamentalists—whether extremists like Khomeini or Smith or moderates like Colson—see themselves as political activists, called upon to resist the destabilizing authority of a radical liberal state, especially when it interferes with religious jurisdiction over matters of faith and morals. And just as Mohandas Gandhi and Martin Luther King Jr. justified acts of civil resistance against particular government policies because of their strongly held religious convictions, so too many fundamentalists hold that the Constitution gives them a legal right to organize into groups like Operation Rescue and become "autonomous communities of resistance" (Carter, 1993, p. 40) to those state-sanctioned policies they consider morally abhorrent. Hence, fundamentalist political leaders often appeal to the same First Amendment that some left-wing religious and political leaders do as a rationale for acting on their autonomous religious consciences.

Stephen Carter (1993) points out that fundamentalists construct their religious narrative on the central premise that the "authority of God" is always superior to the "authority of the state" (p. 38). Consequently, pivotal to the fundamentalist story is the belief that individuals are autonomous moral actors who owe their religion a separate allegiance, especially when they believe biblical principles are in collision with the state's legal/ political strictures on such issues as capital punishment, homosexuality, evolution, prayer in schools, sex education, and abortion. Carter (1993) captures the extraordinary political force of the fundamentalist narrative with these words:

> Religion ... *matters* to [some] people. ... For some, it is more real than the state. ... The essence of religious martyrdom is the sacrifice that comes from the refusal to yield to what one's society demands. (p. 42)

Thus, in the 1970s and 1980s, Jerry Falwell founded the Moral Majority and organized a number of "I Love America" conferences in order to fight "Godless Communism." Pat Robertson declared himself a candidate for the Republican presidential nomination because he claimed he heard a "direct call from God." And former President Ronald Reagan, fundamentalism's highest political officeholder, declared at a 1984 prayer breakfast in Texas that "those with a religious agenda are faithful to the nation's traditions, while those with a secular agenda are a source of intolerance in the American society" (quoted in Averill, 1989, p. 96). While in office, Reagan subsequently went on to push a religious agenda that included school prayer, strident anti-abortion rhetoric, and demonization of the Soviet Union as the "evil empire."

President Reagan's religious agenda is an excellent example of how easy it is for the fundamentalist narrative to transmute itself into a highly conservative political ideology. In Averill's (1989) words, Reagan had the ability to " . . . deliberate[ly] confuse political ideology with sectarian religion . . . and [to forge] an open, even eager, alliance with Protestant fundamentalism . . . and . . . to abet bitter polarization within the American community as a consequence" (p. 96). Even allowing for the possibility that while in office President Reagan might actually have been motivated more by political polls and horoscope readings than by holy scripture, I maintain that at some level, Reagan believed in the absolute superiority of his biblically based religious principles, and thus was willing to become a potential political martyr in behalf of certain conservative causes.

In this reading, Reagan and other fundamentalists who risk publicly subverting democratic politics and the will of the courts see themselves less as religious fanatics than as devoutly principled believers, rightfully exercising their constitutional rights to act politically on their deepest personal convictions. It is not for them to create an easy (or even uneasy) alliance with the liberal state over such issues as welfare policy, euthanasia, abortion, same-sex marriage, and, perhaps the most explosive topic of all, the usurpation of power by the Supreme and federal courts. Rather, fundamentalists see themselves serving as a radical countercultural force to all the evils of modernism, including humanism, individualism, secularism, rationalism, pluralism, atheism, and hedonism.

Whenever we read fundamentalist Christians such as Jerry Falwell, Pat Robertson, Ronald Reagan, and even the more irenic evangelicals, Ralph Reed (1996) and former President Jimmy Carter, most of my students are willing to grant the truth of the following proposition: *Fundamentalism as a transcendental narrative is potentially most dangerous whenever it encroaches into political territory.* In fact, I, and they, would argue that fundamentalism must, of necessity, always be in conflict with a constitutional democracy because, at least in theory, democracy is meant to be a government of, by, and for the people, and not of, by, and for the Bible and its authoritative translators. For democratic, liberal, nonfundamentalist citizens, the Constitution is always a living document, subject forever to changing political interpretations and social contexts. It is a document amenable everywhere to the interpretive voices of responsible dissenters, to those whose defining texts are as likely to be diversely secular, even irreverent, as they are to be monolithically religious.

Lloyd J. Averill (1989) argues that Christian fundamentalists who attempt to usurp democratic politics have grossly misread American history. For him, the founding fathers were actually pluralists and deists, not monolithic theocrats who believed in a personal creator. John Adams, Thomas Jefferson, and James Madison celebrated the virtues of ideological pluralism, and they argued eloquently for the extension of religious freedom to everyone, including agnostics, atheists, and pagans. Averill goes on to demonstrate that religious fundamentalists actually show great "hostility" to American traditions such as the constitutional separation of powers, the disestablishment of religion clause in the First Amendment, and constitutional protection for criminals.

In sum, what bothers Averill (1989) most about fundamentalism, with its political pretensions, is its disdain for democratic traditions, often masked by a concern for "traditional family values." Averill inveighs against fundamentalism's inherent hostility to the Constitution, because this document encourages ideological pluralism and multiple interpretations. Mostly, though, Averill fears fundamentalism's tendency to polarize people ideologically, on the basis that because there is only *one* truth, and that truth resides in holy scripture, then only the Bible is able to empower individuals (pp. 89–125). Only fundamentalists are able to read the Constitution as the framers intended it, because in fundamentalists' eyes, the framers were God-fearing Christians whose political insights were inspired by the Bible.

As if to confirm the truth of Averill's fears, Peshkin (1988) lets us listen in on a headmaster of a conservative Christian school as he makes a stunning anti-pluralist announcement to his captive students one morning in chapel: "The Word of the Lord is the [only] source of our power. You are to be saturated with it, to sow it; and to know it [alone] is always the solution" (p. 294).

And, sadly, as if to presage the death of a pluralist democracy, and along with it all of its dissenting opinions, Peshkin goes on to remark that not a single student or adult in attendance that morning was able, or willing, to offer one word of resistance to the headmaster's pronouncement. Not one of them, faithful or unfaithful, behaving or misbehaving, was "boldly heretical enough to utter a dissenting word . . . for to do so [was] to risk riding a yellow bus to the nearest tax-supported school" (p. 294).

Finally, while I have never heard a single student of mine declare publicly that religious fundamentalists ought to be legally banned from engaging in political activity in the "naked public square," most nevertheless express great reservations over the efforts of such anti-pluralists as Falwell and Robertson during the last 20 years to conflate the sacred and the secular realms. For me, the overwhelming, and most deadly, implication of the transcendental narrative is, in Peshkin's (1988) words, "to put political power at the service of doctrinal ends" (p. 288). Historically, whenever this happens, sooner or later the orthodox believer and the questioning heretic come to verbal, and subsequently to physical, blows. What we in the United States gratuitously have come to call "mean-spiritedness" in political discourse has all too often ended up in terrible warfare in other countries. Elsewhere, ratcheted-up expressions of religious incivility, mixed in with generous doses of ethnic and racial hostility, occur almost always as an ominous precursor to violence. Soon after comes the actual hell of an Israeli Left Bank, a Northern Ireland, an Iran, a Cyprus, a Lebanon, or a Yugoslavia. The ultimate losers, to be sure, are always peace, pluralism, and democracy.

TEXTS AND HERMENEUTICS

Before I can examine the impact of biblical interpretation on the fundamentalist narrative, I need first to devote this section to a brief discussion of two of my favorite words: *text* and *hermeneutics*. My students hear me use these two words very often during the semester. In fact, if I could give any advice at all to educators regarding the actual teaching of the four religious narratives, I would urge them to first learn the meaning of these two terms. Teachers need not be professional theologians or philosophers to effectively explore religious meanings with students so long as they are knowledgeable about, and assiduously attentive to, the many pedagogical uses of text and hermeneutics. I will go so far as to say that in over 30 years of teaching at the college level, plus several years at the secondary public school level, no two terms have served me better as instructional tools in the classroom.

Although I have never actually taught a formal methods course for teachers in the humanities or social sciences, I know immediately what my first four (admittedly unorthodox) required readings would be if I did: Stanley Fish's (1980) *Is There a Text in This Class? The Authority of Interpretive Communities*; Terry Eagleton's (1983) *Literary Theory: An Introduction*; and two by Robert Scholes (1985, 1989), *Textual Power: Literary Theory and the Teaching of English* and *Protocols of Reading*. Each of these texts is highly accessible to nonspecialists. Each is didactic in the best sense of the word, incisively instructive on matters of textuality and interpretation, while written with elegance and passion. And each text is a wonderful example in itself of how best to use the literary method the author advocates as a pedagogical strategy.

More specifically, in relation to teaching religion, I would also assign two indispensable texts on interpretation written by evangelical Christian hermeneutes: Peter J. Gomes's (1996) *The Good Book: Reading the Bible with Mind and Heart* (especially Chapter 2), and Karl Keating's (1988) *Catholicism and Fundamentalism: The Attack on "Romanism" by "Bible Christians."* In my opinion, Gomes's (1996) chapter "A Matter of Interpretation" is the single best account of biblical hermeneutics I have ever read. And Keating's (1988) entire text is a superb critical dissection of the way Protestant fundamentalists deliberately misuse scriptural proof-texts in order to attack, among others, Catholic doctrines and beliefs. (Also, see an excellent collection of essays on hermeneutics and biblical analysis, McKim, *A Guide to Contemporary Hermeneutics: Major Trends in Biblical Interpretation*, 1986.)

At the outset of every course I teach, I usually assert that a text (L., *textus*, a weaving pattern) is a kind of woven fabric, complex and multilayered, with meaning frequently beyond its own terms. That is to say, a text is "woven" out of other texts (what I call the *inter-text*) in that words, concepts, and paragraphs are fundamentally influenced and surrounded by texts that come before, or accompany the particular text in question. The language, concepts, arguments, and meanings in a text are dynamic: They shift around constantly, and are almost always elusive. Thus, nobody can ever have the last word on what a text means, or what the author actually intended. All meanings are indeterminate. Despite the impossibility of discovering the "final word" on a text's meaning, however, it is still my belief that all texts, particularly the Bible, are eminently worthy of study.

I also specify for my students that when we talk about religion, it is essential that we think of each other as living "texts" as well. Each of us, I submit, is an evolving religious narrative, a story in the process of being constructed, a special container of religious meanings that is complex and multilayered. In order to expose and to understand the religious dimensions of the personal text we are "writing," we must exercise significant amounts of humility, patience, discernment, and sensitivity with each other in our classroom conversations, because in a very real sense we are all "texts," studying other "texts," on the way to becoming a relatively finished "text" ourselves.

Each of us (students, authors, and instructor) is a complex container of meanings. As we encounter each other for the first time in a class, we must realize that each of us embodies a particular *pre-text* (we hold prior religious/metaphysical assumptions), a *context* (we inhabit particular social, political, religious, and educational worlds), an *inter-text* (we draw upon prior textual influences in our lives, including formative readings, persons, and events), *proof-texts* (we reiterate pivotal passages, quotations, and assertions from cherished authors and others in order to prove our points), and a *post-text* (we are always in the process of "writing" our personal [religious] narrative, enlarging, deepening, and enriching the religious language we already possess).

Texts are never simply read; they are always interpreted. *Hermeneutics* (Gr., "skilled in interpretation") is a word named after the god Hermes, the herald and messenger of the other Greek gods. Hermes was a model of eloquence, and the Greeks highly valued his interpretive commentaries on the proclamations of the gods. I continually stress for students that while none of us is a Hermes, I still maintain that we are all "closet hermeneutes," because we are always busily interpreting what we see and hear. We cannot help ourselves. We are incessantly annotating and commenting upon the various texts that come to our attention. We are constantly adding to and subtracting from the texts we study. We are inveterate interpreters, and my message to epistemological realists, who deny the validity of interpretation, is that none of us ever "knows" an uninterpretable, immaculately perceived, objective world. Alas, seeing the world through a set of hermeneutical filters is always and everywhere our inescapable, human fate.

In fact, the only absolute statement I dare make about reality is that it is endlessly and diversely interpretable. Therefore, my, and my students' "ultimate" reality is no closer to a "true reality"—no better or worse, certain or uncertain—than anyone else's. In some cases, of course, a particular interpretation of a text will be more defensible, more eloquent, more aesthetically pleasing, and maybe even more inspiring and persuasive than someone else's. When this happens, however, it is possible to say that the meaning of a text does not reside solely in the text itself, but in a person's unique interpretation of the text as well. In a sense, then, every time we read a text we are also creating a text. Unavoidably, and gloriously, we always add as much to the text in our own right as does the author who creates the text.

Finally, I always issue a warning to my students: Every text also has an integrity of its own, because it has its own autonomy, its own right to exist as an "other," even though the "objective" quality of this "otherness" is virtually inaccessible to us. The text has at least a minimal right to our initial respect, because it exists as the author's special creation. Consequently, in my classes it is necessary for students to clarify what I call their "hermeneutical perspectives/filters." By this I mean that to a large extent, each of us is trapped in our own unique containers of fundamental meanings, beliefs, assumptions, and feelings. Our "hermeneutical filters" shape and color every observation we make about a text. Thus it is essential that we come to terms with each other regarding our own hermeneutical perspectives whenever we are moved to make a judgment about somebody else's text. In the end, what we might think about the worth of somebody else's ideas is frequently the result of either a *coincidence* or a *collision* of hermeneutical perspectives or filters.

In this sense, then, the search for truth is less a matter of appealing to logic, science, experience, intuition, politics, or God to establish the absolute validity of our views. Rather, it is more a matter of understanding, explaining, and integrating our different (flawed) interpretations so that, possibly, some minimal (flawed) consensus might evolve. In class, we spend much time talking about the coincidences and collisions of differing perspectives, because in the end the ultimate purpose of spending our time together discussing different religious narratives is to deepen, enrich, and enlarge the religious languages we presently possess. The readings, guests, and conversations we have with each other serve mainly to focus our many religious coincidences and collisions, and occasionally we even discover common ground, although consensus remains a rare achievement.

IS THE BIBLE ONLY A MATTER OF INTERPRETATION?

Most fundamentalists would heatedly deny everything I have said above about texts and interpretation. For fundamentalists, the Bible is an objectively constituted text that God dictated literally. In all cases, the Bible says what it means and means what it says, *period*, and readers must be ever vigilant to avoid reading between the lines for meaning. No reader commentary is appropriate unless it squares with the authoritative readings of fundamentalist preachers. Moreover, for most fundamentalists, the authors of the various books in both the Old and New Testaments were little more than secretaries who agreed to take God's dictation verbatim. Gomes (1996) relates a humorous anecdote highlighting the extreme to which some fundamentalists can carry their biblical literalism.

For example, in Matthew 8:12, the outer darkness into which the wicked are cast is described as a place where "men will weep and gnash their teeth." A toothless reprobate asked his hellfire-preaching pastor what would happen to those who had no teeth to gnash: "Teeth will be provided" was his answer. (p. 31)

During one class, I remember a particularly explosive exchange—a true "collision of hermeneutical perspectives"—that we had with a group of fundamentalist visitors when I tried to explain "reader response" or "reader reception" theory to my students. Briefly, this theory attempts to shift a reader's understanding of a book from the assumption that a text contains unassailable *objective meanings* to the perspective that a reader actually engages in the *production of meanings* within the reading process itself. Reader response and reception theorists argue that readers actually change the meanings in a text according to their "existing horizons of expectations." In this view (Baldick, 1990, pp. 184–185), readers always produce as much meaning as the author, because readers are actually "rewriting" the text as they interpret it from their unique hermeneutical perspectives.

During that particular class period, I created the following "five-text strategy" to illustrate my point:

Take the gospel of John in the New Testament. *This gospel is actually 5 different texts.* Text 1 is the gospel John thought he was writing. This is the *author's text*. Text 2 is the gospel each one of you thinks John wrote. This is the *individual reader's text*. Text 3 is the gospel that John actually wrote. This is the *objective text*. Text 4 is the gospel that each one of you is "writing" as you interpret this gospel from your own cultural and historical context. This is the *hermeneutical text-in-process*. And text 5 is the gospel you and I might be able to agree on as the gospel that John intended to write. This is the *consensus text*.

None of us can ever know with any degree of certainty the truth of text 1, because we do not know what was in John's mind while he was writing. Neither can we ever fully capture text 3, because there is no such thing as an "immaculate reception" of a text, absolutely devoid of a reader's, or writer's, presuppositions. In fact, to speak of an "objective" text makes no sense at all, because without "subjects" to read and interpret the text, the text has no inherent meaning. The only texts worth studying, then, are text 2, text 4, and text 5; and while text 5 is certainly worth pursuing, universal consensus on *all* meanings in any text is virtually unachievable. Thus, we are left only with text 2 and text 4 as texts to analyze, and because these texts are always subject to very personal readings and commentaries, then, in a real sense, when we study the gospel of John, we are really studying ourselves.

When I finished, the fundamentalist visitors erupted in amazement. "You're nothing but a relativist," yelled one. Another accused me of "undermining" the inerrancy of the Bible by reducing the book of John to a "Rorschach Ink Blot Test" (a diagnostic personality inventory based on a viewer's interpretations of a series of inkblot designs). Still another visitor charged me with the "devil's hubris," because I was arrogant enough to think that my reading of the Bible was "wiser than God's." And a fundamentalist minister pulled out the ultimate "doomsday weapon": He reproached me and the class with the complaint that we were all "atheistic postmodernists" for whom "nothing was sacred," and for whom everything, even "God's Holy Word," was up for grabs. And he added for good measure: "This is exactly what's wrong with universities today and, particularly, with teacher-training programs."

I believe the fundamentalist visitors were deluding themselves in thinking that they alone had unmediated access to a sacred book so historically distant from us in today's postmodern world, a book so diversely translated and interpreted throughout the centuries that its precise intent and meaning are virtually irretrievable 2,000 years later. Who among our visitors could ever know for sure the "literal" meaning of every single biblical proof-text, especially those separate passages that seem to contradict one another on such topics as homosexuality, sex, women, social justice, sin, war, the afterlife, wealth, even love? (See Gomes, 1996, and Spong, 1991, for examples of several proof-texts containing glaringly humorous *and* serious contradictions.) David Blacker, in a personal correspondence with me, notes that claims of unmediated biblical interpretations remind him of the school board member who said against foreign language instruction, "If English was good enough for Jesus, it's good enough for me." Which is to say that whether we wish to acknowledge it or not, alas, we are always "interpreting ourselves" in our *own* "languages," sometimes literally, sometimes allegorically, and sometimes, like the school board member, foolishly.

I believe that Gomes (1996), unlike our fundamentalist visitors, arrives at a felicitous balance on matters of biblical interpretation. He manages to hold all five of my "texts" in a desirable, dialectical tension, by asking his students to "trust the text, trust themselves, trust the people, and trust the Spirit" (p. 34) when reading the Bible. For him, there is an "interpretive triangle" in biblical reading whereby author, text, and reader are mutually interdependent. Because readers seldom read the Bible in isolation; and because the Bible is a text held in high estimation in the community; and because the authors of the Bible always wrote out of the contexts of their particular communities; then, according to Gomes, a "proper reading" of the Bible requires an "interpreter's freedom," along with "some degree of external, corporate authority" (p. 29).

Gomes insists that fundamentalists themselves, in fact, read their Bibles this way because they belong to a particular faith community, and hence they consciously or unconsciously impose the assumptions of that community onto the very texts they claim are beyond personal interpretation. I agree with Gomes that fundamentalists proudly display their interpretive biases without always knowing it. For example, fundamentalists express a prior belief in biblical inerrancy and in original intent (the latter admittedly a worthy ideal to pursue, while empirically unachievable), even though they are unable to cite a single unequivocal biblical proof-text to support these hermeneutical biases. According to one biblical scholar, *there is no such definitive proof-text* (Keating, 1988). Thus, fundamentalists themselves are susceptible to the modernist "errors" of selective interpretation and the construction of self-interested post-texts.

In Gomes's construction, historical biblical *contexts* always, to some extent, relativize biblical *texts*. And while the Spirit is indeed necessary for biblical instruction, so too is serious scholarly study. Finally, while some degree of objective analysis of the Word is called for, likewise a reader's presuppositions appear inevitable, and subjective interpretation must therefore count proportionately. Gomes (1996) rejects reading the Bible "as one would a fortune cookie," because this type of reading is too passive, too hit-or-miss. Rather, he wants readers to "trust" the text, not because it is scientifically verifiable or because it makes them feel good, but because the Bible "in its infinite variety points to the truth" without actually being the "truth" (p. 35).

One danger of a fundamentalist reading of the Bible, for Gomes (1996), is "bibliolatry," by which he means the tendency to substitute the Bible for God, to reduce the full essence of God to what historically situated, fallible human authors had to say about Him. For Gomes, the Bible must always be *less* than the God it proclaims. Another danger for Gomes is "literalism," the temptation to look to the Bible for an absolutely "reliable and fixed content and meaning." Gomes and I are in agreement that literalism is indefensible because the "doctrine of original intent" is an impossibility, given the role that hermeneutics plays in every individual's, and community's, textual reading. Finally, fundamentalists commit what Gomes calls the fallacy of "culturalism," the tempting inclination to use the Bible to support the sociopolitical status quo—this in direct defiance of the revolutionary political content in the Bible itself. Gomes goes to great lengths to show how people have used the Bible through the centuries to justify slaveholding, anti-Semitism, homophobia, and sexism. In Gomes's (1996) disturbing words:

> In the American South of slavery and segregation . . . most people could not be appealed to on the basis of the constraints of conscience because they understood themselves to be good and faithful people who were simply doing God's will. They read the Bible, they heard their preachers, they said their prayers, and they knew in their hearts that they were right and justified by the Bible. . . . Yet the very gospel they used to maintain the status quo would eventually destroy that status quo, and that is the story that remains to be told. (p. 51)

CONCLUSIONS

The fundamentalist religious narrative ultimately fails, not only because it is anti-intellectual and dangerously political, but because it is starkly antithetical to the spirit of independent thinking required by a democracy. If a critical-minded hermeneutic is out, then biblical authoritarianism (what Stephen L. Carter [1993] calls a "hermeneutic of literalism") must be in. Somewhere a centralized force, a political or religious magisterium, will decide for all of us what is to be the "right" sacred text to read, what is to be the "right" meaning of the "right" scriptural proof-text, what is to constitute the "right" truth as designated by the "right" God, and who among us must be marginalized, or worse, terrorized, as heretics. In fact, this may already be happening in some public school systems in the United States. In response to political and educational pressures from the Christian Coalition, school boards in communities such as Fort Myers, Florida; Charlotte, North Carolina; Des Moines, Iowa; and Ramona, California have mandated that high school curricula must include both elective *and* required courses on what they call "Bible history." One fundamentalist school board member (reported in Baker, 1997) in Fort Myers, Florida, remarked: "In Florida, we must teach black history and the Holocaust. It's mandatory. So why not the Bible as an elective? It's the oldest textbook I know of" (p. A22). And Charles Haynes (reported in Baker, 1997), a conservative Christian scholar at the First Amendment Center at Vanderbilt University, supports this move to teach Bible history in the public schools. He contends:

> A new consensus is emerging. . . . There is much more agreement than disagreement [on teaching the Bible], but we have been shouting past one

another for so long about prayer that we have missed opportunities to transform how public schools deal with religion. (p. A22)

What is potentially alarming to me about this fundamentalist educational initiative is that some secular school boards with biblically inerrant leanings are currently acting in a quasi-magisterial capacity, deciding that, first, the Bible is indeed a *historical* document, and second, that public school students *must read* this document because it represents world history. While I support teaching the Bible as one type of religious *literature* (pointing out its peculiar narrative strengths and weaknesses), I worry that the next step in some of these counties will be for school boards to require that teachers adopt a hermeneutic of strict literalism in teaching the Bible as a historical chronicle. Moreover, at least one critic (reported in Baker, 1997) of this biblical initiative agrees with me, charging that "the Bible isn't history. Nobody believes it accurately reports world history. It doesn't even acknowledge a world outside the Middle East, where it takes place" (p. A22).

While I readily acknowledge that in an *intellectual* sense, the fundamentalist mentality remains alive and well in all of us, religious or nonreligious, premodern or postmodern, conservative or liberal, capitalist or socialist—and, I believe, is one that educators ought to check, even discredit, at every opportunity—I still find the fundamentalist mentality of the *religious* believer to be particularly alarming. In the 17th century, John Locke, British philosopher and author of the monumental *An Essay Concerning Human Understanding* (1690/1959), depicted religious zealots in a way that forcibly captures the fundamentalist style that today I find so disturbing:

> They see the light infused into their understandings, and cannot be mistaken; it is clear and visible there, like the light of bright sunshine; shows itself, and needs no other proof but its own evidence: they feel the hand of God moving them within, and the impulses of the Spirit, and cannot be mistaken in what they feel. Whatsoever odd action they find in themselves a strong inclination to do, that impulse is concluded to be a call or direction from heaven, and must be obeyed: it is a commission from above, and they cannot err in executing it. (Quoted in Rauch, 1993, pp. 93–94)

The fundamentalist religious narrative, despite its understandable seductiveness during times of social upheaval, culture wars, moral decline, and postmodern nihilism, is ultimately a perilous perspective, because in Rauch's (1993) words, "purges, jihads, crackdowns on the independent minded, and violent schisms are common" (p. 9). Whether an ayatollah or pope, a cult leader or a Jimmy Swaggert, those who feel the "hand of God moving them within," and who see their "crackdowns" on apostates as a "commission from above," are genuinely to be feared in a democracy. If it is true, as I contend, that religious fundamentalism is a powerful counter-discourse in the world today, primarily because it appeals to those among us who are profoundly disenchanted with the false promises of modernism and secularism, then the educational antidote is clear. What schools and colleges ought to be offering students at this time is a number of alternative religious discourses—"counter-counter" discourses, if you will—that effectively refute the false claims of the fundamentalist narrative, *and* the modernist and secularist narratives as well. As an educator, I for one do not intend to exempt the latter two orientations from close critical scrutiny.

In the next two chapters, I explore the viability of the prophetic religious worldview in becoming an effective counter-narrative to these other worldviews.

CHAPTER 4

The Prophetic Narrative

If fundamentalism tends to be the religious narrative of biblical premodernists, then the prophetic narrative is the religious inclination of many politically disenchanted modernist/liberals. A few years ago, one of my students brought to class a couple of *Doonesbury* comic strips depicting a very liberal, New Age kind of Protestant pastor who presided over the "Little Church of Walden." In one of the comic strips, the liberal reverend is reporting on the upcoming weekly events to his church community. After the listing of such church-sponsored activities as holistic nutrition, drug- and sex-addiction 12-step groups, organic co-gardening, and aerobic male bonding, one of the parishioners asks if there will be a church service. The pastor reluctantly acknowledges that the service has been cancelled due to a conflict with the self-esteem workshop.

In the second comic strip, the same reverend is interviewing a couple who are inquiring about becoming members of the Walden church community. In response to their question about his particular approach to the gospel, the pastor remarks that he is a 12-step Christian minister who sees his flock as a group of recovering sinners needing to overcome denial, and to seek redemption and re-commitment. The couple, obviously upset with the pastor's notion of sin and redemption, express their concerns over being made to feel guilty. Both assert that they are looking for a supportive community where they can feel good about themselves, not one where they have to deal with sin and guilt. And even though the church at Walden offers racquetball, the couple decides to shop around some more, and perhaps visit the Unitarians.

The student confessed to the class that these comic strips symbolized, for her, everything that was wrong with liberal Christianity. Raised a Methodist, she deeply regretted the turn in her own church, during the last decade, toward what she called a "psychologized Christianity"—a notion of sin as being in denial, and "yuppie self-esteem workshops." She refused, she said, to join the fundamentalist church community in the next town because these people went to the other extreme—"pounding their Bibles, speaking in tongues, holding healing services, and singing sappy hymns." "Where," she asked, "is there a religion with flesh on its bones, that stands for something against the self-centeredness of yuppie/ generation-X life, that is not so open-minded that its brain falls out, nor so close-minded that its brain implodes?" Her final question was a challenge to all of us: "Is it possible for me to be a religious person in the mainline liberal churches without making personal compromises, without losing my intellectual and spiritual integrity, and without becoming a dropout who, out of desperation, joins these know-nothing fundamentalist groups?"

THE PROPHETIC WORLDVIEW, FUNDAMENTALISM, AND MODERNISM

I find that the majority of my students have given up the religions of their childhood precisely because they believe these religious traditions are either too "open-minded" or too "close-minded," too permissive or too authoritarian. Although a few students manage to find what they are seeking in the fundamentalist story, some abandon Christianity or Judaism all together and look toward an "alternative spiritualities narrative" (see Chapters 6 and 7) to satisfy their religious needs. A small minority even become what I call "post-theists" (see Chapters 8 and 9), more than happy to move beyond a traditional, or even a New Age, conception of God and spirituality to a postmodern agnosticism or atheism. However, for those students in my classes who continue to seek spiritual sustenance in the more liberal, mainline (Jewish, Protestant, and Catholic) churches of their youth, the *Doonesbury* comic strip is an unsettling caricature of liberal theology whose basic truth comes a little too close for comfort.

In contrast, what I am calling the "prophetic narrative" appeals to some students' social idealism, to their sense that the religious experience does not always have to be doctrinally hidebound or spiritually ethereal, neither a self- nor world-denying experience. Many of those students who were raised in more liberal religious traditions want their churches to become deeply involved in the social and political struggles of the day, especially in the search for social justice. They yearn for a religious account that is utopian, political, and hopeful, one that is personally liberating *and* socially transforming. Many resonate with Segundo's (1976) assertion that all religions are political, always implicated, in some way, in maintaining the established status quo. Thus they refuse to look for "scapegoats," choosing instead to acknowledge full responsibility for their own (and their churches') complicity in maintaining systems of injustice throughout the society.

The prophetic worldview shares some things in common with the fundamentalist worldview (Skillen, 1990), substantive political, theological, and philosophical differences notwithstanding. Both can be equally contemptuous of modernism's excesses, particularly the enthronement of individual autonomy, progress, efficiency, productivity, capitalism, bureaucratization, and scientific rationalization. Both are highly critical of the rampant ethic of hedonism that pervades consumer-driven, capitalist societies. Both emphasize the significance of community in restoring the desired religious vision. Both refer to common traditions in the American historical heritage whenever this suits their own religious, educational, and political purposes. Both possess a transcendent, utopian ideal for what they believe the state, and education, ought to be. Both appeal to a concept of the "common good" in order to rally people to their causes. And both readily use the gospel to critique what they perceive to be "sinful" social structures.

Where the worldviews diverge sharply, of course, is that the fundamentalist narrative appears to be more accepting of the existence of *economic stratification* throughout American society, in the name of a valorized individual liberty, while the prophetic narrative more easily tolerates the loss of *common moral standards* in the society, in the name of a valorized pluralism. The prophetic worldview, in contrast to the fundamentalist, and even the modernist, is more likely to interpret its mission as *pro-justice*. Its primary function, therefore, is to expose the evils of social, political, and economic oppression throughout the social order. This worldview frequently speaks the language of civil rights, peace, justice, equality, solidarity, liberation, and social democracy. Dietrich Bonhoeffer (1944/1967) accurately captures the prophetic intent. He advances a worldview that "sees the great events of world history from below, from the perspectives of the outcasts, the suspects, the maltreated, the powerless, the oppressed, the reviled" (p. 134). For Bonhoeffer and other prophetic thinkers, we must always read history from the perspective of the sufferers, rather than that of the privileged.

Actually, the prophetic religious perspective is an ancient one, and most students are genuinely surprised when they learn of its influence on the world's major religions. Prophets show up in a number of religious traditions, including the Native American, Jewish, Islamic, Babist, Baha'i, and Christian. In these traditions, a prophet, always charismatic, is a highly variegated person, at times a respected professional, at other times a socially marginal figure; often very political; and occasionally a shaman or a cultic personality. At various times, prophets have engaged in telling the future, social protest, millenarian preaching, healing, and preparing the way for the eventual appearance of some divine presence on Earth.

Despite their different emphases, though, what most prophets have in common is their tendency to act as *social critics*—emissaries on a mission from God to hold people accountable whenever their social actions are antithetical to their professed religious ideals.

The Jewish educational scholar David E. Purpel (1989) writes eloquently of what he calls the "prophetic tradition" in his well-received *The Moral & Spiritual Crisis in Education: A Curriculum for Justice and Compassion in Education*. Some of my students find this text to be profoundly disquieting when we read it because, for the first time ever, an educator is willing to openly discuss spiritual matters with them, in the context of their everyday work in the schools and colleges. Inspired by the two-volume work of the Jewish intellectual Abraham Joshua Heschel (1962), author of *The Prophets*, Purpel asserts the following:

> The prophetic voice speaks most directly to issues of justice and righteousness; it is a voice that not only roars in protest at oppression, inequity, poverty, and hunger but cries out in pain and compassion. (p. 81)

And later, quoting Heschel himself, Purpel (1989) declares that a prophet's

> images must not shine, they must burn. The prophet is intent on intensifying responsibility, is impatient of excuse, contemptuous of pretense and self-pity.... his words are often slashing ... designed to shock rather than to edify ... [the prophet is concerned with] wrenching one's conscience from the state of suspended animation. (p. 81)

Whenever we read Purpel, who gives the impression in his text (1989) that he thinks of himself as a kind of modern-day educational prophet, some of my mainline religious students find a spiritual voice they can genuinely respect. While it is true that Purpel makes many of my students very uncomfortable—because they see themselves as the guilty legatees of a middle-class American privilege he indicts—his voice does manage, very effectively, to shake the foundations of their comfortable liberal/ modernist worldviews. Along with his message of social responsibility and justice, Purpel delivers a religious message of hope and faith to students. As an educator, he believes that teachers, like the ancient prophets, must speak out against oppression and inequality wherever these evils occur, and they must do this both critically and compassionately. Mohandas K. Gandhi and Martin Luther King Jr. serve as Purpel's religious models, each coming from distinctively different prophetic traditions.

Both of these prophets combined their struggle for social justice with such universal religious themes as love, compassion, hope, faith, and forgiveness. Not only did Gandhi and King righteously denounce oppression and corruption in all social institutions, they also called for direct political action in these settings based on a Hindu-Christian strategy of nonviolent resistance (Skt., *ahimsa*). They incorporated into their political philosophy such Hindu virtues as self-control (Skt., *dama*), detachment (Skt., *vairagya*), fortitude (Skt., *virya*), compassion (Skt., *daya*), self-understanding (Skt., *swayam-gyan*), self-sacrifice (Skt., *tyag*), and self-transformation (Skt., *swayam-parivartan*). For Purpel, this strategy of nonviolent resistance (Skt., *satyagraha*) is calculated to raise the consciousness of all of us, both participants *and* observers, by alerting us to possibilities for transformation in our own lives.

Because each of us lives in a dominant culture that continues to tolerate certain types of injustice and exploitation, Purpel reminds us that as prophets, we too must work relentlessly to restructure those systems of injustice in all areas of the society in which we are directly involved, including, of course, schools and colleges. Once again, Purpel's words both disturb and inspire many of my students, particularly those who were reared in mainline churches:

> [Prophetic education] involves sharp criticism, dazzling imagination, a sacred perspective, commitment to justice and compassion, hope, energy, and involvement. Freedom does not come, according to the prophets, from adaptation and acceptance, nor does freedom emerge out of numbness and callousness to injustice. Freedom for the prophets emerges from caring, and lies in hope, possibility, and commitment. (p. 85)

EARLY PROTESTANT AND CATHOLIC
PROPHETIC SOURCES

One early mainline version in this country of what I am calling the prophetic worldview flourished from 1880 to 1918 among liberal Protestants in America. The Social Gospel movement in 1907, spearheaded by the theologian Walter Rauschenbusch (grandfather of the postmodern philosopher, Richard Rorty), attempted to respond to the crises generated by modern industrial society and by a laissez-faire capitalism. Rauschenbusch emphasized the Bible's prophetic call for social justice as an important way to redress the grievances of impoverished urban workers and their families. For Rauschenbusch, God's kingdom is "a social hope . . . a 'collective conception' with political overtones" (quoted in Skillen, 1990,

p. 109). Utopian in spirit, these social reformers took a postmillennial (a thousand years of peace and harmony in a future time) view of Protestantism, and they pushed for progressive social and political reform in order to create the kingdom of God on Earth. The Social Gospel movement eventually founded a national interdenominational agency, the Federal Council of Churches of Christ in America, in 1908 (Smith, 1995, p. 1007).

In spite of its success in the liberal Protestant churches, though, the Social Gospel movement actually had little impact on American Catholicism. But it is noteworthy that Catholics later began to construct their own kind of social gospel, beginning with Pius XI's encyclical *Quadragesimo Anno* (*After 40 Years*) in 1931. This encyclical replaced the Aristotelian/Thomistic idea of *legal* justice with that of *social* justice. Now the Catholic church began to challenge social institutions according to their willingness to respond to the social, legal, economic, and political rights of all citizens. Since *Quadragesimo Anno*, the church has become a strong advocate for *economic* justice, and has urged all citizens to accomplish this goal through strenuous, organized political activity rather than through fragmented individual action (all of the encyclicals mentioned here and below are cited in McBrien, 1995, pp. 1203–1205).

Subsequent papal encyclicals, *Pacem in Terris* (*Peace on Earth*) (1963), *Populorum Progressio* (*Progress of Peoples*) (1967), and *Centesimus Annus* (*The Hundredth Year*) (1991), encouraged a movement toward "international social justice" in behalf of an international common good, whereby a just international economy was now seen as one that provided adequate distribution of goods and services to people in developing countries. J. Bryan Hehir, a noted Catholic scholar on the social teachings of the church, remarks that

> The influence of teaching on social justice may best be assessed in light of the fact that the entire social ministry of the Church is today often described simply as the work of social justice. (in McBrien, 1995, p. 1204)

As a pedagogical aside, I have never met a single Catholic student, undergraduate or graduate, who has read even one line from a papal encyclical. In fact, I cannot remember anyone who could define, even in simple terms, the meaning of an encyclical. An encyclical is a formal pastoral letter, usually written by the pope on matters of morality, doctrine, and church discipline, and addressed to people of good will everywhere (O'Keefe in McBrien, 1995, p. 465). A papal encyclical contains the latest thinking of the pope on church matters, and it has become the standard tool for the pope to exercise his teaching authority and to speak to the universal church. Sadly, though, because the encyclical as a usable text remains virtually nonexistent to most of my Catholic students, few are capable of making an informed interpretation of its contents; worse, few Catholic students seem to know anything about the content of official church doctrine. Therefore, students usually end up lampooning the idea of an encyclical rather than trying to understand its purpose, function, and teaching on its own terms. Their hermeneutic on encyclicals is one of suspicion and mistrust based on ignorance.

I usually surprise Catholic students when I point out that contrary to popular misbelief, the Catholic church does *not* consider an encyclical *per se* to contain infallible teaching. Thus in many cases the church tolerates respectful dialogue and dissent on moral, doctrinal, and disciplinary issues covered in an encyclical (Kaufman, 1989). In fact, the eight social encyclicals (1891–1991), dealing with such issues as capitalism, human rights, social justice, subsidiarity, individual liberty, the common good, and peace, were ecumenical in nature and addressed to the whole world, not just to faithful Catholics. All the social encyclicals were meant to engage the world in open-ended dialogue on significant social themes (Curran, 1985).

Even more shocking to me, and eventually to many of them as well, is that few Catholic students in my classes ever know anything about the church's past and present teachings on the issue of social justice. Beyond being able to mouth a few well-worn clichés concerning what they believe to be papal oppression and injustice against its own members *inside* the church structure itself, in my experience, Catholic students are stunningly illiterate regarding biblical, stoic, Aristotelian, Augustinian, and Thomistic conceptions of social justice *outside* church structures. Thus they remain embarrassingly oblivious to the 2,000-year link that exists between these and current Catholic social teachings, many of which are genuinely revolutionary, even Marxist, in nature.

Similarly, I would add that through the years I have had very few liberal Protestant or Reform Jewish students who grasp the social teachings of their respective religious traditions. Consequently, whenever we take the time in class to explore the historical, theological, and political backgrounds of the prophetic narrative, most students are truly amazed at the pro-justice richness of their respective religious heritages. Some Catholics choose to read the papal encyclicals on social justice for the first time (O'Brien & Shannon, 1977). Reform Jews start to engage in disciplined Torah study on the topic of social justice. And liberal Protestants begin to read the Bible "from below," from the perspectives of the politically disenfranchised and of the sufferers of economic injustice, especially those who are radically poor. And along the way, Protestant students also learn something about the Social Gospel movement.

TWO LATTER-DAY AFRICAN-AMERICAN PROPHETS

The ultimate surprise for students occurs, however, whenever we read the writings of two African-American modern-day prophets—Martin Luther King Jr., and Jesse Jackson. As a teaching device for motivating my students to examine the prophetic worldview as two contemporary social justice activists understand it, I once circulated two excerpts (from Skillen, 1990, p. 120) from the writings of King and Jackson. I was at once struck by how the uncompromisingly strong *religious* allegiances of the two thinkers startled both my religious *and* secularist students. While most students were at least vaguely aware that these civil rights activists were Christians, and a few even knew they were ordained ministers, almost all were unaware of the overall impact that King's and Jackson's prophetic religious faith actually had on their social reform efforts.

First, I asked my students to reflect on Martin Luther King Jr.'s response to a white minister who scolded him for confusing the faithful with all of his talk about civil rights:

> We too know the Jesus that the minister just referred to. We have had an experience with him, and we believe firmly in the revelation of God in Jesus Christ. I can see no conflict between our devotion to Jesus Christ and our present action. In fact, I can see a necessary relationship. If one is truly devoted to the religion of Jesus, he will seek to rid the earth of social evils. The gospel is social as well as personal. . . . As Christians we owe our ultimate allegiance to God and His Will, rather than to man and his folkways. (Skillen, 1990, p. 120)

Then I asked them to think about Jackson's comments on religious liberty in his *Straight from the Heart* (1987):

> Most of us still live in a three-tiered cosmos: there is God's domain, the human domain, and land—a material domain. When we remove God from his domain and engage in the cosmic domains as though we're self-sufficient, then human beings project themselves into God's domain and play God. People can only play God; they can't be God. . . . But when human beings play God, then land and materialism rise up and are valued at the level where man and woman, boy and girl used to be. As a result, we now respect and revere cars and rings like we used to respect boys and girls . . . If children will not give deference to God—the origin, Creator of creation—ultimately, those children will not give deference to their parents, their teachers, their brothers, or their sisters. (Skillen, 1990, p. 120)

In response to my questions—"What central assumptions do you think each thinker is making about what he believes is the primary purpose of religion in a secular pluralist society like the United States?" "And in what senses, if any, do you think the two African-American leaders can be called prophets?"—I got reactions from students approximating the following:

- "King is really saying that, while religious teachings are important, social justice comes first."
- "It's all well and good to profess your Christian faith publicly, but when it is in conflict with your social principles, the social principles override the religious ones. At least this is what I think King means."
- "If I didn't know better, I'd say that Jackson sounds more than a little like some of the fundamentalists we studied."
- "King obviously has no patience with religious hypocrites who claim they believe in Jesus Christ but who fail to act when racism rears its ugly head in our society."
- "Are you sure this is *the* Jesse Jackson? What do cars and rings and 'deference to God' have to do with the civil rights struggles he's been involved in all his adult life? I'm disappointed with this reactionary excerpt. Couldn't you come up with anything better? He doesn't sound like a prophet to me."
- "I like these two excerpts very much. What both men are saying, I think, is that civil rights reform begins and ends with faithfulness to the biblical message. For King, Jesus Christ was a social reformer who himself tried to 'rid the earth of social evils,' witness his execution by the state for being a revolutionary. And, for Jackson, whenever human beings play God, they forget that they can't be God. Then God's message of love and respect for the dignity of all human beings, both black and white, gets lost. Cars and rings, prestige and power, wealth and possessions, wrongfully become our idols, because they take on a dignity of their own. We refuse to give to God what is due God, and, in the process, we give nothing to our children, our parents, our siblings, our neighbors, or to people who look different from us. In my mind, this is truly a radical, prophetic message. Only God has dominion over His Kingdom, and we are here to serve God and others as best we can. He doesn't serve us."

From my perspective, this last response adequately summarizes what I think is both uniquely Christian *and* prophetic in the King-Jackson social vision. The student responses that precede this latter one simply miss the mark because, in my estimation, they totally ignore, or misunderstand, the intimate relationship that inheres between both men's profoundly Christian-centered religious convictions and their lifelong struggle for social justice and human equality for all Americans. Most black Christians want a piece of the American dream, and they want to be treated fairly as equals. King and Jackson realize, each in his own way, that hope for social justice resides foremost in Jesus Christ, because for them only he is able to bring new life to all segments of the human community. In the end, God's domain remains supreme.

In the view of King and Jackson, Jesus is truly lord of all politics, all social struggles, all personal efforts to overcome pride and sin. And everything we do in the struggle to bring about social justice, and to end discrimination and oppression, we must do according to the principles of God's Word. "Deference to God" is a necessary precondition to deference to our brothers and sisters, including those of different skin color. And deference to *all* of our brothers and sisters is what it means to be genuinely Christian. King and Jackson believe that one cannot be a true Christian without living and acting in several realms, the social and personal, public and private, political and spiritual. In Harvey Cox's (1984) words,

> The exemplary saints of the postmodern world include a black preacher (Martin Luther King Jr.), a woman (Dorothy Day), and a Latin American (Oscar Arnulfo Romero). These were all persons of profound religious faith who instead of looking for a cave, or accepting the institutional insulation that separates most of us from the agony of the world, immersed themselves in that world. They did so, however, not just as "activists" or "change agents" but as followers of Jesus who were willing to run the risks of discipleship. (p. 211)

In my opinion, this message, as Cox and the last student I quoted above understand it, effectively captures the essence of the prophetic worldview.

THE PROPHETIC NARRATIVE

The prophetic narrative is a compelling one, and most of my students, even the secularists, receive it with enthusiasm when they first hear it. I have used several authors over the years who narrate the prophetic story with unique vision and power. Whenever we read Robert McAfee Brown's (1978) *Theology in a New Key: Responding to Liberation Themes*, students are captivated by the author's presentation of liberation theology (a prophetic movement I will discuss later in this section) as a new "musical key" within the "established harmonies" of liberal Christian theology. For Brown,

Christian theology should be a song to God that celebrates a "liberating love." And Brown's "song" in support of human rights, political and economic justice, and solidarity with the oppressed in all countries, including the Third World, hits just the right "notes" with my students, particularly those who are tired of the same old liberal or conservative "melodies."

Another text that weaves a trenchant narrative for my students is Harvey Cox's (1984) *Religion in the Secular City: Toward a Postmodern Theology*. Not only is this Harvard Divinity School professor a wonderfully accessible theologian for the religiously illiterate student, but Cox is also amazingly prescient on religious matters. Most of the predictions he made in the early 1980s regarding the need for a new theology "from the bottom and the edges" (p. 21) have since come to pass. My students read his text as a very credible critique of fundamentalist and modernist religious worldviews, and many applaud his view that religion will remain viable only if it becomes a potent social force in furthering the cause of social justice throughout the world.

I have already mentioned David E. Purpel's (1989) *The Moral & Spiritual Crisis in Education*, and I will return to this text later. For now, though, I wish to note that Purpel has the distinction in my classes of inspiring many students, including even the most intransigent secular humanists, to see themselves as prophets; and he does this without once censuring or belittling their previous educational endeavors. Purpel has the rare ability to avoid a narrow sectarian approach in telling his prophetic story, and when students finish reading him, many speak enthusiastically of developing curricula in the schools and colleges that foster a special appreciation for love, justice, community, and joy.

Another deeply prophetic educational text, Paulo Freire's (1985) *The Politics of Education: Culture, Power, and Liberation*, includes an essay, "Education, Liberation, and the Church," that never fails to capture the full attention of my students whenever they read it. For Freire, teachers become truly human only when they experience their own "Easter," when "they die as elitists so as to be resurrected on the side of the oppressed" (pp. 122–123). What makes this particular essay so exciting for students is that Freire is able to recast a politically rejuvenating philosophy of education in the language of the Christian Resurrection narrative. Along the way, the author charts the "new Exodus" the Christian church must take if it is to move away from the elitist pretensions of colonialism and modernism and advance toward liberation. Freire's image of a "prophetic," "utopian," and "hopeful" church succeeds in whetting the interest of all my students, religious or otherwise.

If the mark of a good religious narrative is to stir our imaginations and to give us a satisfying account of why we are here, how we should deal with the presence of evil, and how we can make things better, then, I contend, Dorothee Soelle, a German feminist theologian, has written the definitive prophetic *story*. At different times I have used two of her texts, *Thinking About God: An Introduction to Theology* (1990) and *Theology for Skeptics: Reflections on God* (1995), and because she writes so personally, descriptively, and authoritatively, my students generally respond well to her trademark theological "skepticism." They are moved by her remarkable authenticity, her ability to ask the right metaphysical questions in everyday language, and her understated eloquence in offering simple antidotes to the conditions of apathy, acquisitiveness, and spiritual numbness that plague the postmodern world. She is also a gifted storyteller.

I once asked students to refashion what they thought was Soelle's basic prophetic message in *Theology for Skeptics* (1995) into the form of a simple story, one that any bright middle school student might understand. I, too, participated in the exercise, and what follows is my own effort to capture the substance of what I believed to be Soelle's prophetic message. When I first read Soelle, I was struck by her simple attempt to explain the mystery of good and evil from within the framework of liberation theology. (I discuss this framework later, in somewhat more technical language.) And so I started my little story at that point:

> Once upon a time, people thought that God was all-powerful and all-knowing, but they could never reconcile this picture of God with the senseless suffering and premature death of innocent human beings that happens everywhere. After all, if God is all-powerful, they reasoned, why does he step aside and watch people suffer needlessly, especially when they might be guiltless children? Why doesn't He stop the pain? If He won't or can't, they asked, then doesn't this mean that God is either mad, weak, or a monster in the face of human suffering? How, then, can we believe in this kind of a God?
>
> Some other people thought that God might, indeed, be all-loving and all-knowing, but, because we are only human, and because God is God, then we can't hope to understand God's ways. That is, God will always be a puzzle to us. His ways are a mystery, and they will make sense to us only after we are dead and reunited with Him. These people eventually gave up this picture of God, though, because after awhile He stopped having any meaning to them. He was so remote and distant, so mysterious, that

they lost all human feeling for Him. He simply dropped out of their lives, never to be heard from again.

Then some people thought that, perhaps, God might not be all-knowing, all-wise, or all-powerful, but He still might be all-loving. This is not a super-God, after all, but one who cries when people suffer, and He is always on the side of the victims. He suffers with the poor, the outcast, the weak, and the innocent. He is partial to the poor in El Salvador, the hungry in Africa, the political prisoners in Cuba, the persecuted in Bosnia, and the homeless in Washington, D.C. God's church exists mainly to give hope to the poor and to the wretched all over the world. In fact, God's people have much to learn from the poor and the powerless, because they give us hope by the way they manage to live lives of quiet dignity and love, even when it appears to us that they have nothing worth living for—no VCRs, no luxury cars, no credit cards, no cellular phones, and no computer games.

In spite of their poverty and destitution, however, many of the poor love their God with enthusiasm and joy. They read their Bible in a very special manner, as a book that favors poor people. Their "good news" for us is that God has a special place in His Heart for their suffering, and the only way we who are privileged in the United States can ever know God is through the suffering of his beloved poor. The God we come to love and serve is not the old God who knows everything and who is so mysterious that He is beyond our puny understanding.

No, the God we come to know and revere is like our mother, who sympathizes with us when we hurt, who might even cry with us, offer us unlimited affection, and feel our anguish and torment in Her own body. God is connected to each and every one of us the way a loving mother is. God is vulnerable just as a kind and loyal mother is. God weeps for us the way our mother does when we are sick or hurt or injured, through no fault of our own, like Jesus's mother, Mary, did when the Romans crucified and killed her son. In fact, we could say that God possesses more of an emotional mother's qualities than an unemotional man's qualities. This is why some people believe that God might even be a woman.

But even though God can't stop all suffering, He is not entirely helpless when it comes to dealing with human suffering. In the Bible (John 16), Jesus promises that our struggles will eventually turn into joy, just as a pregnant woman's birth pains soon disappear and are replaced with happiness when her child is born

(Isaiah 42:14). Our sufferings become bearable whenever we help those less fortunate than we are. When we see the torment in others, our own pain becomes more tolerable. When we see those people we think are our enemies, at first we want to hurt them. But God wants us to try to understand their own sorrow and weakness and to convert them with love, if we can. If our own sorrow is too great, or if it is too difficult to love our enemies, then God wants us to let His pain absorb our pain. We (God, ourselves, our friends, even our enemies) can work together in our struggles to create a better world for all people, not just a privileged few.

Please understand, though, that God is not saying we shouldn't stand up and fight for what's right. Jesus Himself stood up and defended the rights of the poor, the homeless, and the social outcasts. God knows that there are plenty of mean and selfish individuals around, and a lot of mean and selfish governments too, who hurt others for their own gain. God wants us to get angry, and confront the wicked, and get them to change their lives. But, first, He wants us to change our own lives, and to work closely with others, especially those who suffer, for we have much to learn from them about our own suffering. He wants us to look into our own hearts to acknowledge our prejudice, our unfairness, our pride, our greed, and our own selfishness. The best way to change others is to admit that, first, *we* need to change, and that politics really has very little to do with creating a better, more just world. You see, justice starts at home, and when it does, it beams upward, downward, sideways, and outward.

Mahatma Gandhi and Martin Luther King Jr. knew all about the power of human suffering to free us from the mistaken belief that we are God-like, and to help us realize that it is only in community with others, and with God, that we become really free. We never suffer alone, but always with others. If we really believed that our suffering is also God's suffering, and that sharing our suffering with others can create connections far more loving and lasting than most relationships in our lives; and if we really believed that God has a special affection for the poor and the hurt, and, in the end, that special love will conquer any earthly evil, then what earthly sense does it make to say that suffering is always and everywhere a terrible thing? Suffering, you see, can change the world.

I ended my story with the following questions for my students to consider:

- What is there in this story that you think is particularly religious?
- What do you especially like or dislike about this way of thinking about religion?
- What special qualities does the God in this story possess, and in what ways does this image of God agree or disagree with your own?
- What kind of relationship does the story say we ought to have with God?
- Let's say you don't believe in a God. Could you still be inspired by this religious story?
- How do *you* explain all the terrible suffering in the world? Do religious stories help us to understand suffering better? Does this one help?
- Why do you suppose this story puts so much emphasis on social justice? Why doesn't it say more about prayer, sin, salvation, and the church?

Because I was able to tell a provocative little story about a highly controversial religious account (the prophetic), I was able to get my students to talk a little more freely than usual about very difficult, and very loaded, religious and political questions. The story reached out and grasped them, in spite of their previous awkwardness in knowing how to discuss such topics in an education class. Many of my middle school teachers reported to the class that when they read their little narratives to their own students, the students responded to the prophetic narrative with the same kind of enthusiasm displayed in our graduate seminar.

In my opinion, the story format demystified the complexities of theology and made it easier for young adolescents to talk with one another about religious topics that today the public schools consider mostly out of bounds. Ironically, as little as 15 years ago, most public schools in this country ruled the subject of *sex* outside the pale. Now, of course, sex education is *de rigueur* in curricula at all school levels throughout the United States, because sex is held to be a universal human theme with significant implications for all of us, regardless of age. I have been arguing throughout this book, of course, that the study of religion ought to be *de rigueur* for students for the same reason.

I believe the prophetic narrative, in particular, is an attractive one for students of all ages, because it speaks empathically to people about such universal human themes as good and evil, suffering, poverty, oppression, privilege, injustice, community, liberation, hope, joy, justice, and compassion. In the next section, I will discuss some of these issues in more depth.

LIBERATION THEOLOGY AND FEMINIST THEOLOGY

Soelle's (1990, 1995) special take on the prophetic narrative, as well as the little story I narrate above, encompasses key elements of *liberation theology* and *feminist theology*, and many of my students, even the nonbelievers, respond with heightened interest to these orientations. The prophetic authors we read are steeped in the primary-source literature on these two movements, and educational theorists such as Paulo Freire (1985), Nel Noddings (1993), Warren Nord (1995), and David Purpel (1989) refer to them often. On the subject of liberation theology, I have, in the past, asked students to read the seminal thinker on this topic, Gustavo Gutierrez, *A Theology of Liberation: History, Politics, and Salvation* (1973/ 1983), along with Matthew L. Lamb, *Solidarity with Victims: Toward a Theology of Social Transformation* (1982). And on feminist theology, I have used Letty Russell, *Human Liberation in a Feminist Perspective* (1974), and Sharon D. Welch, *A Feminist Ethic of Risk* (1990). Although these texts are difficult to read for theological novices, because they deal with complex, even strange, religio-philosophical ideas, most of my students are quick to see the parallels between their own liberal political agendas and those of the theologians they are studying. In fact, most appreciate appropriating a new (theological) language to articulate their political views on such issues as the environment, social justice, and diversity.

Whenever we study the prophetic narrative, many students have an opportunity to examine for the first time controversial political issues from the perspective of *liberal/left* religious thinkers. This often comes as a revelation to students, given that for many their only previous contact with the combination of politics and religion has been through the eyes of prominent *conservative/right* fundamentalists, as presented in the media (see Carol Flake, 1984, *Redemptorama: Culture, Politics, and the New Evangelicalism*, for a thorough analysis of this phenomenon). If nothing else, students now start to understand that depending on one's religious hermeneutic, the Bible can be read as either a politically emancipating or a politically conserving text; moreover, they soon realize that regardless of the partisan political views of its proponents, religion always has a vital policy-shaping role to play in the public square. Most of my students, unsurprisingly, prefer the liberal/left slant of prophetic politics, and when we read authors like Gustavo Gutierrez (1973/1983) and Sharon Welch (1990), few ever complain about mixing religion and politics in order to influence public policy agendas. These complaints are more likely to surface when we examine the fundamentalist narrative.

Just what is this liberation theology that has so profoundly influenced the prophetic narrative? Paul Wojda's (in McBrien, 1995) account of liberation theology and spirituality succinctly parallels Soelle's, but without the narrative élan. For Wojda, liberation spirituality is a religious style of "prayer, piety, and discernment" (p. 768) based on God's preference for poor people, as demonstrated throughout the Hebrew and Christian Bible. The definitive Hebrew liberation proof-texts describe the exodus of Hebrew slaves from Egypt (e.g., Exodus 3–12), and the Christian liberation proof-texts describe Jesus's ministry to the oppressed peoples of his time (e.g., Matthew 25: 31–46). Liberation theologians encourage a critical reading of the Bible from the perspective of the "least among us," so that a new way of experiencing God's presence comes to light.

Liberation theology originated in Latin America in the 1960s as a spiritual and political reaction to the collective suffering of the illiterate, disenfranchised, and impoverished people who lived throughout the region. Liberation theologians urged Christians in Third World countries to identify with the plight of the oppressed poor and, as an active expression of Christian witness, to join in the struggle to transform unjust political structures. Under the influence of Paulo Freire (1971), pastors in small and large parishes taught peasants how to read by helping them to understand that literacy confers power, and that reading the Bible reveals God's special preference for poor people. Now people were enjoined to see themselves as political actors, as "active subjects" in their own lives, and to take direct political action against the wealthy landowners in behalf of their family's and community's best interests. In addition to learning the truth of the gospels, Latin American peasants started to put into practice the biblical insights they were learning.

One important insight was the understanding that economic and social privilege keeps existing structures of power in place, and hence those who are in power turn a deaf ear to the entreaties of the poor and oppressed for social justice. Even the bourgeois church, in this construction, is seen as complicit in oppressive systems, and liberation theologians believe that the church must be made to hear the complaints of those who are suffering unjustly within its structures. Reading the Bible in community with others—in what some call Christian "base communities"—becomes genuinely liberating, in that finally Jesus is seen as taking the side of the people who are most vulnerable and weak. This is reading the Bible "from below," from a perspective that offers critique, hope, and a context for grass-roots political action.

A gifted prophetic narrativist like Harvey Cox (1984) sums up a number of central liberation themes:

> Liberation theology is biblical and experiential. . . . From these two sources [liberation theologians] derive a picture of the world as the theatre of both

human and divine action; as a place where sin expresses itself in patterns of institutional injustice more than in individual failings; as a drama in which the principal actors are not single persons but corporate entities—classes and social groups. Liberation theology postulates a world marked by collective conflict, but moving toward both spiritual and terrestrial salvation in a kingdom of God that will eventually come to be "on earth as it is in heaven." (p. 138)

What, in turn, are the core beliefs of *feminist theology* as they continually show up in prophetic thinkers, and how do these beliefs relate to liberation theology? I think Mary Daly (1973) appropriately communicates the impact the feminist perspective has had on contemporary Christian theology. According to her, the major function of feminist theology has been to "transform . . . patriarchy into something that never existed before. . . . Beliefs and values that have held sway for thousands of years [have been] questioned as never before" (p. 135). Feminist theologians, particularly the more radical thinkers, believe that the traditional Christian church has been oppressively androcentric and patriarchal. They contend that church leaders through the centuries have so grossly minimized or ignored women's religious contributions that today feminist theologians are calling for a drastic redefinition of symbols, rituals, sacred texts, and traditions, *to be understood now from the perspective of women.* This includes the creation of entirely new religious organizations that are equalitarian, nonhierarchical, nondogmatic, caring, and nondiscriminatory, for example goddess religions and women-church worshipping communities (see Regina Coll in McBrien, 1995, pp. 523–524).

In addition to its Protestant and Catholic forms, feminist theology also appears in Judaism, Hinduism, Buddhism, and Islam, among other world religions (see J. Z. Smith, 1995, pp. 359–360). Jewish feminist theologians write *midrash* (Heb., interpretation or exegetical study of the Hebrew Bible) from a woman's point of view, and argue that women should be full participants in all aspects of Jewish religious life. Hindu and Buddhist feminist theologians discuss goddess worship, and some undertake a social analysis of Asian cultures based on first-person narrative accounts of women who have been oppressed in these countries. And Islamic feminist theologians are trying to construct new identities for women that are different from the Western, yet still manage to break the grip of male-dominated Islamic religious practices. Finally, many *mujerista* theologians (women of color ["womanists"], and women from non-Western cultures) have criticized the bourgeois Western ethnocentrist bias of so much feminist theology today (e.g., Gloria Anzaldua, 1987), and they try to create a theology more in touch with poor women's concerns.

Feminist and liberation forms of Christian theology come together in a revivified interpretation of the Bible. In this radical reconstruction, liberation feminists expose androcentric and patriarchal interpretations of key biblical texts, and they reinterpret these texts in a way that highlights the positive religious contributions of women. Above all, however, liberation feminists argue that the work of restoring social justice for all the oppressed throughout the world, including women, must take place in the here and now, rather than waiting for full consummation in God's kingdom. According to liberation feminists, the Bible tells the stories of a number of powerful, liberated women (e.g., Deborah, Judith, Esther, and Mary Magdalene), and these women, read now through the eyes of a revisionist hermeneutic, can serve as prophetic models for all of us (see Carolyn Osiek in McBrien, 1995, pp. 524–525).

Finally, to summarize the liberation feminist message, I cite Rosemary Radford Ruether's (1972) hopeful words:

> We need to build a new cooperative social order out beyond the principles of hierarchy, rule and competitiveness. Starting in the grass-roots local units of human society where psycho-social polarization first began, we must create a living pattern of mutuality between men and women, between parents and children, among people in their social, economic and political relationships, and finally, between mankind and the organic harmonies of nature. (pp. 124–125)

CONCLUSIONS

I do not usually ask visitors representing the prophetic worldview to come to class, as I sometimes do the fundamentalist. So many of my students each semester like to think of themselves as "prophetic educators" that the presence of an outsider would seem superfluous to them. Therefore, my task in teaching this perspective is not so much to open up students' minds to possible *truths* in this particular account in order to counterbalance all the media distortions (something I try to do in teaching the fundamentalist story), but to help them look more closely at the deeper, more challenging religious and political meanings in a worldview they are inclined to take for granted as having undeniable value. Jarring to many of them, after some study, is the insight that living a genuine prophetic life goes way beyond the vapid pieties of "political correctness." Students begin to understand, some for the first time, that the biblical message, at least according to the prophetic hermeneutic, is unequivocally political and activistic. To be a true Christian, for example, necessitates direct grass-roots work in behalf of the poor, the politically oppressed, and all those whose human and civil rights have been violated, including women, children, and the aged and infirm throughout the world.

When read closely, liberation and feminist theologies make serious demands on believers: Political activists must find a way to operate in two realms, the religious *and* the secular, without letting either realm overpower the other. For example, Christians will need to know how to act Christlike while confronting un-Christlike practitioners of political and economic oppression. One of the unsettling implications of this paradox, of course, has to do with the question of whether violence is ever justifiable in a confrontation with unyielding militaristic, capitalistic, or racist systems of injustice.

As we have seen, the Gandhi-King response to injustice is a nonviolent one—*satyagraha* (Skt., truth-grasping, holding firmly) and *ahimsa* (Skt., non-injury, not desiring to harm)—an appeal to self-restraint, patience, love, and fortitude. Gandhi and King realized that genuine liberation comes about only when people overcome such personal vices as lust, anger, greed, pride, and malice, and when they are willing to put their bodies on the line for social justice in a nonviolent manner. In Skillen's (1990) Christian words: "Liberation comes not by means of government-enforced policies but by learning to live without appeal to force. It comes via the Cross, not the bomb" (p. 156).

For those teachers in my class who might wonder how they can translate the prophetic narrative into actual classroom teaching, I find that placing educational theorists such as Nel Noddings (1993), David Purpel (1989), and Paulo Freire (1985) on a *prophetic continuum* puts things into practical perspective very quickly. Teachers can then choose their own points of prophetic entry on the continuum whenever they discuss this religious perspective with their own classes.

Noddings (1993), a nonbeliever, but sounding very much like Christian feminist theologians Rosemary Radford Ruether (1972), Letty Russell (1974), and Dorothee Soelle (1995), delivers a *moderate* prophetic message to my students, particularly in regard to liberation theology. She contends that teachers ought to engage students in discussions that

> lead to thoughtful examination of life-styles in the United States, the selfishness of continual striving for more and more material goods, the ways in which religion sometimes soothes our consciences when they should remain disturbed, and the enormous risks taken by a few who are willing to give up both personal and spiritual comfort. (p. 131)

Noddings's own approach to raising these prophetic issues with
students is via a "pedagogical neutrality," always asking provocative
religious questions in a respectful way, being careful to cite opposing
points of view, and giving sound reasons when taking a specific moral
position herself (pp. xv–xvi). She encourages teachers everywhere to "disturb" students' consciences whenever they appear too contented with
their middle-class lifestyles, and to call attention to those secular saints
who have given up so much in order to minister to the impoverished
and the marginalized among us.

Purpel (1989) advances a *reformist* prophetic message to my students.
Upping the ante over Noddings's more moderate, "pedagogically neutral"
approach, Purpel asks teachers to emulate the religious prophets'

> passion and commitment to persisting values—justice, compassion, and con-
> cern from the oppressed; the strong authority that their criticism provides;
> their courage in expressing their convictions so loudly; and the energy and
> hope that they inspire. *It is important to remember that the prophetic voice is one
> that speaks not only to criticism; it is also a voice of transformation* [emphasis
> mine]. (p. 81)

Throughout his text, Purpel (1989) tries to get teachers to think of
themselves as social reformers whose mission is to provide, and to live
out, an alternative prophetic story to the dominant capitalistic culture.
This story would include "sharp criticism, dazzling imagination, a sacred
perspective, commitment to justice and compassion, hope, energy, and
involvement" (p. 85). Purpel is being entirely consistent as a prophetic
reformer when he urges teachers to cultivate "attitudes of outrage" in the
face of injustice and oppression (p. 118), and to teach and act accordingly.

And Freire (1985) sends a *revolutionary* prophetic message to teachers.
He believes that educators must both "denounce" leaders who exploit
the people, and "announce" the dawning of a "revolutionary utopia."
For Freire, a committed Christian, the "denunciation" is the equivalent
of Christ's Crucifixion, and the "annunciation" of Christ's Resurrection.
Ever mindful of the "internal contradictions" that often compromise revolutionary utopias, resulting in tyrannies far worse than the ones they
supplant, Freire advocates the establishment of a certain type of "revolutionary utopia," one that

> tends to be dynamic rather than static; tends to life rather than death . . . to
> living together in harmony rather than gregariousness; to dialogue rather
> than mutism; to praxis rather than "law and order"; to men who organize
> themselves reflectively for action rather than men who are organized for

passivity; and to values that are lived rather than myths that are imposed. (p. 82)

For Freire, teachers everywhere, in both First- and Third-World countries, must be harsh critics of all reactionary social institutions, wherever these are located; moreover, they must situate their religious beliefs in a biblical God who favors the poor and oppressed, and they must view the Kingdom as something to be created in *this* world, rather than in the *next*.

Finally, recall the student at the beginning of this chapter who brought the *Doonesbury* cartoon strips to class because she was looking for a religious experience more visionary and uncompromising than the one portrayed in the Little Church of Walden. I must add that not all students are like her—eager to pursue a different religious narrative from the mainline church story they know so well. Prophetic discourse on liberation and social revolution bothers them for the same reason that fundamentalist political rhetoric about "family values," "prayer in schools," and "right to life" does. They are uneasy over the conflation of religion and politics in America, the transformation of the biblical message to what could be merely one or another plank in the Republican or Democratic platforms. In reaction, these students tend to raise a very different kind of question after studying the prophetic perspective: "Is the prophetic narrative a story I truly want to live my life by?" In the next chapter, I examine the downside of this story.

CHAPTER 5

The Failure of the Prophetic Narrative

The prophetic narrative has many more supporters, by far, in my classes than does the fundamentalist account. Intriguingly, though, what most of my students refuse to admit is that each worldview actually has some things in common with the other. As we have seen in previous chapters, the differences between the two are obvious: On the political right, fundamentalist believers celebrate individual liberty, patriotism and nationalism, conservative political causes, inerrant scriptural understandings biased toward established sociopolitical systems, and capitalism. On the political left, prophetic believers advocate for cultural pluralism, social justice, equality, religious diversity, a biblical hermeneutic suspicious of the status quo and biased toward the interests of the poor, and "base" communities. In spite of their considerable political differences, however, I believe each narrative is alike in being religiously iconoclastic: Both attack the cherished beliefs and images of mainstream (liberal) theology and politics, along with the "religious" pretensions of secular humanism.

Furthermore, according to Harvey Cox (1984), both movements have drastically reshaped the old religious organizations by emphasizing small, face-to-face worship communities rather than large denominations. Both claim they have retrieved the original intent of the biblical authors, and both strive to place their readings of scripture beyond the relativistic reach of a liberal/modernist hermeneutic. Both stress the importance of active political involvement. Both are attracted to charismatic religious leaders who claim to be the true defenders of God, the faith, and the people. But most important is the fact that both are succeeding in bringing people together in rare unity, despite the several internecine rifts and cliques that have historically divided religious denominations.

I mention the similarities in both worldviews in order to point out that the dangers they pose to free inquiry in a secular, pluralist society are also remarkably similar. Where I think the prophetic story fails is that, like the fundamentalist story, it too is alarmingly authoritarian and anti-democratic, but coming from an opposing political direction. The prophetic orientation runs the risk of repressing intellectual freedom because in its admirable zeal to help the oppressed and to redress injustice, it refuses to consider even the remote possibility that its particular political pre-text on religious truth might simply be wrong, or at the very least ideologically biased. Left-wing prophets who "burn" with the truth as God's chosen messengers run the risk of overstating the case against the sociopolitical status quo, or of misinterpeting a "sacred" book or proof-text in order to push pet political causes, or of recklessly blurring the line between religion and politics in a way that calls down the wrath of God on whole groups of people whom they stipulatively specify the "oppressors."

Historically, this kind of prophetic authoritarianism has sometimes led to tyranny, particularly in its more Marxist forms (Ellul, 1988). Prophetic authoritarianism brooks no religious or political dissent, allows for no ambivalence, and in Jonathan Rauch's (1993, p. 150) words, refuses to distinguish between "propositions and persons," between debatable biblical proof-texts and people it designates as heretics. Thus, in the inevitable revolution that always seems to follow an era of prophetic authoritarianism, it is persons, not propositions, who most frequently end up as fatalities. For 2,000 years, throughout the world, whenever prophets have aligned with one political force or another—reactionary/conservative, liberal/modernist, progressive/radical—the result has too frequently been the erosion and ultimate loss of religious faith (Johnson, 1976).

As I will argue later, I believe the religious prophet's—and the educator's—primary mission ought to be to mount a radical critique against *every* political ideology (including the very idea of ideology itself), privileging none, challenging all, and remaining hypersensitive to religion's own ideological biases. Historically, whether intended or not, these biases have often become the insidious source of centuries of religious malevolence and maliciousness.

A HEATED CLASSROOM CONVERSATION

One day in class, impatient with the favoritism my students were showing the prophetic narrative, I asked this question: "Why do you persist in finding the prophetic worldview to be more palatable and less blameworthy than the fundamentalist? Given the broad similarities between the two accounts, including the particular strengths and weaknesses each share, why are you so quick to discover *error* in the fundamentalist story and so eager to find *truth* in the prophetic?" The subsequent class conversation between the students (Ss) and me (RJN) went something like the following:

Ss: The prophetic voice is a religiously and educationally inspiring one, in spite of its weaknesses. The fundamentalist voice is religiously narrow and judgmental, and, frankly, its supposed strengths elude us, particularly for the work we do as educators.

RJN: But isn't the prophetic voice narrow and judgmental in its own way? And isn't the fundamentalist voice inspiring in its own way? Doesn't it depend on the reader's hermeneutic? How do you suppose Charles Colson would "read" the prophetic story? And how would Paulo Freire "read" the fundamentalist story? Isn't each "believer" trapped in his own "container of meanings," his own "taken-for-granteds"? Do you remember the time we talked about the concept of "textual equivocality," the notion that there is always more than one way to interpret a story? Why can't we try to read the fundamentalist narrative from the perspective of its committed and convinced believers rather than from its skeptics and detractors? Will you try to read the fundamentalist story from the point of view of some of your students' parents? Or will you impose your own view on their story?

Ss: One thing that bothers us about your "textual equivocality" concept is that it makes *all* religious interpretations appear equally valid. When is it ever possible for us, as educators, to say that one story—for example, the prophetic—is clearly superior to another story—say, the fundamentalist? Why shouldn't we judge religious claims according to their social consequences, according to the political outcomes of the story? Look around the world. Fundamentalist leaders, whether religious or political, usually end up oppressing or stigmatizing people who disagree with them. In this country, religious fundamentalists tend to be zealots who are anti-everything: anti-abortion, anti-gay, anti-environment, and anti-poor. The prophetic believers, in contrast, especially the liberation and feminist groups, are *for* something: They realize that because religion is always deeply political, and because most believers usually end up on the side of the power elite rather than on the side of the weak, the poor, and the powerless, then they must advocate for the side of the powerless. Aren't prophets supposed to remind us of injustice and inequity in society, and call us to task whenever we say one thing and do another? Be honest, who do *you* want in the classroom talking to *your* children about religion, its meaning and purpose in America, David Purpel or Charles Colson? What, pray tell, do the fundamentalists know or care about injustice, oppression, or suffering?

RJN: But isn't the prophetic narrative as politically biased in its own way as the fundamentalist? Don't people like Mary Daly, the feminist theologian, and Gustavo Gutierrez, the liberation theologian, take political sides? In fact, aren't they proud of their politics and disdainful of the opposition's? Don't they stigmatize those who disagree with them as being on the side of the oppressor, or of the patriarchy, or of the power elite? Can't the case be made that prophetic believers are anti-capitalism, anti-wealth, anti-liberty, anti-middle-class, even anti-family? How can you be so sure that prophetic believers will treat all people justly? In the cause of social justice, won't some people (e.g., the wealthy) need to be treated unjustly if their wealth is to be equally redistributed? Won't certain basic freedoms (the right to hold property, to make a profit, to speak out against left-wing totalitarianism) have to be abridged, at least initially, in order to establish the just society? Also, isn't it true that prophets of all persuasions around the world, religious, political, or educational, have often overstepped their bounds and become self-righteous tyrants when they call the rest of us to task? Why, pray tell, do you want *anyone* in your children's classrooms talking about religion in the first place? And if you do, why not let your children hear *all* the religious points of view, even those you dislike?If you encourage only the religious stories you find politically acceptable, aren't you sowing the seeds of religious bigotry later on?

Ss: You are missing the important point in a really infuriating way. Isn't religion supposed to help us make a better world? Don't all the sacred books of all the religions, each in their own ways, give special attention to the plight of the outcasts, the mistreated, the victims of greed and misfortune, the reviled? In Christianity, isn't Jesus Himself a prophet, a liberator, who gives up his life in the cause of those who are materially destitute and politically oppressed? Fundamentalism tells essentially a selfish story, one where sacred books like the Bible are used to prop up the perquisites of the privileged. In contrast, the prophetic orientation tells a genuinely humanitarian story, one where the church is invited to accept a voluntary poverty as a way of identifying with the marginalization and silencing of the disenfranchised classes. We ask you: Which story do you think is more likely to teach students of all ages the religious message of patience, love, sacrifice, redemption, and solidarity with all peoples, regardless of social class?

RJN: I admit you make many good points. But I also have to remind you that even fundamentalists have been known to work with society's outcasts, to reach out to pregnant teenagers, to the homeless, to prisoners, and to the physically disabled, in gestures of love, sacrifice, assistance, and solidarity. I'll bet some fundamentalist parents in your own communities are highly involved in social activities that benefit the less well-off. You haven't convinced me yet that one or the other religious story is more or less selfish on *its own* terms. Can't the case be made that the class conflict encouraged by people like Freire and Soelle is itself selfish, because it assigns a preferential option to the poor, and then favors them in the class war that is bound to follow? Also, how exactly is it being "generous" to consider the poor, not as individuals capable of creating better lives for themselves, but as an aggregate entity—helpless, angry, and envious—and dependent on messianic-like liberators to advance their cause? Is it always selfish to point out that in some cases at least, an absence of personal gumption and individual shortcomings might better explain poverty and injustice than structural causes? Isn't this a message your students need to learn? Is systemic social causation to be the only biblically certified explanation for human suffering? Who says so? I can read these sacred books, particularly the Bible, in such a way that just the opposite message comes through. And, so, isn't it a matter of textual equivocality after all?

Ss: We know that you want us to look at all these religious narratives with some kind of equanimity and balance, and to further this end, you are playing devil's advocate; we sometimes play this game with our own students, too. But your philosophical relativism and theological skepticism only confirm what prophetic thinkers are saying about middle-class American intellectuals in universities. Of course, you can accuse the prophetic thinkers of "politicizing" religion, of mixing up the secular and the sacred, because your theological hermeneutic, if you will, is suspicious, dispassionate, academic, and abstract. What do *you* know firsthand about the struggles of the poor? You ought to visit *our* schools sometime and really see some poor children: kids from trailer parks, inner-city slums, and rundown rural farming communities. Let us put it this way, and we don't mean to offend you: If fundamentalists were to come to power in this country, you would have little to lose; if prophetic believers were to come to power, though, you would probably lose almost everything you value, particularly your privileged intellectual status to remain above the fray without taking sides.

RJN: What can I really say to this personal attack? This type of *ad hominem* assault, the ultimate weapon of those who are convinced they alone possess the truth, is what disturbs me the most about the prophetic story, as it does with the fundamentalist story. Depending on who's in power, all the rest of us must toe the right ideological line or be stigmatized as miscreants, oppressors, privileged, or worse. In the United States, we have seen only too well what the "politically correct" mania has done to freedom of speech and thought in the university. Some of you have even complained about the presence of political correctness in the public schools, and how it distorts and trivializes the courses you teach. But the biggest loser, I submit, is religion itself, because now religion's ultimate worth is made dependent on its ability to support revolutionary political systems. Throughout history, religion has allied itself with the Holy Roman Empire, with capitalism, with socialism, with democracy, with the Enlightenment, with various "people's revolutions," among a host of other political movements. You history teachers know these facts all too well, and if you don't, I strongly suggest you do some rereading. When these regimes fail, and most do, religion fails right along with them, and the fullness of God's alleged truth falls by the wayside as well.

Ss: There you go again, presumptuously and patronizingly talking about God's "alleged" truth and telling us what to reread! What about the everyday struggles of people right now, *outside* the ivy-covered walls of the academy, to make better lives for themselves, in the face of all those corporate forces committed to keeping them powerless: repressive political regimes around the world? capitalism with its single-minded emphasis on profit, consumption, and competition? middle-class churches with their bourgeois values and "cooling-out" therapeutic ideals? educational institutions, particularly in the cities, that continue to miseducate, label, sort, and classify, and, in the end, destroy the dreams of the youthful underclass? Many of these people believe in God's *actual*, not "alleged," truth. Where are the latter-day prophets who will speak of the presence of God amidst the sufferings of all the disinherited peoples of the world? We know one thing for sure: We cannot find them among the fundamentalists!

IS THIS THE STORY I TRULY WANT TO LIVE MY LIFE BY?

This section heading was the student's question I used to close Chapter 4, and I believe it effectively sums up the ambivalence at least some of my students feel about the prophetic narrative. In spite of the black-or-white, either–or tone of the class conversation above, there are always students in my classes, like this one, who remain genuinely perplexed regarding the actual value of each of the religious stories for their own lives. These students are the "seekers," and they remain at least moderately open to the claims of all four religious accounts. Underlying this student's candid question, I suspect, is the concern that something is deeply troubling, even though strangely appealing, about the prophetic story. Perhaps I captured some of this student's ambivalence in my own comments above, perhaps not. But I do sense there is something in the *prophetic* narrative that fails to mesh completely with the *personal* narrative that gives this student's life a special order, purpose, and direction.

On the one hand, my students in the above conversation accurately point out that injustice, inequality, and great disparities of wealth and opportunity permeate cultures everywhere. They wonder, for example, when all is said and done, what the traditional Christian, Jewish, and Islamic religions have really accomplished to improve conditions for society's have-nots. Many of my students remind us that religion, if it serves no other purpose, must take up the cause of the poor as its first responsibility. From their view, the mainline churches, wittingly or unwittingly, have too often allied themselves with repressive political regimes, and consequently they have provided an invidious religious justification for poverty, persecution, and oppression.

But what I think mostly concerns my students in the previous dialogue is the huge gap that exists in the mainline churches between religious rhetoric and social deed. They contend that the kind of world the great religious figures have proclaimed throughout modern history is the virtual antithesis of the actual world we live in today. Centuries of religious teaching about love, justice, peace, and hope appear to have produced a world of hate, injustice, violence, and hopelessness, especially for the poor and the excluded. What those students with a translucent social vision believe with all their hearts is that unless the church is willing to mount an incontrovertible, justice-based challenge against the powers of greed and exploitation at the highest political levels, then religion is effectively neutered as an active, worthwhile force in people's day-to-day lives.

Absent this militancy on behalf of society's castoffs, these students tend to dismiss the institutionalized church as merely an impotent, spiritualized refuge from the grittier, more troublesome political realities of everyday life. No wonder, then, that the writings of Paulo Freire (1985), David Purpel (1989), Dorothee Soelle (1990, 1995), and Sharon D. Welch (1990) strike such a responsive chord in so many of my students. To them, these thinkers are social activists, prophets, who strive to rescue religion from its system-conserving dogmas and doctrines, its anemic and disembodied spirituality, its stripped-down understandings of the sacred texts, and its overall social irrelevancy.

On the other hand, what I was trying to demonstrate in the dialogue with my students is the strength of Wade Clark Roof's (1993) observation that religion always serves at least a dual purpose in society: It is both system-maintaining and system-disturbing. This is an important understanding for teachers, I contend, because it helps them to realize that religion, like education, serves multiple functions in a society. Religion, like education, is "world-maintaining" in that it provides a way for people to deal with disorder, instability, and chaos, and it does this by rising above social and political upheaval, and by offering people a metaphysical and psychological anchor amidst the storms of protest and change. But religion, like education, is also "world-shattering," in the postmodern sense of reminding people that the present society is only a flawed, human construction, that better ones are possible, even desirable, and that *all* political systems are, at best, poor replications of superior (divine?) arrangements to come.

Roof believes that religion, as a "world-maintainer," "legitimates and creates" the status quo; but as a "world-shatterer," religion "relativizes, demystifies, and debunks" (p. 237) that world, making way for the new. The trick for religion, and for education, I believe, is to "maintain" and "shatter" in such a fashion that one function does not trump and overwhelm the other, or that religion, or education, itself is not obliterated in the process. As I tried to point out in the above conversation with my students, however, the larger tragedy is that religion, whatever its function in the social order, always ends up reacting to what *is*, and in the process it inadvertently protects established political interests. This is in dramatic contrast to standing autonomously for the greater supernatural truth the church predicts will materialize in some distant eschaton.

H. Richard Niebuhr (1951/1975), the brother of Reinhold, a noted Christian theologian, once wrote an important text on Christian social ethics that, I believe, accurately states one of the major problems my students and I were addressing in the conversation we had: How should the church and culture interact so that the interests of each are adequately satisfied? Should religion always stand *against* the culture it inhabits, or does it do its best work when it stands *with* the culture? When is the prophetic (or fundamentalist) role in a society counterproductive to the democratic process? These are questions, I propose, that teachers ought to be raising with their students in the public schools and colleges, because they strike at the heart of how difficult, yet necessary, it is for religion and society to coexist with each other in a secular pluralist democracy.

H. Richard Niebuhr contended in his classic, *Christ and Culture* (1951/

1975), that there are five ways to think about how Christ is relevant to the cultures in which Christians must live today. But because Niebuhr's analysis is Christocentric, and thus not applicable for all believers, I will change his focus from Christ and culture to religion and culture, and I will ask essentially the same questions he did, but in a more generic way. The five questions I suggest teachers ask students are these:

1. Should religion exist in *opposition* to the culture?
2. Should religion exist in *agreement* with the culture?
3. Should religion exist in a dualistic way, that is, both in *continuity* with the culture and in *discontinuity* with the culture?
4. Should religion exist both in *deference to culture* and *in deference to God*?
5. Should religion exist as a *converter* or *transformer* of culture?

Some of my students believe that questions 2, 3, and 4, the more moderate liberal questions, offer believers the best opportunity both for living a personal spiritual life and for forging a peaceful religious coexistence with secular powers. This, for them, is how religion ought to function as a "maintainer" of society. Some other students, especially those attracted to the prophetic narrative, opt for question 1, while those who are intrigued with the fundamentalist story prefer question 5. Prophetic and fundamentalist seekers see the function of religion to be the "shatterer" of society. In the case of prophetic adherents, religion's destiny is to debunk and to critique, to stand against the dominant culture, in order to make a rightful place for the disenfranchised and the neglected. For fundamentalist believers, the objective is to transform culture, to get it more in line with traditional biblical teachings, to build the religious state of Christendom. (This is the case that "theonomic reconstructionists" [those who advocate the constitutional establishment of God's law in society] make. See Greg Bahnsen's *Theonomy and Christian Ethics*, 1984.)

As we will see in the following chapters, students predisposed to the *alternative spiritualities* narrative are far less interested in the *social* functions of religion than they are in *personal* spiritual transformation, and so Niebuhr's five questions are largely irrelevant to them. And those students who are experimenting with the *post-theist* narrative are more likely to pit *society* against religion, rather than the other way around. The particular appeal of these latter two narratives to students today is that each, in its own postmodern fashion, challenges the very validity of religion itself, particularly the construction the institutionalized churches have created. Many of these students are quick to critique the old paradigm of supernatural religion (its world-maintaining or world-shattering qualities notwith-standing), including all the myths, doctrines, rituals, liturgies, sacred books, songs, doctrines, and practices that accompany this construction.

THE IDOLATRY OF THE PROPHETIC NARRATIVE

In the world's major monotheistic religions, idolatry (Heb., *abodah zarah*, alien cult) is considered the ultimate sin. For example, in the Hebrew Bible, the prophets, Hosea, Jeremiah, and Ezekiel, condemned the use of false images in the worship of Yahweh. (See the major criticism of idolatry in Deuteronomy 6:4–9.) In the Christian Bible (1 Cor 8:1–13 and 10:14–22), Paul denounced those Christians elected to public office who willingly participated in emperor-worship ceremonies. And the greatest sin in Islam is when someone places more trust in lesser beings than in Allah. The word for idolatry in Islam is *shirk*, which means literally to associate other beings with Allah. Islamic art, for example, is neither innovative nor original, because God alone is considered the Creator; thus, Muslim artists, working anonymously, and fearful of creating false idols, are happy to be mere artisans, producing traditional and conformist works that confirm God's incomparable goodness and power (J. Z. Smith, 1995).

But there is another sense in which the term *idolatry* can be applied to the prophetic perspective, and I attempted to suggest this meaning in the dialogue I had with my students. I would argue that idolatry in the following context is a concept that teenage students, in particular, might understand, so prone are they to swear absolute, undying loyalty to brand names, sports figures, recording artists, and television personalities, all of which are unsatisfyingly short-lived, but exalted to them nevertheless. Dostoevsky observed once that "a man cannot live without worshiping something" (cited in Tinder, 1989, p. 50). What Dostoevsky was getting at is that people who deny God need to venerate alternative idols—God-substitutes—for example, food, sex, wealth, power, or even a particular political ideology.

The greatest fear I have regarding the prophetic narrative is the tendency on the part of some left-leaning theists to bestow divine honors on one type of political arrangement, usually of a Marxist flavor, and to make this ideology something worthy of worship. Currently, in the field of education, the critical theorists (see, for example, Giroux, 1997) tilt their proposals heavily in this political direction. As I have argued elsewhere (Nash, 1997), critical theory/pedagogy is weakened, because it elevates a particular ideology—democratic socialism—to the status of a sacred icon. And along the way, education is reduced to nothing more than a politically partisan tool for establishing a new kind of social order, one the critical theorists have anointed as blessed for all the rest of us (Sowell, 1995).

I share Glenn Tinder's (1989) grave concern over the ultimate political consequences of this kind of idolatry:

> When disrespect for individuals and political ideology are combined, the results can be atrocious. . . . Consider Lenin: as a Marxist, and like Marx an exponent of equality, under the pressures of revolution he denied equality in principle—except as an ultimate goal—and so systematically nullified it in practice as to become the founder of modern totalitarianism. When equality falls . . . nationalism or some other form of collective pride becomes virulent and war unrestrained. Liberty, too, is likely to vanish; it becomes a heavy personal and social burden . . . (p. 50)

What Tinder is asserting, I think, is that many left-leaning prophets are prone to lose their religious faith in an effort to establish the kingdom of God on Earth. They are so passionately motivated to create a perfectly just society, here and now, that sometimes single individuals get sacrificed, because they do not count as much in the long run as do the aggregate oppressed. The cruel irony of beneficent egalitarian intentions, as history has shown, is that some political saviors are wont to compromise both their religious *and* political ideals in their zeal to create the perfect social order, ostensibly in behalf of the rights of individuals. In Kenneth Hamilton's (1990) words: "It is a frightening prospect for the future when denouncing one's enemies becomes an essential part of being called a Christian" (p. 77).

Hence, the individual is disrespected, and eventually lost, as the revolution heats up, and one God—a particular political regime—eventually replaces the other, more conventional God. Along with Hamilton (1990), I worry about the quickness of some self-declared prophetic thinkers, particularly in the schools and colleges, to categorically denounce the "enemy" as an oppressor (i.e., racist, bigot, capitalist, sexist, homophobe, etc.) simply because some well-intended people may genuinely disagree with the content, style, delivery, and goals of the political vanguard that knows what is best for everyone and will lead us into the future. Too often in the historical chronicle, the pursuit of a perfect equality, always an unrealizable goal, has given way to nationalism, to collectivism, or worse, to totalitarianism. Tinder (1989) and Hamilton (1990) are arguing that this kind of political idolatry is inevitable, once God is no longer available to justify and to exalt the autonomous individual.

CHRISTIAN REALISM AND
LIBERATIONIST/FEMINIST THEOLOGY

Although I have considerable doubts about the theology that underlies it, I am personally drawn to the Christian realism of a Reinhold Niebuhr (1935/1963) and a Glenn Tinder (1989) when it comes to putting the prophetic story in a down-to-earth perspective. By temperament, I am very much a Christian realist (in *my* own agnostic language, I am a post-theist realist/pragmatist), even though, theologically, I reject the whole otherworldly apparatus that accompanies it. I submit that Glenn Tinder's (1989) *The Political Meaning of Christianity: An Interpretation* is the most lucid, and convincing, refutation by a Christian realist of what I am calling the prophetic narrative, especially in its Christian embodiment. I propose to my students that in terms of its own self-understanding, the prophetic account, especially in its Christian liberationist/feminist forms, faces serious, perhaps insurmountable difficulties.

What is Christian realism? Tinder (1989) articulates its meaning in the most concise terms:

> Maintaining a prophetic attitude means looking beyond every historical relationship . . . all political ideals and plans . . . and remembering that nothing in history, nothing human, can be absolutely relied upon. (p. 9)

For Tinder, always the prophetic Lutheran realist, human beings are basically sinful, self-interested creatures whose natural inclinations are to dominate and control others. It is only God's freely given grace, according to Tinder, that allows us to act responsibly whenever we are tempted to overstep our bounds in the temporal, political realm. And because human beings must live both *above* history and *in* history, both in *God's* city and in the *human* city, we are "as individuals inescapably solitary and exposed" (p. 9).

Once again, I quote Tinder:

> Christianity implies skepticism concerning political ideals and plans. For Christianity to be wedded indissolubly to any of them [e.g., Christian socialism, democratic capitalism, social gospel, liberation and feminist theology] is idolatrous and thus subversive of Christian faith. . . . Christianity can indicate only how to stand in the times and circumstances in which—Christians believe—God places us. . . . It can show us how to live in temporal society as citizens of an eternal society. (p. 8)

What Tinder is arguing is an insight that I believe students who delve into history, government, and political science in public schools and colleges have an intellectual right to know, regardless of the teacher's/

professor's special political preference: *All political systems are fallible, subject to human distortion, excess, and self-aggrandizement.* The challenge for prophetic realists, and for students everywhere, is to recognize the inevitable dangers inherent in the historical present without succumbing to apathy, cynicism, or despair. And while it is true that we will never establish the fullness of "God's kingdom" in the temporal present, we are nevertheless responsible, both as believers and as citizens, for doing "God's will" in the here-and-now. Tinder goes on to assert that the good society is not necessarily the most just society, as prophets on the left proclaim. In his words, "Human beings in their passion for justice have not devised institutions that, in their pride and selfishness, they cannot outwit" (p. 12).

For Tinder, and for me as well, many prophets on the left are morally naive, apparently incapable of understanding that utopian adventurism throughout history has always been plagued by paradox and peril. Liberation and feminist theologians give us much cause to hope, it is true. But because so many of them pay such limited attention to their own self-destructive and self-interested tendencies, they have also given us great cause for alarm. For the truth is that in all earthly matters, hope and despair will continue to exist in a dangerously uneasy, paradoxical relationship.

Whenever we read such prophetic thinkers in class as Paulo Freire (1985), Gustavo Gutierrez (1973/1983), David Purpel (1989), Rosemary Radford Ruether (1972), Letty Russell (1974), and Dorothee Soelle (1995), the oversimplified picture we frequently get from them is that if only we have the political will to effect revolutionary social reform in the United States and elsewhere, then the earthly kingdom of God will be a *fait accompli.* Unfortunately, as Tinder has observed, there has not been "a single example in our time of a determined effort to produce immediate and sweeping change that has not ended in tyranny; and these efforts often result in abominations . . . " (p. 12). Examples that come readily to mind are the Soviet Union, Nazi Germany, Cambodia, Cuba, the People's Republic of China, and Vietnam, with their death camps, holocausts, political imprisonments, tortures, murders, and killing fields.

From the institutional church's perspective, liberation/feminist theology, in spite of its commendable compassion toward the world's poor and the silenced, has earned a stern rebuke from several Christian leaders, including Pope John Paul II's right-hand man, Joseph Cardinal Ratzinger (1985). Ratzinger worries that liberation theology, a synthesis of Marxist idealism and Christian neomodernism, pits the rich against the poor, the First World against the Third World, throughout the globe. This polarized oversimplification of geopolitical realities, according to Ratzinger, fosters continual global conflict and instability, despair, class resentment, and a predisposition to resort to violence via the encouragement of "people's revolutions." And where feminist theologians are concerned, liberation theology's "consciousness-raising" technique has precipitated a rage for retribution against the patriarchy in many churches throughout the world. In this regard, Ratzinger is troubled by liberation/feminist theology's grandiose tendency to emphasize *structural* sin over the individual's *personal* responsibility to live a moral life, and the individual's duty to work for social justice and equity in a way more befitting Christians in smaller neighborhood, ecclesiastical, educational, work, and governmental settings back home.

Most disturbing to Ratzinger and other critics, though, is liberation/ feminist theology's sense of its own absolute moral and political superiority—also the bane, as we have seen, of the fundamentalist mindset. This takes the form of claiming a prior privilege for its hermeneutic of suspicion in reading the gospels on behalf of the poor and women, and for its rejection of all distinctions between the supernatural and the natural as an untenable dualism. For liberation/feminist theologians, reality is always political, always in conflict, and always material. In this construction, Christ is not divine; he is a prophet and a subversive. Salvation is synonymous with political and economic revolution. Sin is oppression. And redemption is the triumph of social justice and equality over patriarchal systems of injustice and inequity (Steichen, 1991). For the liberation/ feminist theologian, any other reading of the theological text is obstructionist and reactionary, and must be resisted.

While I am in essential agreement with the general drift of Ratzinger's critique of liberation/feminist theology, I strongly disagree with his transcendental premises. Ratzinger's metaphysical presuppositions are in direct contrast to my own. For example, a Ratzinger sympathizer, Donna Steichen (1991), summarizes what she believes is the official church's understanding of why liberation/feminist theology is anti-theistic and, in the end, unacceptable:

> If God is not a transcendent and incomparably superior Person . . . as neo-modernism maintains . . . there can be no divine moral law, because there is no One "out there" whose nature it expresses. Man is adrift in an existential sea—with no hope of finding the right way home, because there is no right, and no home. [Instead] man "perfects" God by cooperating in the prescribed revolution and establishing the utopian Kingdom. (p. 281)

Contrary to Ratzinger and Steichen, as I have been arguing throughout this book, I believe that religion is risky precisely because it asks us to place our faith and trust in a "transcendent and incomparably superior

Person," *against all the historical, scientific, philosophical, political, and com-mon-sense evidence to the contrary.* While it is true that the following state-ment is as empirically unprovable as its opposite, I believe students in high schools and colleges have a right to consider the equally plausible possibility that, indeed, "there [is] no divine moral law, because there is no One 'out there' whose nature it expresses." It is altogether possible, I suggest, that "man *is* [my emphasis] adrift in an existential sea." But even if this is so, I firmly reject Steichen's and Ratzinger's conclusion that consequently, we have "no hope of ever finding the right way home, because there is no right, and no home." I believe, as resolutely as they do, but from a very different angle, that there is a "right" way to create a better world, and that there is even a "home" worth returning to.

In Chapters 8 and 9, I will develop these ideas in greater depth, from a post-theist point of view. For now, though, let me suggest that any "final" story regarding what is "right" and what is "home" must be a *secular*, as well as a *sacred*, construction, and that the schools and colleges ought to be active participants in writing the narrative. It must take into account the existence of a variety of competing religious, philosophical, and political narratives in the United States and elsewhere, each of which gives a valuable and unique meaning to people's lives in secular, pluralist democracies like our own. And it must recognize that no story will ever be final, because people "read" and "write" their theological and political texts very differently—from their own variegated worldviews and herme-neutics. The Ratzinger/Steichen text represents but one perspective on the world; so too does the liberation/feminist text. What is a reprehensible, "neo-modern" reading of reality to the former is a praiseworthy, realistic reading to the latter.

For me, though, both readings are deficient, because both appeal to a politically interested conception of transcendence in order to bolster their claims to an absolute, undebatable truth. The Ratzinger/Steichen text is idolatrous because, in its subtext, it wants to strengthen the power and influence of the hierarchical Roman Catholic Church. The prophetic narrative, in the liberationist/feminist form, is ultimately dangerous, in my estimation, not because it is anti-theistic, or even utopian, but because, in its subtext, it too is idolatrous. It succumbs too easily to the allurement of political ideologies such as Marxism that promise God-like power and deliverance to the masses (and, by extension, to their leaders), once the social class struggle has been resolved. It does not deny the existence of God; it wants the *poor* and the *oppressed*, and ultimately their *leaders*, to be God.

On the list of the deadliest sins, the prophetic narrative places oppres-sion, not pride, at the top. And in so doing, it refuses to acknowledge

Reinhold Niebuhr's (cited in R. Fox, 1985) sobering insight: "[There is a] deeper sense of the tragic in Christianity, a greater certainty that life on every level may involve itself in self-destruction" (p. 297). Niebuhr's Christian realism recognizes an *ironic* side to life: The tragic sense must always put firm limits on any pursuit of justice, even though it realizes that the quest for justice is a necessity that must challenge any self-serving acquiescence to the status quo. Neither Ratzinger/Steichen nor the liberation/feminist theologians seem remotely aware of how difficult it will be to hold a tragic sense of life and the quest for social justice in a tenuous, dialectical balance. In fact, neither group ever bothers to acknowledge the *existence* of a tragic side of life, except when it can be used as a means to advance one or the other's special ideological agenda.

CONCLUSIONS

The chief virtue of the prophetic account lies in its faith that the truly just society is a desirable, indeed achievable, human project. In spite of David Purpel's (1989) soaring utopian idealism and his tendency to downplay such grisly human vices as guilt, arrogance, and self-deception (three vices, among others, he does mention—but only briefly—in his text), *The Moral & Spiritual Crisis in Education* continues to be a remarkable prophetic statement of hope for some educators in my classes. His "Educational Credo" (pp. 113–119) always moves many of my students. They appreciate his attempt to blend such curricular goals as getting students to contemplate the awe and mystery of the universe along with encouraging students to work for peace, justice, compassion, caring, and interdependence in the real world. Purpel speaks often about the need for educators to cultivate "attitudes of outrage and responsibility in the face of injustice and oppression" (p. 118), and this he is able to accomplish with those socially active students in my classes.

Likewise, Paulo Freire (1985), in his own prophetic fashion, and in spite of his penchant to express his ideas in an arcane philosophical/theological vocabulary, often inspires certain students to translate their attitudes of moral outrage into tangible community action. Because of his influence, I have had some students over the years engage in grassroots literacy projects in rural and urban areas, both in the United States and in many Third World countries.

Also, inspired by the "prophetic" work of a religious agnostic, Nel Noddings (1993), a number of students in my own Northeast region of the country are currently working to establish "communities of caring" in their churches, schools, colleges, state departments of education, and human service organizations. Many take Noddings's ethic of caring one step further. I know of several educational administrators in my state who have systematically attempted to create an ethos of caring in their elementary and middle schools. To this end, they hold frequent student assemblies and sponsor many teacher-parent workshops on the nature and practice of caring in educational settings.

Although the prophetic narrative obviously has its upside with some of my students, with others it poses a number of insuperable difficulties, many of which I have discussed throughout this chapter. At this point, however, I would like to summarize the downside by briefly discussing a major multicultural protest that occurred on my campus some years ago. I believe the discussion will serve as a compelling *aperçu* for what it is I, and some students, fear most about the prophetic worldview—especially when its influence extends into the secular-educational arena.

I feel it is necessary to add, before I begin, that I consider myself an ardent anti-racist. I am keenly aware of the systemic racism that exists in every institution in America, especially in schools and colleges. Moreover, I realize that unconscious racism among liberals like myself is perhaps the most invidious racism of all, because it is covertly protective of established (white) power arrangements. I also find personally detestable the more overt racial slurs, the verbal and physical violence directed toward individuals who are different in some way, and the shallow and hurtful stereotyping of whole groups of people. This includes, of course, the intellectually fashionable bigotry directed against Protestant fundamentalists and evangelicals, as well as conservative Roman Catholics, Jews, and Muslims. Sadly, many liberal colleagues and students, on my campus and elsewhere, often caricature these politically undesirable groups as religious bigots who deliberately conspire against women, people of color, and homosexuals so as to deny them their rights.

To set the stage: 30 minority students at my university barricaded themselves in the presidential administration offices and issued a nonnegotiable communique demanding, among other things: the establishment of 5 new academic departments; the immediate hiring of approximately 40 professors of color; the reinstatement of a minority professor who was denied tenure after an 18-month appeal process; an increase in minority scholarships; search committees chosen by students, staff, and faculty of color; sanctions against "hate" crimes; the removal of the Ira Allen statue at the center of campus because he was alleged by the protestors to have committed "genocide" against the native people of Vermont; unarmed campus security; a freeze on all university funding from the state until issues of racism were resolved; the removal of Marriott food services from campus because of alleged racial insensitivities, including nondivestment from South Africa; and no disciplinary action to be taken against the occupants of the administrative suites.

In the space of three short weeks, the campus hummed with political and media activity. Reporters and cameras were everywhere. Daily ultimatums circulated back and forth between the protestors and the president. A Black Panther revolutionary and a rock band visited the "captured" presidential suite to show solidarity for the protestors. Sympathetic students went on a hunger strike; others took over the Registrar's office; and the president was "assassinated" in a mock revolutionary drama. At a university senate meeting, the faculty overwhelmingly supported a resolution that the president negotiate immediately with the protestors, while non-faculty staff workers argued for their removal as criminal trespassers. Incidents of vandalism escalated around the campus (a bus was burned, a statue defaced, some office locks were glued, and some secretaries' desks were rifled and damaged).

In short, my university was a site of one "nonnegotiable" demand after another, incivility, and turmoil for the better part of a month, until, one quiet spring morning during final exams, university security officers removed the protestors and city police arrested them (all were subsequently released in a matter of hours, and their names expunged from police records per agreement with the university). The president (who resigned during the summer after the takeover and fled the campus in disgrace) earlier appeared at a news conference to express his deepest concerns about why he had to order the forcible removal of the students, and, most important, *to promise a campus-wide, restrained and reasonable dialogue on multiculturalism*, an ideal to which he claimed to be enthusiastically committed.

Predictably, the promised campus-wide dialogue never took place. Instead, the protestors (and their supporters) continued to spend most of their time uttering volatile revolutionary slogans, taking intractable political positions based on black vs. white, gay vs. straight, and poor vs. rich ideologies, and engaging in a number of rhetorical attacks against those they designated the "racist" enemy. The administration, for its part, spent most of the time preoccupied with "damage control," and the faculty and student body disappeared, as final exams wound down and summer arrived. The disgruntled staff members (student affairs personnel, secretaries, maintenance, food services, and office managers) who remained at their jobs throughout the summer found themselves, per usual, to be the only real "oppressed" class at the University. For the most part, they continued to be a faceless, voiceless, and powerless presence on my campus. In my mind, though, the greatest casualty to the university was the death of civil dialogue on extremely important issues that, to this day, remain unresolved, both here and on other campuses around the country. In fact, some years later, students and faculty of color at my university believe that the protestors' issues still have never been sufficiently addressed.

During the takeover, the demise of genuine, open-ended, candid discourse on race and diversity happened on my campus, I believe, because administrators, faculty, and students automatically ceded the moral high ground to the protestors. The protestors were considered by many to be the "prophets" of a new order, calling the rest of us to moral accountability while they themselves remained beyond ethical, religious, or political reproof. While it was true that many of my colleagues and students understandably feared being attacked as racists, they still found it convenient to elevate the protestors to a status that made them morally and politically unassailable. The result was that all of us missed the opportunity to fully understand and, when appropriate, to challenge what have, in recent years, become established political orthodoxies on college campuses throughout the United States. In effect, most of the university granted an *a priori* moral rectitude to the protestors, whose "rage" it certified as fully justifiable, and this effectively silenced those in the community who might have wished to contest some of the more outrageous accusations made against them.

Gone was the opportunity to have a campus-wide dialogue on the following assumptions, all of which, in some form, came up during the student protest, and each of which continues to circulate virtually unchallenged today on my campus:

- The American university is institutionally racist.
- All people of color in the United States are oppressed.
- Cultural diversity is always and everywhere necessary for a good education.
- A preferential affirmative action policy in admissions and hiring decisions levels the playing field, redresses past wrongs, and diversifies campuses in an educationally productive way. Thus, preferential policies in behalf of race, ethnicity, gender, and sexual orientation are a simple matter of social justice.
- A race/ethnic/gender/sexual orientation curriculum must challenge and, at times, discredit the traditional white, male, heterosexist, Eurocentric curriculum.
- Nonviolent resistance to racism, sexism, and homophobia is always a permissible act of moral outrage, the necessary strategy for transforming systemically racist universities.

- The university must require sensitivity group sessions and diversity-education courses in order to stop racism and hate crimes.

Obviously, it is a huge stretch to connect the student takeover on my campus to the prophetic (religious) narrative I have been discussing in these two chapters. There was never an overt religious or spiritual element to the student protest. Nobody explicitly took on the role of prophet. No serious attempts were ever made, to the best of my knowledge, to justify the political activity in biblical, or even in religious, terms. As far as I know, the name of God never came up in negotiations, press interviews, or subsequent campus reeducation sessions. Nobody invoked the writings of liberation or feminist theologians. Not a single Christian cleric appeared to make a statement. Even the local community's group of religious fundamentalists, never before considered camera-shy, stayed conspicuously out of sight of the university and the press.

What is at issue for me regarding this little case study is not whether each and every multicultural assumption I list above is true or false (I happen to believe there is more, rather than less, truth in all of them), but that *a kind of prophetic mood and tone captured my campus, and as a result, these and related issues never got addressed in genuine give-and-take, intimidation-free dialogue*. The prophetic mood, as I have tried to show, is one of absolute moral certainty. It gives automatic moral preference to those whom it designates as oppressed. It bestows unchallengeable moral authority on those whose political pronouncements are somewhat left-of-center, preferably leaning toward a humanistically rejuvenated type of Marxism. It shows a presumptive bias against merit, wealth, individual achievement, and liberty, because it thinks these are capitalist, racist vices. And it insists that those who dissent from the doctrine that social justice entails perfect equality be immediately cast out of the community and declared heretics.

What happened on my campus merely confirmed for me the truth of Tinder's (1989) words: "We have seen again and again that an unyielding determination to achieve perfect justice leads to the use of force on such a scale that the ends are swallowed up in the means" (p. 63). While *physical* violence during the takeover was minimal, the *verbal* and *psychological* violence quotient at times reached the highest decible level and drowned out the more reasonable voice of common sense and compassion. For one, working-class staff and students were effectively silenced, sometimes by being dismissed as "rednecks" by prophetic students. The point still remains, however, that even when outright *physical* violence is held to a minimum, any hellbent pursuit of social justice threatens to give rise to uglier expressions of violence, and these, in turn, generate newer and more terrible forms of injustice.

The proper religious function of the prophetic voice, in my opinion, is to call into question any truth, *especially its own*, that is presented as final, absolute, or exclusive. In addition to calling the rest of us to moral accountability, Christian prophets, for example, need to be open to the possibilities for the renewal of their own traditions. For starters, they might look toward African, Asian, and Oceanic forms of Christianity for ways to revitalize the older language, rituals, and stories. They need to work on lessening the intramural tensions between warring groups within Christianity itself, such as the rapidly expanding fundamentalist/evangelical/Pentecostal communities and the mainline churches in the United States and South America, the Protestants and Catholics in Northern Ireland, and the Catholics and the Orthodox in Ukraine. Christian prophets must look within their church hierarchies to eliminate the injustices rampant in their own ranks. But they need to look outward, as well, to foster a more genuine ecumenicism toward non-Christian faiths. And, above all, Christian prophets must continually bear witness to the truth that religious zealotry of any kind is always injurious, particularly when it is combined with issues of national identity, ethnicity, race, or gender (see J. Z. Smith, 1995, pp. 252–253).

Regrettably, during the student takeover, there were few prophetic *educational* voices on my campus, my own included, who were willing to call the student protestors to account. During the student contretemps, moral courage was at a premium, while moral cowardice was the order of the day. I readily admit that there are times when the prophetic stance must be justifiably loud, intemperate, and even moralistic. (The horrifying policies of Nazi Germany should have evoked this type of response throughout the world; so too should the less obvious, but no less deadly, acts of actual discrimination and violence committed against *all* kinds of people in many American settings every day.) At times, prophets must be able to claim a defensible right to name, and to condemn, the transgressor in the most contumacious manner. But a prophet's moral outrage can also be lethal: No matter how righteous, moral ire can be one-sided, uncharitable, and ultimately ruinous, *especially in an educational environment*. The special mission of a school or college ought to be to foster respect for the virtues of a mutually beneficial, rational, problem-solving dialogue, where nobody has a premium on moral outrage or moral certainty.

In recent years, too many prophets on too many college campuses throughout the United States have been more than willing to engage in self-vindicating expressions of moral anger on behalf of social justice. At least to me, their moral indignation frequently lacks humility, a sense of limits, and patience. In an educational setting, I find that most expressions of moral wrath, while often inspiring, end up being counterproductive. Their end result is to silence opposing views by trying to shame dissenters, and in the process, valid dissent is driven underground. Thus, the public dialogue is terminated, and the prophet is then left to issue the moral ultimatums that may or may not result in the use of force to implement them.

I would suggest that the prophet needs to guard against the ever-present temptation to foment revolution rather than rebellion. In Albert Camus's (1954) language, *revolution* seeks total social transformation, and in some cases the end justifies the means; while *rebellion* seeks the termination of a particular injustice, and the means always justifies the end (see Tinder's [1989] discussion on this topic, pp. 66–67). As an educator, I believe that rebellion seems the more realistic, and ethical, choice in the face of palpable social injustices; but, more important, I hold that the means I use to make things right must always be consistent with the moral ends I hope to bring about. The danger of the prophetic perspective, I contend, is when the prophet chooses to ignore the connection that must exist between moral means and moral ends, in pursuit of some lofty political objective.

In the next two chapters, I intend to examine what I am calling the *alternative spiritualities narrative* as one type of response to effect personal transformation. Its adherents will argue that *personal* transformation must always be the necessary precondition for *social* change.

CHAPTER 6

The Alternative Spiritualities Narrative

According to Harold Bloom (1993), "temperament, and not theology, determines the self's stance in religion" (p. 33). As we have already seen, while very few of my students are temperamentally disposed to the fundamentalist narrative, more are drawn to the prophetic narrative, albeit with some reservations. If temperament is the combination of unique intellectual and emotional traits that predisposes us to act in some ways rather than in other ways, then I would have to say that the majority of my students, particularly the younger ones, are intellectually and emotionally attracted to what I am calling the alternative spiritualities orientation, over all the others. And it has been this way in my classes for more than 30 years. The religious stance that has seemed most salient to students throughout the years is the one under consideration in these next two chapters, because it is the one they consider to be the most personal, spiritual (as opposed to religious), holistic, and self-transforming. A few have yearned to combine personal spirituality with a prophetic intention to engage in social action and community life, to be sure, but these types of students, while vocal, have still represented a minority view in my classes.

AN OFFICE VISIT

Whenever students sing the praises of alternative religious spiritualities, they make several stated and unstated assumptions about what a post-modern, late-20th-century religion ought to look and feel like, what beliefs and values it should profess, what epistemology it ought to advance, and what human needs it must fulfill in order to be a living, transformative force in people's lives. My alternative spiritualities believers, a hard-core group of students who always manage to show up in force in every class I teach, have a distinct religious worldview, and they are not afraid to express it. Generally, these students can be articulate, well read, somewhat abstract (at times annoyingly ethereal), and far less zealous, even laid back, in their conversational style than the fundamentalists and the prophetic believers. They exhibit no less resolve or enthusiasm, however, in propounding their worldview.

By way of introducing the alternative spiritualities worldview, I will recount a memorable experience I once had with a student who, I think, typified this religious mindset, at least in the rough. A young woman came to my office at mid-semester several years ago, shortly after we had finished studying the fundamentalist and prophetic narratives, and at a time when I had not yet created a distinct unit on alternative spiritualities. A new high school English teacher, and obviously somewhat disenchanted with my course, she engaged me in the following conversation. I will call her Donna, and what follows is the dialogue that occurred between us as best I can remember.

Donna (a little cautious but determined): "I don't want to sound hyper-critical, but I can't connect with much of anything we've talked about so far this term. We've spent too much time on Christianity and Judaism, it seems to me, and even though you've tried to steer us away from the traditional churches at times, we always seem to get back to the same old religions. Do you know that whenever I bring up our course content with my own students back at the high school where I teach, they get turned off? One of them even asked me the other day why we're wasting time on 'dead issues.'"

RJN (gulping): "Nothing we've studied so far is interesting to you? None of your *own* students come out of these backgrounds? Do *you* think we are spending time on 'dead issues' here?"

Donna (more self-confident now): "I won't speak for my students, but I will speak for myself. I see Western religion as being a very destructive force in society by and large. My parents were deeply involved in the political activism of the 1960s, and my mom always says that was the time when she felt the most religious, and the most connected, in her whole life. She and my dad experimented with hallucinogenic drugs big-time, along with mescaline and mushrooms, during those days, and while she doesn't try to sell me on the virtue of psychedelics, she does say that drugs were a way for her to get away from the smothering and restrictive atmosphere of her church with all its uptight teachings. My dad says the same thing about his temple upbringing. They often claim that doing drugs helped them to go through the pains of religious withdrawal better than any deprogrammer could provide. They grew up hating religion, and so they never raised me in any church. And yet, I really admire my parents' spirituality. They don't do drugs anymore (in fact, they don't approve of my smoking pot), and they are devoted to a number of social causes, especially animal rights, environmentalism, and holistic health. My mom is into Buddhism, and my dad does yoga, and both of them live really healthy lifestyles. They have been a great influence on me, and I credit them with turning me on to meditation.

RJN (happy to change the topic from class to parents): "What did your parents particularly dislike about the mainline religions, if I may ask?"

Donna (enjoying this immensely now): "They think their childhood religious upbringing stressed the head more than the heart, reason more than feeling. Their early religious experience was much too otherworldly, too distant from their own personal concerns. And they feel organized religion in their day separated people rather than uniting them. Either you went to church or temple or you didn't; and if you didn't, you were *persona non grata* in the community. Their religions seemed to be far too comfortable with middle-class values like striving and competition and the accumulation of worldly goods. The church rituals themselves were sterile. Everything was so unimaginative, so mechanical, so predictable, so hierarchical. To this day, they still talk about their neighbors and colleagues who attend religious services every week but whose personal lives seem to be in shambles. Everybody is so neurotic, driven, cutthroat, and dependent on antidepressant medications like Prozac to get through the day. I myself see this hypocrisy all the time in the teachers and parents at school. It seems to me that organized religion today is either so bent on comforting people and giving them a sense of guiltless, middle-class security, or in scaring the hell out of them, that it ends up being empty and boring. I think this explains why my own students' eyes glaze over whenever I try to get a discussion going with them on religion. I know this is why my own eyes glaze over in your class."

RJN (gulping again): "I'm really sorry that the course is such a turnoff to you. How might the two of us salvage something for you this semester so that the experience isn't a total loss?"

Donna (now the self-confident teacher): "Do you think we could spend some time on non-Western forms of spirituality? Why don't we talk about Eastern religions, macrobiotics, ecology, Native American spiritualities, the Gaia movement, even some of what people call the 'New Age' beliefs? I know a lot of adults like you put down New Age thinking as 'cotton candy for religious yuppies and Generation-Xers' [RJN—I did say this once in class, regretfully], but I think New Agers have something important to offer. I know some of my own high school students are really into the *I Ching*, witchcraft, the occult, tai chi, astrology, herbal medicines, and reincarnation. And I like many of these things, too. I only wish I knew more about them. This is what really turns on some of *my* students about religion."

RJN (needing to change the subject again): "Could I ask you a personal question about all of this?"

Donna (defiantly): "Sure, if you let me ask you one back."

RJN (a little wary): "Okay. Do you believe in anything that one might call a God? I ask you this question not because I'm prying, but because it will help me to understand more clearly what you mean by religion and spirituality, and what your own students might mean, too."

Donna (finally coming to the point, victoriously): "I don't want to sound snide, but I took this course hoping to come up with some new images and words for what I believe. So far, I feel as tongue-tied about answering your question as before I took this course. But let me try to respond anyway. My God certainly isn't like the fundamentalist God. I've got no Bible to consult for the final revelation. And my God isn't political, isn't a Reagan Republican. Neither is my God interested in punishing non-Christians, or in turning people against each other, if they don't toe the line according to some sacred scripture. On the other hand, my God is not the prophetic God, although I like some things about this image, this 'story,' as you say. My God isn't some social justice fanatic from on high who's always trying to start socialist revolutions on Earth. And my God isn't politically correct, because politics doesn't really matter when you get right down to it. Right? Somebody's always going to be on top and somebody's always going to be at the bottom, and that's just the nature of capitalism and politics, as far as I'm concerned. Isn't the point to be happy and self-confident and spiritually fulfilled as individuals, wherever you are on the social pyramid? Who am I responsible for? you are probably asking. Well, I'm here to tell you, I am accountable to myself, because the way to others and to my God is first through myself. If that sounds selfish, I'm sorry. No, my God, if you want to call it that, is a kind of Unifying Presence, a cosmic force that is neither male nor female, human nor inhuman, but a spirit that links us to each other, that is present in everything, that inspires us to realize our higher selves. My God doesn't need churches, temples, or synagogues to inhabit, because this Unifying Presence is everywhere. You might say my theology is a mystical one, because I am on a journey to find my God in myself, and in the people and animals and nature I love, and in the few social causes that are important to me. This Unifying Presence flows through me and through others, and there are times when my creative energy is so cosmic it frightens me. At this point, I think each of the world's monotheistic and polytheistic religions have a piece of the story about God, but I think pagans and even nonbelievers do, too. I love something one of my students said to me in class the other day: 'God is every religion and no religion, because no single religion can hold God in captivity. God is the ultimate escape artist!' I guess I can't do better than this. And now I have a question for you. Have you ever felt anything like what I've just described, or is this a generational thing?"

RJN (unsure of correct protocol here but pulling out a few pedagogical stops, nevertheless): "Whew! You don't sound inarticulate to me at all. It's obvious you've been thinking about religion, God, and spirituality for a long time. Can you recommend any readings for me and the class on this topic? And by the way, I hope you decide to remain in the course. In answer to your question, I have felt some of what you are saying, especially when I was present at the birth of my two daughters and my two grandsons. I felt the existence of what you are calling a Unifying Presence, a natural force, during these experiences that was exceptional. I felt truly connected to the people I loved and to the whole of nature and even to humankind in general, as birth and death are probably the most elemental natural experiences that human beings in all places and times share in common with each other. I would not call this connection 'God,' or a 'Unifying Presence,' however. To be honest, I don't know what I would call it, but it did feel spiritual."

NEW AGE, RELIGIOUS, AND SECULAR SOURCES

In our conversation, Donna raised a number of issues that frequently come up in class whenever we study the alternative spiritualities worldview. This narrative is actually the most difficult for me to teach, because, like the conversation I had with Donna, it is so wide-ranging, often ephemeral, in its aspirations and so eclectic in its content. It is not strictly New

Age, even though it contains New Age elements. Neither is it primarily a melange of alternative American, European, and Eastern religions, although it contains major elements of these as well. And neither is it mainly a secular phenomenon, although it draws generously from the new physics, left-right brain research, environmentalism, feminism, and humanistic psychology for its intellectual base.

Consequently, whenever I teach this orientation, I choose (somewhat arbitrarily, I admit) to narrow the subject matter by concentrating mainly on the *Eastern* (e.g., Buddhist, Hindu, Sufi, Confucian, Taoistic) foundations of this orientation. Although I try, if only cursorily, to introduce students to New Age thinking, to some of America's alternative religions (e.g., Native American spirituality), and to some key secular influences such as humanistic psychology, I believe Eastern religion, whether or not its adherents are aware of it, is the single major philosophical and religious influence on alternative spiritualities thinking in the United States today, as it has been for decades. In fact, most of the time in class, I can very quickly detect a strong Eastern assumption (implicit or explicit) underlying a student's profession of faith in alternative spiritualities.

Actually, according to Smith (1995), the *New Age* movement originated in the 1960s, even though a number of occult and Spiritualist (those who believe that it is possible to communicate with the spirits of the dead via mediums and spirit mentors, often women) groups have used the term since the 1800s in this country. New Age spirituality is a loose, all-purpose designation meant to describe a higher consciousness. New Age is an eclectic synthesis of such disparate beliefs as reincarnation, karma, paranormal powers, UFOs, holistic healing, pantheism, astrology, channeling, biorhythms, shamanism, and trance induction, among others. In Ted Peters's (1991) words, New Age philosophy moves in two directions:

> One [is the direction] of the inner life, but this eventually opens out into the whole of the cosmos. It leads to an identification of the self with the whole of the cosmos and with God. It also leads to the idea of transformation, of transforming oneself as well as the whole of society. (p. 51)

While at this time the movement has dissipated somewhat in intensity in the United States, and has since become the target of comic page satire, I find that many of my own students (some *sub rosa*) still subscribe to particular New Age beliefs and practices, and they inform me that the movement is undergoing a kind of renaissance with their own students in the middle schools and the high schools. But even if the expansion of New Age initiatives and the growth in the number of converts have diminished in recent years, I would argue that the New Age influence in the culture at large has been remarkable and promises to be long-lasting. Smith (1995) has summarized the core of New Age thought whose impact, I contend, can still be felt throughout the culture in a number of ways:

> New Age philosophies ground their diversity in the truth to be found in immediate personal experience, seeking the spiritual transformation that will shatter the limits of mundane life, initiate a new awareness of the bonds among individuals, and enable the creation of an enlightened global community fully integrated with its earthly environment. (Smith, 1995, p. 768)

The *alternative religion* spirituality in America, dating from the late 17th century and largely non-Christian, includes, among other phenomena, African-American and Native American forms of worship. This spirituality also takes in Theosophy and Spiritualism. Theosophy is an eclectic religion, based on Brahmanic and Buddhistic teachings, that sees the universe as a single entity, a matter-and-spirit unity, and through the mediation of angels or Masters, people can make direct contact with the spiritual world. And Spiritualism is a combination of Gnostic, Tibetan, and Rosicrucian beliefs that emphasize reincarnation, group meditation, mediums, angelology, and demonology. The alternative religion spirituality also includes such "inner-awakening" groups as the Scientologists (ca. 1953, those who use a special technique to recall the identity of the true self over successive incarnations), the neo-Pagans (who practice the faith of ancient Egyptians, Greeks, Celts, and Norse), Goddess and Wicca worshippers, Buddhists (Zen, Vajrayana, Tibetan, Shoshu, Theravada), Hindus, Unificationists ("Moonies"), Sufis, and Black Muslims, among others. What all the alternative religions have in common, despite their significant differences in philosophical and theological content and worship style and practices, is that unlike many New Age religions, they are rooted in some form of community, they feature distinctive spiritual techniques and disciplines, they are influenced by charismatic personalities or masters, and they manifest a mystical interest in the occult (Miller, 1995).

The *secular* influences on the alternative spiritualities narrative have been humanistic and Jungian psychology, holistic healing therapies, the ecology movement, recent developments in physics, evolution, right-brain theory, astrology, and holism and systems theory. More specifically, in the field of psychology, the major secular influence has been the work of Abraham Maslow, Fritz Perls, and Carl Rogers. These pioneers ushered in what is known as the human potential movement (originating with G. I. Gurdjieff, 1877–1949), a holistic philosophy that stresses self-realization and creativity, heightened perception, and spiritual well-being. Human potential professionals often refer to a "revolution in consciousness" as their main objective. The human potential movement gained a huge following in the 1960s and 1970s among a number of human-service professionals in America, especially among educators, and to this day its impact can still be felt in state departments of education, teacher training programs, schools, and colleges across the country (Peters, 1991).

It is my contention that the alternative spiritualities narrative incorporates key elements of New Age thinking, alternative religions, and selective secular influences, and I present this particular religious orientation to my students as an important postmodern discourse. In general, I would argue that the *narrative as a whole* has four major components in its worldview (see Phillip Lucas in T. Miller, 1995, p. 360):

1. Adherents believe that a global spiritual transformation is going to occur wherein human consciousness will be elevated significantly.
2. Before this transformation can happen at the societal level, however, self-empowerment and self-healing must take place in each individual.
3. No longer can science and religion (reason and faith) remain enemies. This traditional dualism must give way to a "higher synthesis" that enhances life spiritually and materially throughout the planet.
4. The alternative spiritualities movement is strongly anti-institutional, decentralized, leaderless, and geared primarily to individual self-enhancement as a precondition for cultural transformation. It is also deliberately syncretic in its embrace of holistic healing therapies, Eastern and Native American religious beliefs and practices, and even millennial hopes.

In summary, the alternative spiritualities story has established itself as a viable countertext to what some perceive to be the drab, more traditional beliefs and practices of the mainline religions. This is essentially what Donna was saying to me in our little dialogue. To this day, publishing houses and bookstores, speakers and workshops, and groups and networks continue to push the alternative spiritualities agenda, with great success. In any given semester, I can enter a classroom fairly certain that I will find among my teachers several deeply committed, outspoken proponents of this religious account, along with open-minded seekers like Donna. And many will have actually attended alternative spiritualities workshops sponsored by their churches, schools, and professional associations.

Some of these students concentrate primarily on their own personal, religious, and creative growth, and they tend to emphasize metaphysical ideas and the spiritual practices of the East over direct social action. A minority engages in overt political activity, promoting social agendas related to international relations, peace, and the environment. And still others become involved with the holistic health and animal rights movements. I should acknowledge, however, that I have actually had very few students in my classes who indulge in channeling or who use crystals, two New Age practices that have earned the ridicule of critics everywhere.

THE ALTERNATIVE SPIRITUALITIES NARRATIVE

As I attempt to identify what I think are pivotal beliefs in the alternative spiritualities story, and their impact on my students who teach in public schools and colleges, I will frequently refer to some representative texts on alternative spiritualities I have used in class at one time or another. All the books I mention in this section are very readable, more or less open-minded in tone, and most of the writers are profoundly convinced of the personal and social worth of this worldview. Most important, though, students have told me that many of the books read like novels, so compelling are the personal and religious testimonials they present. In fact, I believe these texts lend themselves to narrative analysis much better than readings in the other three narratives, because the authors purposely use a story format to depict their journeys of personal discovery and religious revelation. (For example, see Diana L. Eck's powerful account of her own spiritual journey in *Encountering God*, 1993.) I am, of course, grateful to students like Donna for recommending many of these readings to me through the years. And I am also thankful for their willingness to share their own spiritual revelations with me and the class. I will save my analysis of the weaknesses of the perspective until the next chapter.

It is important to remember that in what follows, I will be highlighting what I believe are key Eastern assumptions that form the substratum of the alternative spiritualities story. I find that the following nine interrelated "plot" elements sum up the core of the alternative spiritualities narrative, as I have heard my students talk about this perspective over the years.

1. The purpose of life is not only action and performance
   but contemplation, surrendering, and being.
   According to this view, the spiritually educated person takes time to explore those dimensions of psychic life usually denied or ignored in the hustle and bustle of everyday living. To be truly educated means to play with ideas, to bracket preconceptions and accept situations as they are without forcing meaning on them, to declare moratoria on performing

in the world in order to step back to observe the diversity and richness in that world. To be spiritually educated is to be able to live part of life in the *passive* mode, in a spirit of compliance and surrender of the ego, to be nonattached, rather than to experience life exclusively in the *active* egoistic mode of attachment, control, and dominance.

One book I have used recently by Ram Dass and Mirabai Bush, *Compassion in Action: Setting Out on the Path of Service* (1992), is a particular favorite of my students. Dass and Bush make a strong argument for the importance of providing service in a passive, noncontrolling, nonattached way, while also remaining deeply committed to helping others. (Also see Ram Dass and Paul Gorman, *How Can I Help? Stories and Reflections on Service*, 1985). Several brief chapters in the *Compassion in Action* text offer such down-to-earth tips for human service professionals as "acting from the heart," listening to those who are the recipients of the help, the importance of "starting small," the need to "start right where you are," "doing your homework," "staying awake to suffering," and continually "reflecting on your motives." Dass and Bush (1992) state the overall theme of their text in these words:

> People on the path of action may seem goal-oriented, but they also have a peacefulness that comes from non-attachment. The *Bhagavad Gita* says that as we progress on the path of action we come to "work as one who is ambitious, respect individual life as one who desires it, and are happy as those who live for happiness." But through it all we are, as the *Tao Te Ching* suggests, travelers who are enjoying the journey because we are not intent upon arriving. . . . In the *Bhagavad Gita* . . . Krishna, who represents higher wisdom, reminds the seeker not to be caught up in thinking of himself as the doer. He says, "Only the fool whose mind is deluded by egoism considers himself to be the doer." (p. 144)

Another helpful text in getting educators to understand the concept of "total seeing," the ability to do away with such arbitrary separations and divisions as the doer and the one done-to, subject and object, teacher and student, is J. Krishnamurti's *On Education* (1974). Krishnamurti is conversational, eccentric, and crystal clear in his delineation of difficult Eastern ideas, and my students warm to his distinctive personality and his storytelling gifts. Another popular text on the subject of "total seeing" is Sri Aurobindo's *On Education* (1953/1973), because Aurobindo manages to blend both Western *and* Eastern insights on teaching and learning without totally derogating the worth of the intellect. Aurobindo acknowledges the pragmatic need, at times, to foster "separations and divisions" when one must teach, advise, or counsel, but he is also forthright in declaring that when education is done right, the separations and divisions dissolve naturally. The teacher becomes the student, the student becomes the teacher, and during these times, the designations *student* and *teacher* disappear simultaneously, replaced by a process called mutual, un-self-conscious learning.

2. *While truth is endowed with endless forms and modes of expression,*
   it is at the same time one and universal.

While there are multiple ways of satisfying them, human beings everywhere share the needs to be competent, creative, loved, and committed to fostering something cosmic in themselves. Truth is also universal in the sense that beyond its idiosyncratic expression, there is a "right" way to live. All the world's major and minor religions possess pieces of this one universal truth, this right way to live. For example, Buddha's Four Noble Truths hold for all cultures and all times: There has always been suffering and dislocation; selfish craving and desire cut individuals off from their fellows; release from the narrow constraints of self-interest is essential for community; and the Eight-Fold Path (Buddhism as a religion) is a way to enlightenment.

Three texts on non-Western religions that I have found illustrate both the variety and universality of religious truth are Paul G. Johnson's *God and World Religions: Basic Beliefs and Themes* (1997); Arvind Sharma's *Our Religions* (1995); and Huston Smith's *The World's Religions* (revised ed., 1991). These texts are a challenge to most of my students' media-driven preconceptions about the more exotic differences among the world religions. The books compare and contrast, in a highly agreeable manner, the major religions of the world, without ever once losing sight of the transcendental needs human beings have in common everywhere.

Johnson's (1997) text has proven to be the most entertaining for students to read, because it is a quirky, somewhat provocative, thematic analysis of major and minor religions, complete with many opinionated references to contemporary events, as well as incisive questions for reflection and discussion at the end of each chapter. Johnson's forte is to show, in jargon-free language, how all the world's religions are more similar than dissimilar in their notions of good and evil, mercy and grace, morality and ethics, eschatology, sense of divinity, and virtue, even while he points out definitive, indeed irreconcilable, differences in the various faith traditions.

Sharma's (1995) edited text is the most detailed and experientially based, because each author actually believes in the religion being examined. Thus my students get a bird's-eye view of each religious tradition from the perspective of a noted international scholar who is also a devout practitioner. In Sharma's text, students experience a firsthand understanding of the unique appeal of seven very different religious traditions. And they learn that pluralistic religious orientations such as Hinduism, Buddhism, Confucianism, Taoism, Judaism, Christianity, and Islam can each be both charming and inspiring, rather than fearsome and divisive. I have even had a few students seriously consider converting to one or another of the religions Sharma presents, so engrossing, and inspiring, are the firsthand accounts in his volume. Noteworthy here is the fact that not a single account comes close to propaganda or indoctrination.

And Huston Smith's (1991) text is a classic, first published in 1958, reprinted an amazing 90 times, and as readable as ever for the neophyte in the study of comparative religions. My students are always grateful for Smith's meticulous sense of balance, keen insight, and general good will as he surveys the world's major religions. Smith has since added new material on the primal religions—the native traditions of the Americas, Australia, Africa, and Oceania. And unlike the former two authors, Huston Smith (1991) covers the oral traditions, because, in his words:

> for the bulk of human history, religion was lived in tribal and virtually timeless mode. . . . Recent decades have witnessed a revival of concern for the feminine and the earth, concerns that the historical religions (with the exception of Taoism) tended to lose sight of, but which tribal religions have retained. (p. xiii)

As an afterthought, I would also add two popular commentaries on non-Western religions that I have assigned in past years: Harvey Cox's *Turning East* (1977) and Jacob Needleman's *The New Religions* (1970). Both texts are very reader-friendly, and they give students a look at how two respected Western scholars, one a theologian, the other a philosopher, predicted in the 1970s the extent to which non-Western religions would take hold in the United States in the next 20 years. Both scholars have proven to be able prognosticators regarding the Eastern influence, but, ironically, neither anticipated the sizeable impact New Age ideas and practices would have on mainstream America.

3. *The ultimate goal of life is to integrate action, love, wisdom,*
   and peace into a dynamic, unified lifestyle free of nagging contradictions
   and fragmented aspirations.

One way to achieve integration is to look for the mystical elements in everyday experience, or, in Peter L. Berger's (1970) terms, the "signals of transcendence" in the humdrum. Perhaps the single most popular text I have used in recent years in any of my religiously oriented courses is James P. Carse's *Breakfast at the Victory: The Mysticism of Ordinary Experience*

(1994), because it demonstrates, up close, how incredibly hard, but how essential, it is to create an integrated, unified lifestyle. Carse, a university teacher, writes a great deal about his experience as an educator, and because he discusses the alternative spiritualities narrative within the context of his successes and failures as a classroom teacher, he speaks in a very poignant way to my teachers.

Carse's special challenge in his book is to integrate all the conflicted components of his always interesting personal life into some kind of harmonious whole. Because he is a fragmented Westerner, but, more importantly, because he is an insecure and troubled human being like the rest of us, he is not always successful. He is always engaging, however. By way of summarizing the special appeal of the alternative spiritualities narrative to so many of my students today, I will try to encapsulate elements of Carse's particular story in the next few paragraphs. My younger students are forever talking about "getting themselves together," creating authentic, integrated lives, and finding harmony and balance in all their activities. They resonate with Carse's efforts to find this proportion in his own life.

Carse, director of religious studies at New York University, host of the WCBS-TV program *The Way to Go*, and author of several books on religion, begins *Breakfast at the Victory* (1994) with a story about Charles, a friend who was dying from cancer. While away on vacation, Carse mailed Charles a photograph of an old boot he found on a hiking trip in the Cantabrian mountains. When Carse arrived home, he went by to see Charles and, surprisingly, he found the photograph proudly hanging above Charles's bed. Charles delighted in telling Carse that the old boot could well have been his own, as he had lost one in the very same mountains years before.

Carse uses this little story to demonstrate the point that modest events in a person's life rarely "announce [to us] that they are special" (p. x). But each event that occurs in the unwinding narrative of a person's life opens a path into the unknown. "All experience . . . is bounded by the boundless. Every step on our journey adds to what we know, but it also reveals there is no end to knowing" (p. xi). And with this parable, Carse begins to tell the story of his own journey to discover the extraordinary in the ordinary, and, along the way, to find some kind of unity in both the sublime and the ridiculous events of his life.

Throughout the book, Carse relates a number of similar experiences where he is able to discover an element of mysticism hiding in the prosaic. For example, in reflecting on the closing, and razing, of his favorite breakfast diner in New York City, the Victory Luncheonette, Carse realizes how much he will miss Ernie, the short-order cook and owner. What is most impressive about Ernie, according to Carse, is the effortless ease, the total absence of self-consciousness, with which Ernie manages to fill all the customers' breakfast orders every morning at the grill. Ernie is an unflustered master at doing many things at once: cooking eggs, slicing bagels, frying bacon, flipping pancakes, and filling cups at the coffee spigot. The spiritual lesson for Carse is that sometimes it is best not to think too much, not to plan too far ahead, not to be so fully preoccupied with one's motives and actions.

Carse, echoing the *Tao Te Ching*, believes that when *this* and *that* are no longer separated—the ego from the object, the thought from the deed, Ernie's food orders from the act of cooking—then we can find the "still-point" of the Tao, where the infinite resides. For Carse, Ernie found his still-point at the Victory grill in the midst of a frenetic breakfast schedule, and his work became a beautifully harmonized, virtuoso performance of skill, efficiency, and grace. And Carse realizes that he occasionally discovered his own still-point in teaching, especially on those days when he stopped consciously trying to make the extraordinary happen in the classroom. In his words, "The classroom looks very different when I take a mystical view of it. If there is anything truly extraordinary in my teaching it is found in its ordinariness" (p. 17).

Throughout his extended spiritual narrative, Carse is able to glean transcendent religious meaning from the quotidian ordinariness of his day-to-day life—whether in a boating experience on Lake Michigan, or in gutting a fish, or in a golf match with his brother, David, or on a duck-hunting excursion, or in avoiding an ugly classroom encounter with a surly student whose three notebooks for Carse's course were sarcastically entitled "Shit-1," "Shit-2," and "Shit-3." Carse draws important theological lessons from these ordinary vignettes, and laces them with the wisdom he finds in such alternative spiritual sources as the *Tao Te Ching*, Islamic mysticism, Buddhism, Sufi teachings, the *Upanishads*, and Meister Eckhart.

For example, one day, while sitting at the desk in his study, Carse became suddenly aware that he and his beloved cat, Charlie, his soulmate, did not need spoken language to communicate with each other. "Although Charlie's face has the same absence of both comprehension and incomprehension as the Buddha's, it does not suggest an ocean of words needing to be spoken" (p. 20). There is meaning in silence, according to Carse, because it is the way to the "still-point" of Tao, and to the "presence of the unutterable" within each of us. Carse resolves, from that moment on, to help his students understand that only in the "speechlessness that precedes speech" is it possible to know God, indeed, to know anything at all. Language is impermanent, while silence and solitariness are constant reminders that the knowledge of most worth is that which issues from our ignorance, our unknowing. This, for Carse, is the "higher ignorance" that all teachers and learners must learn to cultivate, if they are to truly know anything at all.

Perhaps Carse's most moving spiritual revelation, though, happened a few weeks before his wife, Alice, died in his arms, after a horrible year-and-a-half-long struggle with cancer. One day, as Carse was soothingly massaging his wife's feet, she suddenly, and uncharacteristically, made the following assertion: "You know what I have learned about myself, about life, from these moments of illness, especially now that I know I won't survive it? . . . Nothing, not a goddamn thing" (p. 49).

As an initial, sympathetic response, Carse was tempted to agree with his wife that yes, perhaps life does come to nothing after all, and, of course, rarely is there anything startling to learn about life while one is dying—dramatic movie script endings notwithstanding. But then, after looking at Alice's face closely and seeing no tension or sadness there, Carse reflects:

> Clearly I hadn't got it. I realized suddenly that it was the ego in me that had been listening, still regarding it all as a matter of struggle, seeing death as something that stood over against us, as a hostile force we needed to oppose. But Alice had moved beyond the struggle and was speaking from another place. . . . Her life in that lucid moment meant nothing else other than what it was. I felt the effortlessness in her. It was the unmoving center, it was soul, pure presence. (p. 50)

In my opinion, this little, heart-wrenching story about living and dying dramatically captures the essence of the alternative spiritualities narrative and, along with it, its strong visceral attraction for so many of my students. Carse never preaches. While he frequently cites a number of "sacred" texts from many different religious and philosophical traditions, he never treats them as inerrant or infallible. He has no particular social, religious, or political agenda to advance. He is interested primarily in his own self-understanding, self-improvement, and self-transformation. He wants to work on his own project: to tame his own relentless ego, to plunge into his own inwardness, to find the meaning in his own ignorance and solitude, and to discover the "soul," the "unmoving center," the Tao, in his own teaching. He wants to become a whole human being.

The tone and substance of Carse's story are strikingly different from what we have seen in the fundamentalist and prophetic narratives, and my students are quick to notice the discrepancies. I will close this section with the one proof-text my students always find most captivating in Carse's narrative; and, by extension, I will make the claim that his anti-authoritarianism, humility, and ironic insight are also the outstanding features my students find in the alternative spiritualities account at its best. Carse fully understands that the more desperately we pursue integration and wholeness, for all their worth, the less likely we are ever to achieve them:

> But there is something more important than getting it right: not knowing exactly what getting it right is. . . . We are always wrong in some essential way about what our story is. We are never living out exactly the story we mean to be. But to be wrong in these ways is what makes it a story, openended and unpredictable, instead of a fixed plot rolling out to its foreknown conclusion. . . . *Knowing that we don't know is not only a higher ignorance, it is the basis for all our hope.* (p. 185; my emphasis)

4. The satisfaction of human wants is not always the equivalent of happiness.

Many human desires must be transformed, not satisfied. Authentic success is attained when a person is able to create and nourish a rich inner life, maintain a perspective of nonattachment toward the phenomenal world, find a "true vocation" as opposed to a "successful career," and arrive at self-knowledge through continuous self-observation and development.

The second most popular text I have used over the years in my religiously oriented courses has been Sheldon B. Kopp's *If You Meet the Buddha on the Road, Kill Him! The Pilgrimage of Psychotherapy Patients* (1976b). Kopp is easy to read, very quotable, and a psychotherapist who considers himself, first of all, to be a teacher. An intelligent and passionate exponent of Zen Buddhism, Kopp speaks profoundly, via a series of short "tales," to teachers on matters of vocation, authentic success, the inner life, the difference between wants and needs, and the vital importance for professionals to nurture a respect for the everyday experience of teaching. I consider Kopp to be both a philosopher of education and a philosopher of religion, and this is the way I usually approach his work with my students. (Also see his *Guru*, 1976a.) Some of his aphorisms (what Kopp calls his "eschatological Laundry List" in *If You Meet the Buddha . . .* , 1976b, pp. 223–224) that my teachers find extremely relevant to their own work are:

- "There is no way of getting all you want."
- "You can't have anything unless you let go of it."
- "You only get to keep what you give away."
- "The world is not necessarily just. Being good often does not pay off and there is no compensation for misfortune."

- "You have a responsibility to do your best nonetheless."
- "It is a random universe to which we bring meaning."
- "If you have a hero, look again; you have diminished yourself in some way. If you meet the Buddha on the road, kill him!"
- "Evil can be displaced but never eradicated, as all solutions breed new problems. Yet it is necessary to keep on struggling toward solution."
- "We must live within the ambiguity of partial freedom, partial power, and partial knowledge."
- "All of the significant battles are waged within the self."

I have heard a number of my younger students recently talk about the futility of trying to engage in "macro-change" efforts to transform this country politically. While they remain acutely critical of the competitive, greedy, consumer-driven aspects of American culture, they grow increasingly pessimistic about ever turning this society around. Opting out of social change efforts on a grand scale, as have most political radicals from the 1960s, many students today strive, instead, to take control of their own lives, to change themselves from within, and to work on transforming their own "micro-environments." They appreciate Kopp's (1976b) advice because, as one of my students said, "He sees life small, he keeps it all in perspective, and he works, first, on himself." For my students, Kopp's observations that we can never get all we want, and that the secret to happiness is to let go of what we think we need, come across to them as an epiphany.

This understanding that wants are not always needs, and that happiness must amount to something more than a mindless accumulation of adult "toys," sparks some of my younger students to want to live lives of "voluntary simplicity." This ideal plays itself out in a rejection of what they call the "supermarket culture," and some of my younger students make it a point to grow their own organic gardens, live close to the Earth, wear simple, unpretentious clothing, minimize waste, and take care of the environment.

5. *The principal cause of so much suffering and earthly destruction is the deeply ingrained Western belief that there is an individual, disembodied ego.*

This individual ego persists unchanged through time and space, and is considered superior to other egos and the natural world. This has led Western civilization to the neurotic belief that it must secure and control the natural world and other egos in order to shield itself from the unpredictable, and the fortuitous, aspects of life. This has also led to extreme forms of competition, aggressiveness, individualism, and striving.

This insight into what might be called "non-duality," so central to Zen Buddhism, is ultimately the most perplexing for many of my Western students to understand, mainly because Western epistemology is thoroughly grounded in the irreducible difference between subject and object, observer and observed, "in-here" and "out-there." Also, Western ethical and moral systems stress the supreme value of individualism, self-realization, and individual salvation. And much of Western psychology is premised on theories of ego differentiation and identity construction. Even a few contemporary Eastern thinkers appear to be at odds over whether there is a "lower" and a "higher" ego, the "higher" being important enough to retain because it is less contaminated by grasping, material desires. It may be that the principle of non-duality will never be fully amenable to the Western worldview, and hence will be ignored or watered down in any final East-West synthesis.

Many of my students, in contrast, who are drawn to the alternative spiritualities narrative are *monists* who believe in the underlying unity of all aspects of life. They try to be authentic non-dualists. Often they talk about being overwhelmed by a sense of connection with everything in the natural, human, and physical world. They are ill at ease with any lifestyle that alienates the individual from the majestic beauty of nature, the warmth of communal sharing, and the oceanic experience of feeling a unity of body and spirit in physical exercise, lovemaking, and bonding with friends and family. For these students, *illusion* is separation, independence, false distinctions, and the fragmentation they undergo on the job, at school, or at home.

The reality for these students happens during those times when they can live their lives monistically, when their Atman (the individual self) is consistent with their Brahman (the primal source and ultimate goal of all human beings). Brahman, in Hindu metaphysics, is God, a shared oneness, an interconnected creation. In the observation of an anonymous Sufi, "God" is not only everywhere, but we become more aware of God when we try to see everything as God might see it, that is, when the self stops *seeking* and instead becomes the *sought*. The Sufi's insight is that each of us is at once both seeker and sought, separate but interconnected, neither one in flight from the other, reaching fulfillment only in complementarity (Carse, 1994, p. 139). In this sense, we are all "higher selves."

Kenneth Cragg's *Wisdom of the Sufis* (1976) helps my students to get "inside" the Sufi (an ascetic, mystical Muslim sect) story for another perspective on how to transcend what philosophers call the "subject-object distinction." And Chogyam Trungpa's *Cutting Through Spiritual Materialism* (1973) provides an illuminating analysis of separation, independence, and the illusion of objectivity.

6. *Life is a continually flowing, causally determined process of becoming, developing, and unfolding.*

Practices like yoga, meditation, breathing, energy awareness, centering, and fasting are meant to free individuals from the misguided need to intrude aggressively upon the natural environment and the world at large in order to get into the natural flow of living. The experience of meditation, self-hypnosis, and visualization involves a "letting be"—an absence of struggle with the external world, a profound respect for the natural environment, a "going with" the flow of personal energy, and a radical alternative to the medical model as a way to experience a robust "holistic" health.

Many of my students regularly attend stress-reduction workshops, and they teach these strategies, in turn, to their own students. They learn the principles of mind-body healing. They practice breathing techniques, such as the relaxation response, that are self-soothing. They learn how to become "mindful," how to commit themselves wholeheartedly to a task, how to do it completely, and how to be fully present in their personal and professional relationships. One of my students recently became a disciple of Thich Nhat Hanh (1976, 1991), author of two major works on mindfulness, and she has introduced many of his meditation activities to her high schoolers, both in formal school assemblies and in her work with athletes as a soccer coach. Some of my students have even learned to do hypnotic trance work, a kind of self-hypnosis, and one of them has found this strategy effective in working with addicted youth in a detention center.

The purpose of all these activities, in Csikszentmihalyi's (1988) terms, is to help distracted and fragmented Westerners to move into a "flow experience," a way to merge subject and object, the part and the whole, to experience time and space in a very different manner. John P. Miller (1994) is one educator who has written extensively on how best to use the meditative disciplines in schools and colleges in order to enhance learning, and I mention his work in Plot Element 8 below. So, too, the work of James Moffett (1994) is worth mentioning in this regard, as are the educational publications prepared by the Seva Foundation for *The Project on the Contemplative Mind in Society* (1996).

Marilyn Ferguson's *The Aquarian Conspiracy: Personal and Social Transformation in the 1980s* (1980) and any number of works by such thinkers as Herbert Benson (1987), Norman Cousins (1984), and Bernie S. Siegel (1989) develop the truly revolutionary idea in the West that health is a positive state and not simply the absence of disease—a fundamental tenet of the Western medical model. My students appreciate using the term *wellness* to describe something qualitatively different from most conventional American physicians' understanding of *health*. For many of my students, health connotes a strong autoimmune system; a state of incredible spiritual exhilaration, creativity, and joyfulness; and a sense of harmony and balance with the human, natural, and spirit worlds.

To this end, more and more of my students have tried, at one time or another, homeopathy, acupuncture, biofeedback, meditation, touch therapy, root medicines, macrobiotic food diets, aerobic and yoga exercises, such martial arts as tai chi, and even various forms of massage therapy. According to Peters (1991), what all of these holistic health techniques have in common is that they "capitalize on the 'wisdom of the body,' which is alleged to be innate" (pp. 20–21). If this is true, then the new "wellness paradigm" (Ferguson, 1980) teaches that the responsibility to heal derives from the *inner person*, not from the physician who resides in the hospital or HMO office, but from the real "doctor" who resides in each of our private selves.

On another note, Native American religious traditions are gaining a strong following among certain educators in this country, mainly because of the neo-shamanism currently popular among some groups in the New Age Movement. More than a few of my own students in the rural state where I teach are attracted to the Native American's special attunement to the forces of nature, and they prefer this natural mysticism, the spirituality of the medicine man, to the otherworldly mysticism of the major religions. I know firsthand of several young teachers who have taken my courses who actively teach various kinds of Native American spirituality in their classes, even in the elementary grades. This, of course, infuriates fundamentalist parents in their communities who resent what they perceive to be the privileging of one "trendy" religious orientation over another, more conventional one, Christianity.

Wade Clark Roof (1993) describes a young woman who is drawn to Native American religious traditions because of their sense of "connectedness" to the land and to people. She says:

> I just love the way that [Native Americans] make that sacred, in a time like this when so much destruction has happened on the land, the pollution in the air and the mountains and strip-mining and all that. I feel like that energy is very healing. (pp. 22–23)

Roof (1993) goes on to add that this woman "goes to medicine wheel gatherings and has a sweat lodge in her back yard" (p. 23). I must admit that so far, not a single student of mine has admitted attending a medicine wheel gathering or sitting in a sweat lodge, although I have had a few students who experimented with peyote in Mexico, not as a drug but, in their words, as a "sacred medicine." One student, after doing some research, was surprised to learn that the peyote religion in Mexico and the American Southwest actually incorporates Christian symbols (Jesus, the Bible, the cross) into the traditional native elements (divination, visions, healing, rites of passage, and hunting). According to one scholar (J. Z. Smith, 1995, p. 761), many Native American religions came into existence *after* contact with the Christian West, and thus Christian elements are bound to appear in some Native American religious ceremonies, as do other influences.

7. There is a divine, cosmic spark in all of us.

All individuals carry a cosmic consciousness within them, an internal God and a Goddess every bit as powerful as the transcendent God of the traditional religions. This God/Goddess also lives within our communities, nature, and intimate relationships, and, in Nord's words, this divine spark "resacralizes the cosmos" (p. 192). Perhaps the most succinct yet comprehensive treatment on cosmic consciousness that I have ever assigned to students is Ted Peters's *The Cosmic Self: A Penetrating Look at Today's New Age Movements* (1991). Students appreciate Peters's generally sympathetic critique of much that calls itself *New Age* in the United States, because they know he is a nontraditional Christian theologian who understands well the spiritual hunger of disillusioned and disenfranchised Christians. Peters is highly aware of Christianity's failure to remind young people of their own divinity and goodness, preferring instead to talk of sin, suffering, remorse, and redemption; he publicly acknowledges the New Age vision to be a "noble and edifying" one.

One renegade Catholic theologian, Matthew Fox (1988), has written a book, *The Coming of the Cosmic Christ*, in which he argues that Christ is a pre-Christian symbol of the God who is present in each person. Christ, as archetype, represents the divinity of all human beings, the transcendent "I Am" in every one of us. While Jesus incarnates the Cosmic Christ, according to Fox, each one of us is also an incarnated Christ. For Fox, life is an "original blessing," not an "original sin," and because God dwells within each of us, and in the natural environment as well, we need to accentuate not sin but self-love, joy, and fulfillment. We need to look for the Cosmic Christs everywhere. Fox's work is filled with alternative spirituality language: He speaks about paradigm shifts, ecological disasters, right-brain thinking, meditation, reincarnation, goddess worship, Jungian archetypes, harmony, and the glories of panentheism (the belief that everything is in God and God is in everything).

I mention the work of Matthew Fox here because his "creation theology" is an excellent example of how one very controversial alternative spirituality has infiltrated, and enlarged, Roman Catholic theology for millions of his followers who choose to remain in the church. And his work has great resonance for those of my students who have given up on their childhood religions as too depressing and punitive, but who now consider returning. Fox's work, and others like it, also gives new hope to the agnostics and atheists in my classes. Thanks to writers like him, they are able to find a way to be more attuned to a spark of divinity existing within them, without having to profess an allegiance to what they think is a repressive, "pie-in-the-sky" theism. (In 1994, Fox left the Catholic Church to become an Episcopal priest. He recounts his reasons for becoming a "post-denominational" clergyman in *Confessions*, 1996.)

The concept of cosmic consciousness is a good example of the *kataphatic* spirituality I mentioned in the first chapter. Kataphatically, God is immanent, present in all created things, a horizontal presence rather than a vertical one. This perception of God has enormous appeal for some of my students, because it reverses *apophatic* conceptions of God as a transcendent otherness, absolutely separated from creaturely existence. Kataphatically, God and I are now perceived to be the same. Both of us are infinite and eternal. God serves and defines me; I serve and define God. There is no significant qualitative difference between me and God. We are both human and divine, and we each struggle to improve ourselves. We are each in the process of unfolding.

8. The intellect alone is not enough to know reality.

An overemphasis on conceptualization as the supreme mode of cognition leads people to categorize the world, to concoct ideologies and systems that too often explain the world away, even while they provide personal identity, useful rules of action, and succinct sociopolitical interpretations. Concepts too easily act as filters to screen out direct perceptions of the world. A spontaneous, intuitive, and direct experiencing of the world, as in contemplation and meditation, is a type of knowing as powerful and valid as the intellective.

In this regard, the *contemplative* practices of Eastern and nontraditional American religions are making something of a comeback in this country. Contemporary educators such as John P. Miller (1994) are presently devoting entire textbooks to the effectiveness of contemplation and meditation in the helping professions. In fact, one could say that there is an ongoing "meditation revolution" in the United States. These meditative practices are basic to Siddha Yoga (the highest stage of Raja Yoga that the practitioner can reach on the way to spiritual enlightenment), and are the key to a number of alternative religious rituals in this country. It is important to understand, however, that while the meditation revolution has made some adaptations to modernity in the United States, non-Western meditative philosophies "hold that the highest and final authority is the spiritual master or guru, whether honored as a maharishi, swami, gurudev, or gurumayi" (Thursby in Miller, 1995, p. 207). Thus, the true meditative experience is "charismatic" rather than "technical," tied to a guru and not a technology.

9. All things and experiences are manifestations of a basic oneness.

This oneness is an ultimate, indivisible reality, called Brahman in Hinduism, Dharmakaya in Buddhism, and Tao in Taoism. Differences and contrasts are relative within an all-embracing unity; good and bad, pleasure and pain, life and death, and masculine and feminine are merely two sides of the same reality, extreme parts of a single whole, what Jung called *enantiodromia* (Jung, 1968). All opposites must be seen as polar, and thus as a unity, different aspects of the same phenomenon. What can sometimes be a very painful experience in my class is to hear believers in this narrative trying awkwardly to explain the notion of *oneness* to the rest of us. So much of their disquisition on this concept ends up sounding trite and ingenuous to Western ears.

I think what these students are searching for is a way to talk about "holistic" thinking. In my mind, they are declaring adamantly that *moral perfection* is not the quintessential goal of life, as it is in the mainline monotheistic religions; rather, *psychological completion* is, in the sense that one needs to be psychically, spiritually, and physically together, whole, integrated, balanced, "in touch" with both the shadow and light sides of the personality (Peters, 1991). What Westerners "see" as "obvious"—separate objects and events—is actually a function of a discriminating and categorizing intellect. In contrast, these students believe with all their hearts that at some level of consciousness, opposites are interdependent and always held together in a dynamic tension; thus, the best state of mind is one that is an integrated, rather than a fragmented, consciousness. In this sense, then, these students strive for a oneness, a wholeness, and even though they do not mean to leave the impression that they are inflexible, they can come off sounding doctrinaire about the value of what Donna, in her office visit with me, called a "Unifying Spirit."

CONCLUSIONS

Of the four religious orientations I teach, the alternative spiritualities narrative is the easiest to parody, particularly the New Age elements. Some of my students enjoy poking fun at what they think are its airy, cosmic pretensions and its "elitist," quasi-mystical vocabulary. A nationally syndicated cartoonist, Garry Trudeau, creator of *Doonesbury*, has made a virtual career out of burlesquing such esoteric New Age practices as channeling (contact between a human and a spirit), the use of crystals (the belief that crystals vibrate at the same rate as brain waves, store and transmit energy, and join people to the universe), and divination (using Tarot cards, *I Ching*, Ouija boards, and tea leaves to learn the future of hidden knowledge). And on a more serious note, a Jesuit scripture scholar, Mitch Pacwa (1992), laments that New Age spirituality, especially the Eastern religious influence, poses the single greatest threat today to the Catholic faith in America, because young people are so highly susceptible to noncultic, nonauthoritarian, highly individualistic appeals to "awaken the divine energy within each person" (p. 16). Thus, according to Pacwa, youth abandon the Catholic Church in droves in their search for the ever-elusive "cosmic self."

While some of the more exotic beliefs and practices in the alternative spiritualities orientation may be in decline today, I always warn my more skeptical students to avoid consigning this narrative to the dustbin of passing religious fads. One study, the Roper Reports (reported in Graham, 1997, p. 6C), found that baby boomers are forcing the mainline Christian churches in America to adopt such practices as meditation and "sacred labyrinth walks." And in some Reform and Reconstructionist Jewish congregations, Zen and Eastern mysticism are starting to find a place alongside traditional Jewish beliefs and practices. Nord (1995) claims that polls show that 20% of Americans believe in reincarnation, 25% put their faith in astrology, 28% are certain that witchcraft is true, 31% place their confidence in magic, and a whopping 46% rely on ESP (p. 193). Moreover, self-esteem and human wellness agendas continue to influence school and college curricula throughout the United States. Eastern religious practices are prospering in this country in the form of stress reduction workshops, mind-body healing, relaxation and imagery training, acupressure, yoga, mindfulness training, meditation, sensitivity, and hypnotic trance work. And Native American spirituality is becoming increasingly attractive to environmentalists and holistic health enthusiasts.

Like the fundamentalist and prophetic perspectives, the alternative spiritualities narrative can be read as a valuable counter-discourse to the dominant secularist and modernist religious texts. One scholar, J. Gordon Melton (in Miller, 1995), has gone so far as to assert that this perspective is a

> clear, mature religious vision that combine[s] the centuries-old Western meta-physical tradition with new (to the West) Eastern wisdom traditions. . . . The movement's beliefs and practices remained under new names that . . . actually better describe the community of transformed, spiritually awakened, compassionate, earth-loving persons of which the movement consists. (p. 351)

This narrative works for many, I believe, because it is a story that takes place *outside* the mainstream religious text. There will always be religious dissidents who prefer alternative forms of belief and worship. Orthodox Catholicism, Protestantism, and Judaism are examples of main-line monotheistic religions wherein, over time, dissidents have actually modified many conventional practices and beliefs in these faith traditions, sometimes even breaking off into new sects. Why do dissidents continue to look for alternative religious texts? Some dissidents struggle with major life transitions and seek the excitement, and succor, of innovative religious communities, while others find the practices of the mainline churches intellectually, theologically, and morally bankrupt, and pursue what they believe are more authentic religious frameworks. And a few are in such distressing states of personal psychological and religious upheaval that any change that promises inner peace and harmony seems beneficial.

Some of these religious dissidents will continue to experiment, some will find a stable home in newer forms of spirituality, and others will return to the faith communities of their youth; but spiritual alternatives to the mainline denominations will continue to attract people, including many of my students, and *their* students as well. Some scholars estimate that currently there are upwards of 3,000 alternative religious groups in the United States, with 10 million members (Larson, 1982), although J. Gordon Melton (1993) claims that the actual number is closer to 600 groups with 200,000 practicing members. Whatever the true number, I am convinced that some spiritually sensitive people will continue to challenge religious orthodoxy and orthopraxy in this country, either as individuals seeking relief from the hegemony of modernism and secularism, both in the churches and in the society at large, or as members of kindred spiritual groups who desperately crave religious and global transformation.

In my opinion, the best one-volume encyclopedia of alternative spiri-tualities published in this country is *America's Alternative Religions*, edit-ed by Timothy Miller (1995). Miller's Introduction (pp. 1–10) is a nicely balanced overview of the unintended consequences of "diversification and decentralization" in the American mainline churches during the 20th century. Miller and his co-authors refuse to use the terms *cult* or *sect* to refer to less popular religions, because they are pejorative. For them, the modifier *alternative* more fairly describes a wide spectrum of religions that "differ from their mainstream counterparts, [without presupposing] an inherent inferiority" (p. 2). Miller's (1995) book covers over 100 alternative religions currently being practiced in the United States, each described in a series of very understandable, brief essays, written by respected religious studies scholars primarily for nonspecialists. It is a volume that should have great appeal for educators in secondary public schools and colleges, because it is a convenient guide for understanding the alternative religions that engage the attention of so many young people today. The coverage includes such religions as Hare Krishna, the Unification Church, Baha'i, Sufism, Santería and vodun, Rastafarianism, People's Temple, Neo-Paganism and Witchcraft, a number of Native American spiritualities, and Satanism, among others.

Before I close this chapter, I would like to identify what I believe is especially noteworthy about the alternative spiritualities stance *in regard to teaching*, and the unique challenge they pose to modernist and postmodernist educational theories. In what follows, then, I will present a series of straightforward educational assertions that, I submit, constitute a countertext to modernity every bit as vigorous (and no less serious) as the two we have examined in previous chapters:

- Often, a tranquil mind is an understanding mind. Krishnamurti (1974) and Carse (1994) argue that educators tend to confuse *intelligence* with *intellectualism*. Intellectualism, for them, is *not* tranquil. Instead, it is the feverish preoccupation in American schools and colleges with learning high-tech skills, the business logic of bottom-line reasoning, and personality packaging, to the exclusion of other kinds of understandings, often found in the arts, humanities, and the natural and social sciences. Intelligence, as I understand these writers, is less driven, less narrowly focused; intelligence happens when students awaken to the power and imagination of their own thinking, when they are able to make wise judgments about the most moral ways to apply technological and scientific insights, and when they can balance the beauty of the analytic intellect with sensitivity to the beauty of the outer world, including the natural environment.
- An education that helps students to determine for themselves what higher ideals to live by, what commitments larger than themselves

they need to make, is a "spiritual" education in the truest sense of the word, because it inspires students to construct an ethical framework, to care deeply about love and compassion, and to respect all of creation, including animals and the natural environment.

- There is in Taoistic thought an important principle for educators, *wu-wei*. Wu-wei is not intellectual passivity, inertia, or "thought stoppage." Rather, it is a "letting go" of cognition at the appropriate moment, a tranquil watchfulness, a creative quietude. Teachers who jog, or do aerobics, or meditate, or fast, often talk about the brilliant flashes of intellectual and emotional clarity they experience in the afterglow of an intense physical experience. There are apparently two incompatible conditions in human consciousness, cognitive activity and cognitive relaxation. Both are necessary for creativity to occur. Sometimes we must allow the working intellect to follow its own directives; this is the way of the scientist. At other times, we need to let the conscious mind relax, and stop standing in its own light. Wu-wei is the freedom that flows when a student "works without working," achieves clarity without disproportionate effort and strain.

- When taken seriously, the alternative spiritualities narrative can provide a rich educational model for the school and university classroom. For example, a seminar that embodies a *dharma* (Skt., a higher principle, a disciplined body of spiritual practices), a *sangha* (Skt., a group, a community of loyal and trusted friends who will support, criticize, and challenge the bodhisattva, the seeking student), and a *guru* (Skt., a venerable person, a spiritual friend who is an intellectual superior, mentor, and spiritual companion) is a vast improvement over much that passes for education in the schools and colleges today.

- Prophetic and fundamentalist educators run the risk of dissolving religion and learning into the political cause of the moment, and in the process, private life threatens to disappear in an ocean of political confrontation. While social engagement is necessary, so too is the "life-giving quiet at the center of the relentless social storm" (Roszak, 1975, p. 192). It is this deep inwardness that is as crucial to human sanity as political action. This "deep inwardness" is not antisocial; it is trans-social, above and beyond the political cause of the moment. It is not reactionary; it is realistic, in that it recognizes there may be political situations that cannot be changed, in spite of a long history of Western technological optimism and Christian-Marxist theories of moral and social perfectibility.

- The alternative spiritualities orientation reminds us that what is crucial in education is, in the end, the quality of the relationship between teacher and student. The teacher must *be* the way as well as *point* the way. The teacher must become a living example of someone pursuing enlightenment, holism, and tranquility. The best teacher is one who has an unobtrusive good will, who is willing to "let be" in the classroom, when the situation requires that students find their own answers to the universal question, What is the right way for me to live in the world? While the hunger for quick fixes and magic bullets is insatiable in the modern world, the best that any effective teacher can do is to stop giving easy answers to complex questions, to help students get on with their own growing, and then to disappear from the picture with dignity, style, and grace.
- Finally, education with an alternative spiritualities flavor asks *why* as well as *how*; it deals with *meaning* and *wisdom* as well as with *data* and *information*; it is concerned with *subjectivity* as well as with *objectivity*; and it is directed more toward *understanding* than it is toward *acquisition*. Good teaching, then, stems not from a flurry of outward activity, but from quiet, resolute contemplation about the larger purposes of education and its desirable relationships.

But, alas, in addition to identifying what I consider this narrative's strengths, I must also discuss the dark side of the alternative spiritualities orientation. Each of the above assertions, as we shall see, contains within it the ominous seeds of its own negation. In the next chapter, I will analyze the hidden dangers in this worldview in a manner that, I hope, takes its central claims very seriously; and I will try to do this without intentionally making fun of its more obvious deficiencies and excesses, as so many other critics do.

CHAPTER 7

The Failure of the Alternative Spiritualities Narrative

In class, occasionally, an exasperated critic will try to sum up the alternative spiritualities orientation with the following type of derisive comments:

> Who really takes this stuff seriously anyway? To me, it's an intellectual vacuum filled with self-indulgent snippets of everything from Shirley MacLaine, Dalai Lama, ashrams, new paradigms, inner bliss, rhythmic breathing, and guided imagery to Hindu swamis, Muslim imams, cosmic selves, eco-feminism, Wicca, and goddess worshipers. It's ridiculous. How can we ever consider this religious hodgepodge to be a viable counter-discourse to modernism and secularism? In fact, I would argue that the whole program is symptomatic of exactly what's *wrong* with modernism and secularism today: It's shallow, self-centered, exploitative, and trendy. And it shamelessly commercializes the wisdom and practices of many of the major religious traditions throughout the world. Every time we challenge their assumptions, these alternative folks come back with the charge that we are stuck in "Old-Paradigm" thinking; this seems to be their favorite putdown.

In many ways, I think this narrative is even more rigid than the others we've studied. At least the fundamentalists and the prophetics make an honest, up-front effort either to convert me or to make me feel guilty, but these flaky navel-gazers look down their noses at me, and tell me I'm just not with it. I'm sorry, but this narrative just doesn't do it for me. It's anti-intellectual, naive, self-righteous, self-centered, pretentious, and dangerous. I say it's a dangerous story because it's reactionary and elitist. It's completely out of touch with the nitty-gritty worlds of people I know who live in the inner cities, in small, rural farming communities, and in the working-class ethnic neighborhoods. The so-called "New Paradigm" has no realistic political mission at all, as far as I can tell. Exactly how will the navel-gazers help the poor and the struggling middle class find this perfect bliss? What politicians, pray tell, are going to "transform the cosmic order"? This has got to be the pipe dream of an elite professional class of therapists, probably located in the universities, and all it's going to do is exaggerate even more the economic and political differences between the haves and the have-nots!

The biggest losers, in my opinion, though, are the easily fooled teachers and professors, and their students, in whose institutions this alternative spiritualities agenda has fully taken hold. In my school, for example, we talk the alternative talk all the time: new paradigms, global thinking, student-centered learnings, holistic education, emotional literacy, right-brain learning styles, stress reduction techniques such as centering and relaxation exercises, healing, self-esteem, cooperative learning, and recycling. No teacher dares mention *God* in class, of course, but we do hear a lot of talk about the Great Spirit, the Life Force, and Mother Earth, particularly in those classes that feature an environmental agenda. One of my colleagues, a science teacher, has just completed a unit on "eco-spirituality" with his seventh graders. So far this year we have had just three school assemblies, and would you believe that each one has had an ecological twist? I'm convinced that ecology has become the substitute religion for many public schools and colleges. My colleague has several copies of *The Whole Earth Catalogue* and *Natural Health* in his classroom for students to read, but you can be sure there is no other "sacred" text available.

THE THREE FAILURES OF NEO-GNOSTICISM

While the above tirade is obviously overstated, and definitely uncharitable, I believe it contains more than a germ of truth. In my estimation, the alternative spiritualities orientation is, despite its strengths, an incoherent and aesthetically unpleasing narrative because it contains so many internal inconsistencies. What I will examine briefly in the pages to come are three of what I think are the major weaknesses that often accompany this narrative.

First, I maintain that the alternative spiritualities story is dangerously *Gnostic* (Gr., *gnosis*, special knowledge) in the sense of being esoteric and self-indulgent. Its ultimate purpose is to acquire a transcendental knowledge of the self and, by extrapolation, of the cosmos and of God. This kind of knowledge, for the Gnostic, is considered a "higher" knowledge, and, as such, is said to be preferable to all other forms of knowing. I will argue that essentially this is an elitist and anti-intellectual approach to knowing, and ends up reinforcing some of the worst aspects of a self-centered, secularist society.

Second, because of its dominant Gnostic tendencies, this narrative is politically reactionary, notwithstanding its professed, and laudable, interests in achieving world unity, fighting for animal rights, and encouraging respect for the natural environment. The alternative spiritualities political agenda is unrealistic and naive, because, ultimately it is caught between pursuing two incommensurate objectives, self-enlightenment *and* cultural transformation. Since the 1960s in the United States, it has never been made clear exactly how the former will lead to the latter, and as a result, many socially idealistic youth tend to lose their political faith entirely, choosing instead to work on their own "inner" projects and personal lifestyles. This self-concentration, for all of its reputed personal benefits, leaves intact a larger society plagued daily by concrete instances of injustice, corruption, exploitation, and political oppression. A preoccupation with self-enlightenment and self-help, I suggest, unwittingly puts this orientation in the same conservative camp with the Christian fundamentalists.

And third, because the alternative spiritualities narrative tends to make excessive, undocumented claims in behalf of its putative spiritual, health, and psychic benefits, it finds itself vulnerable to widespread dilution, commercialization, and trivialization. Worse, some ethnic traditionalists, Eastern religious leaders, and aboriginal peoples on the North American continent have accused adherents of this perspective of practicing a subtle form of racism and imperialism, because they seem to exploit culturally endemic religious practices for their own financial gain.

ELITISM AND ANTI-INTELLECTUALISM

Gnosticism as a theological term first appears in early Christian times, and it refers to a number of religions (Christian, Jewish, Greek, Iranian, etc.) that stress the importance of knowledge as critical to salvation. Through the centuries, Gnostics have borrowed ideas and practices from such religious traditions as the Hellenistic mystery cults, Jewish cabalism, Iranian dualism, Babylonian and Egyptian mythology, and the Christian Bible. Although each of the Gnostic religions has a particular theology, cosmology, cosmogony, and series of rituals, I am using the term here generally to refer to a distinct way of interpreting the world. It is my contention that those who identify with the alternative spiritualities account are Gnostics by temperament and hermeneutic. The early Christian church had an axiom: *Extra Ecclesia, nulla salus* (Outside the Church, there is no salvation). I maintain that Gnostics tend to drastically modify this assertion to read: *Outside of self-knowledge, there is no salvation; and with self-knowledge there is no need for a church.*

Temperamentally, Gnostics tend to be anti-institutional, anti-dogmatic, and anti-authoritarian—each stance premised on their firm belief that *inner* enlightenment rather than *external* doctrine is the necessary prerequisite for salvation. Gnostics also tend to demean the material world while valorizing the inner world and the spirit world. They believe ultimate truth exists outside of space and time in some kind of Divine World of Light and Goodness. They also strive to be counted among those superior human beings who alone have special knowledge of God, and, by implication, of God's Kingdom of truth, goodness, and beauty. For the Gnostics, only a minority is ever saved, because only a few people are qualified to receive this divine illumination. Those who are not among the enlightened are condemned to live out their days in ignorance, in illusion.

Because Gnostics in the second and third centuries placed such a high value on knowledge of the divine as the only key to salvation, and because some even went so far as to assert that Jesus Christ was more of a spirit than an enfleshed human person, the Roman Catholic Church condemned this kind of thinking as a heresy. According to the Church, *docetism* (Gr., *dokein*, "to seem") is the false belief that because anything material (e.g., human flesh) is evil, then Jesus Christ must have been fully spiritual rather than human (see McBrien, 1995). According to the Gnostic scholar Elaine Pagels (1981),

> . . . some gnostic Christians went so far as to claim that humanity created God—and so, from its own inner potential, discovered for itself the revelation of truth. The gnostic, Valentinus, taught that humanity itself manifests the divine life and divine revelation. The church, he says, consists of that portion of humanity that recognizes and celebrates its divine origin. (pp. 146–147)

Today's Gnostics—whom I will call the *neo-Gnostics*—particularly those in the Eastern traditions, believe that most suffering comes from ignorance, and that only self-knowledge brings relief from suffering and results in ultimate enlightenment. Despite the appearance of a kind of spiritual populism among the adherents of alternative spiritualities, there is an undeniably exclusivist element hidden in the unstated, but widely prevalent, assumption that because most people choose to live in self-ignorance, they will be doomed to a lifetime of deficiency. While, admittedly, adherents acknowledge the pursuit of gnosis to be a solitary, complex, and challenging process, even for those who are among the chosen few, still, one unmistakable impression remains clear: The unenlightened among us must be content to dwell in deficiency until our final end arrives—self-annihilation. Only gnosis can save us, it is true, but only the few are able to pass "from this ephemeral world of darkness into the eternal realm of light" (Peters, 1991, p. 80).

Besides being elitist and exclusivist, I contend that neo-Gnosticism is anti-intellectual, in the *literal* sense. While it is true that neo-Gnostics place supreme value on knowledge, unfortunately for educators, the knowledge they value most is personal, intuitive, esoteric, and salvific. They prefer the tranquil intelligence over the busy intellect. In spite of talk about balancing right *and* left sides of the brain, feeling *and* thinking, heart *and* head, neo-Gnostics can barely conceal their disdain for scientific, logical, theoretical, pragmatic, and analytical forms of knowledge. This type of cognition is branded as "linear," "either-or," "subject-object" thinking (Ferguson, 1980). For neo-Gnostics, this kind of knowledge is ignorance, unless and until it gives way to knowledge of the divine. The knowledge that takes us inward, the knowledge of the "third eye," is the only knowledge that eventuates in divine wisdom; the knowledge that delivers us outward to the material world, the knowledge of the "blind eye," is knowledge of a lesser, partial reality. According to Peters (1991), only the newer mystical "paradigms" can change our vision and give us a "direct knowledge" of the "whole" cosmic reality.

I believe the anti-intellectualism that permeates the literature on alternative spiritualities is serious enough for teachers to confront directly in their classrooms. Today, the wide-eyed fascination that many people of all ages and educational backgrounds express for out-of-body experiences, UFO abductions, angels, and sun-sign astrology is evidence of the anti-intellectualism, and critical naivete, that typifies too much of American culture. So, too, there should be major cause for alarm among this nation's teachers when hundreds of adults, some highly educated (Heaven's Gate members were experts in computer technology, with their own World Wide Web page), can completely give themselves over—body, intellect, and psyche—to charismatic religious zealots like Jim Jones (People's Temple in Jonestown), David Koresh (Branch Davidians in Waco), and Marshall Herff Applewhite (Heaven's Gate in California). A dose of healthy intellectual skepticism and the ability to engage in critical scrutiny are the proper antidotes, I contend, to those who profess they talk directly to Jesus Christ, or to those who claim to be intergalactic gardeners in need of fellow travelers. I fear that all the neo-Gnostic talk about *losing* one's ego and opening up to understand the divine spark within too easily equates to *losing* one's intellect and falling prey to self-acknowledged gurus and masters who claim to possess perfect wisdom.

Also, the more neo-Gnostics stress the value of a passive, private, intuitive knowledge over an active, public, analytic intellect, the greater, I believe, is the temptation to deny the worth of a democratic intelligence that must be able to refuse, to negate, to challenge, to criticize, to negotiate, and, finally, to resolve. At the very least, educators need to be constantly on guard against *the erosion of the right to criticize* in America, especially in the religious sphere. There is no leader, religious, educational, or political, who is beyond criticism. Critical thinking skills are crucial if we Americans are ever to find common ground on the issues that currently divide us, and if we are to make intelligent political decisions together in a secular pluralist democracy.

Listen to the anti-intellectualism of Krishnamurti:

> The immediate perception of truth is liberating, not ideation. Ideas merely breed further ideas, and ideas are not in any way going to give happiness to man. Only when ideation ceases is there being; and being is the solution. (quoted in Powell, 1975, p. 44)

Also, listen to Ram Dass (1977):

> [The] mind plays too many tricks. . . . Don't sit and analyze or wonder or get preoccupied. . . . It all has meaning. It's all work you're doing on other planes. It is significant spiritually, but you don't have to understand it. (p. 93)

These comments are characteristic of the extreme bias against the cognizing self in the literature on alternative spiritualities. Too many of these writers go to bizarre lengths to reject the value of critical analysis and logical thinking—the skills I believe education ought to be about in Western democracies—in their pursuit of "*dharmakaya*" (raw experience) or the "thatness" of reality.

It should be obvious to all of us in the late 20th century that the act of thinking is neither illusory nor evil in itself. Thinking, like willing and feeling, is a means to an end, and it can be used for good or bad, depending on the thinker's motives and purposes. Moreover, despite the claims of the neo-Gnostics, truth is not always identical with intuition, contemplation, or enlightenment. Ram Dass's and Krishnamurti's assertions above are simply silly. A concept can be a tool for personal liberation at least as powerful as meditation or yoga. As a teacher-educator, I am more than ever convinced that students need an acute awareness of the intellectual complexities of moral and ethical life, a thorough, content-based grasp of history, literature, religion, philosophy, mathematics, and science, and an in-depth, critical understanding of the costs and benefits of a number of political systems throughout the postmodern world. Students need all of this, I submit, if they are to become independent-minded, global citizens, able to resist the blandishments of what might be called the "totalitarian temptation."

Why, I ask, can't thinking be a kind of praying, wherein people learn to think more intense thoughts in order to live their lives more intensely? As an educator, I am more than willing to admit that the rational mode of consciousness is by itself insufficient for the fullest experience of reality. But I am resolutely unwilling to spend my time as a teacher encouraging my students to live predominantly in the passive, wu-wei mode of "letting go." I see many of these same students a little too eager to "let go" of their critical faculties in order to get into the natural "flow" of life. I observe among my students a disproportionate number of budding "Seinfelds," who would rather simply "hang out" than be "hung up" on "bullshit jobs and politics," as one of my students indelicately put it.

Certainly, I am aware that much of our scientific understanding of the universe has been the achievement of some theoretical physicists who have been willing to make inexplicable, intuitive leaps, of astronomers who have remained silent and let the world speak, and of cosmologists who have grasped the power of daydreams, trances, the unconscious mind, metaphorical and analogical thinking, and meditation. But I refuse to go as far as thinkers like Andrew Weil (1973), who, in an earlier, highly influential work, advocated the use of marijuana as a way to ignore the "verbal productions" of the intellect. According to Weil, it was only when he started smoking marijuana regularly that he was able to meditate, and to construe original hypotheses about health and illness. Weil talks again and again about the possibilities of mind-expanding drugs (as well as more natural methods of transforming consciousness), the evils of the Western attachment to intellect, and the deficiencies of an ego-centered notion of consciousness. (See MacFarquhar, 1997, for an account of Weil's latest endorsement of educated drug use.) A few of my younger students consider themselves the grateful heirs of their 1960s parents' dog-eared copies of Weil's *The Natural Mind* (1973), and they enjoy using Weil as a validation for their own mind-expanding adventures with drugs.

Unlike Weil, I find few students today who are overly "attached" to the intellect, but I do see many who are overly attached to the prospect of "getting stoned" or "partying." (My university is consistently named a top-10 party school by the annual Princeton Review.) According to their own self-reports, the only "verbal productions" these students are looking to escape are the "hassles" of parental expectations, job requirements, office-related politics, relationship problems, and academic demands. In answer to my question each semester—"Why do people like to get stoned?"—I often hear the following from students: "We need to let go." "We want to laugh." "We work hard, we play hard." "We want to be free." "We don't want to worry anymore." "We need to relinquish control." "We have to stop the merry-go-round."

I have heard these types of responses from students of all ages, representing a variety of helping professions. Alarmingly, a few of my students have even come to my seminars stoned (an increasingly common occurrence, according to many of my university colleagues throughout the country), and I can attest from firsthand observation that when this happens, their intellectual abilities are seriously skewed. These students, whether stoned during class or the night before, frequently experience delusions of brilliance whenever they write or say something under the influence of drugs. Later, when they are sober (or "straight"), however, they always express extreme embarrassment over the mediocre quality of their work. Moreover, I have found that stoned students have no short-term memory. And their capacity to think logically or clearly is severely impaired, as are their decision-making skills in general. I remember a young teacher with a somewhat vacant look in his eyes solemnly remarking to me after one of my classes that he felt "really close to God in class today" as a result of our "intense religious conversation." This disclosure took me completely by surprise, because the students had spent the entire class taking an examination, with no conversation allowed.

Regarding the relationship of rational cognition and mystical understanding, I prefer to take the neo-Gnostic rhetoric about complementarity seriously, unlike thinkers such as Krishnamurti, Suzuki, and Weil, who frequently contradict themselves. Fritjof Capra (1977), a theoretical physicist, holds that science and mysticism are not oppositional, but rather two complementary manifestations of the human mind, of its rational and intuitive faculties. While the rationalist and the mystical worldviews are essentially different in their approaches to the physical world, Capra argues, in the end, each is mutually interdependent: Mystical experience is necessary to understand the deepest nature of things, while science is essential for describing and understanding physical reality and for negotiating the everyday demands of modern life. The mystical experience helps us to understand that something ineffable and spiritual transcends, or dwells within, all empirical content, while the *rational* experience drives home the truth that without an intimate knowledge of the empirical content of our lives, we are unable to live, or function well, in the world as productive human beings.

Whenever my students get carried away with James Carse's (1994) vividly moving accounts of finding elements of the mystical in his ordinary experiences, I have to remind them that Carse was not looking to flee from the commonplace events of his life into some kind of pot-induced nirvana. Rather, he was hoping to acquire deeper insight into those prosaic events in order to be a more competent human being *in the here-and-now*: a better—more intelligent and compassionate—teacher, parent, son, brother, and, even, mourning husband. One tangible proof of this is the fact that Carse, with all his heightened mystical consciousness, still comes down to earth to be a repeated winner of New York University's Distinguished Teaching Award. He also manages to use his intellect to write scholarly books, moderate television shows, be an expert radio commentator, and lecture worldwide.

I would also add that without language, conceptual categories, and interpretive frameworks—that is, without what might be called a *rational epistemology of mystical experience*—we would know absolutely nothing about what neo-Gnostics call ultimate reality, or the divine spark within, or the still-point of Tao, or God. The post-theists in my last two chapters will argue, among other things, that mystical experiences never occur in an epistemological or hermeneutical vacuum. Each and every human experience, including the religious, is a mediated one. That is, what counts for personal "bliss," or "enlightenment," or a feeling of "oneness with the universe," is always shaped by what the neo-Gnostic brings to a mystical experience by way of a prior theology, personal history, and membership in a particular language community. In the hermeneutical sense, there is no such thing as *dharmakaya* (raw experience). Or in analytical terms I introduced in an earlier chapter, no religious *text* is ever without an accompanying *context*. The neo-Gnostic text regarding the mystical experience is an exceedingly complex one, and students must understand the various *pre-texts* and *inter-texts* that surround ecstatic claims of personal enlightenment and liberation.

In this regard, Harold Bloom (1993), somewhat sarcastically, but no less insightfully, believes that the neo-Gnostic narrative in the United States is incomprehensible, unless we first understand that it has been revived and nurtured in California throughout the 1960s, 1970s, and 1980s. About the California context, he says:

> The Californian God differs in that he is a kind of public orange grove, where you can pick as and when you want, particularly since he is an orange

grove within. His perpetual and universal immanence makes it difficult . . . to distinguish between God and any experience whatsoever, but then why should such a distinction occur to a California Orphic? . . . The absolute immanence of the [neo-Gnostic] God is, I suppose, the inescapable poem of California's climate, the cosmos as one grand orange, consciousness as its juice. (p. 186)

For Bloom, words such as *immanence, cosmic consciousness,* and *inner bliss* are prototypically Californian in tone; being in tune with the infinite, and recalling previous incarnations with prehistoric warriors, are the "fantasies" of Hollywood stars like Shirley MacLaine. Where else but in California, Bloom conjectures, do people devoutly believe that absent a "cosmic rapport" with the universe, a person will never be able to experience spiritual insight, physical well-being, or economic success?

Ironically, as different as they might appear on the surface, neo-Gnostics and fundamentalists share a similar kind of exclusivity and anti-intellectualism. Each renounces the hegemony of intellectual elites, and highlights instead private, spiritual experience and knowledge of the divine, although it is very clear that for the neo-Gnostics, some people are more equal than others in being able to find this divine truth. And both, according to Nord (1995), possess "an apocalyptic vision of the world issuing in a millenial 'New Age'"; moreover, both "emphasize spiritual healing and self-help therapies" (p. 193). The eclectic neo-Gnostics go one step further than the fundamentalists, however, in their rejection of any central, canonical text. The neo-Gnostics pride themselves on being experiential and emotional rather than book-based in their spirituality. And because some neo-Gnostics are antinomian, they reject certain moral laws. They place such a high priority on the life of the spirit that bodily activity becomes morally irrelevant. This moral antinomianism explains why some neo-Gnostics appear to outsiders to be licentious, willing to deliberately flout sexual conventions.

In summary, I believe the neo-Gnostics drive an arbitrary wedge between the intellect and the intuitive imagination whenever they proclaim the glories of helping students to become "de-automatized" (less automatic and predictable in the ways they think and do things), "dishabituated" (able to break habitual patterns of behavior and thought), and "non-attached" (able to be *in* the world but not *of* it). From my perspective, what the Western world needs at this time is *more*, not *less*, of an education rich in what might be called "intellectual capital." Intellectual capital includes a broad range of factual knowledge; higher-order analytical skills (such as Western logic and the scientific method) that translate into real-world critical thinking; relevant background understandings in history, literature, mathematics, science, and, yes, religion; an ability to use language and concepts effectively both in speaking and in writing; and a civic literacy training *for everyone*, guaranteed to produce autonomous citizens able to participate effectively in the politics, economy, and education of the nation (Hirsch, 1996).

The acquisition of this intellectual capital will require teachers to realize, *contra* the neo-Gnostics, that *at times* subjective and objective data must be seen as qualitatively different; that active cognition is preferable to tranquil watchfulness; that the world must be comprehended in parts before it can be apprehended in wholes; that transcendence and verticality (as well as immanence and horizontality) are valuable paradigms for relating to divine reality; and that a certain amount of habit, automaticity, and attachment to the things of this world are actually prerequisites for most learning. For most of us, *the acquisition of data must first precede the deeper understandings of the meaning of that data*. Or in the language of literary theory, there can be no context without a text, no act of interpretation without discrete phenomena to interpret.

In the end, I concur completely with Wendy Kaminer's (1992) irreverent, but accurate, comments on the anti-intellectualism of New Agers:

> Listening to the weird New Age babble of bliss-speak, techno-talk, and personal development proverbs, while the experts bemoan the excessive rationality of our culture, I wonder. Am I the only person who thinks we've gone crazy? Assaulted by sound bites and slogans that pass for political discourse, gossip that passes for news, and anecdotes that take the place of ideas, I never feel surrounded by rationality. (p. 117)

To which I hope teachers everywhere are willing to say: "Wendy Kaminer, you are not alone! We, too, think people all over America have gone a little 'crazy' in their denigration of anyone who is 'intellectual,' who is trying to think seriously, deeply, and critically about the persistent problems that plague us in this society, beyond the shallow media sound bites."

Before I close this section, I must acknowledge an important objection to my charge of neo-Gnostic anti-intellectualism by David J. Blacker, in a personal correspondence. He says: "It doesn't strike me that the neo-Gnostics are any more susceptible to the anti-intellectual critique than the fundamentalists and the prophetics. . . . Almost by definition, any spiritual tradition could be described as having its anti-intellectual moments . . . " Blacker goes on to remark that the real failure of neo-Gnosticism lies in its "ersatz quality"—the tendency of so many neo-Gnostics to think they can create new historical traditions at will, with total disregard for their own cultural and historical situations.

While I certainly agree with Blacker's assessment regarding the "hubristic and shallow" inclinations of so many neo-Gnostics to assume they can blithely "leap out" of their historicity, I nevertheless take a different view of their hubris. For me, the inability to recognize their historical and cultural situatedness is simply one more peculiar manifestation of the neo-Gnostics' anti-intellectualism. In fact, despite their own hermeneutical blind spots, an unmindful disregard for the force of particular traditions, myths, doctrines, rituals, and ethical teachings on *all* individuals is *not* a condition that fundamentalists and prophetics share with the neo-Gnostics. The arrogant presumption that one can leave behind one's culture, one's community of memory—*at will*—signals to me a special kind of hermeneutical ignorance that educators ought to teach their students to avoid at all costs. (See Blacker's brilliant *Dying to Teach: The Educator's Search for Immortality*, 1997, for his own take on this topic.)

THE INCOMPATIBILITY OF SELF-ABSORPTION, GLOBAL HARMONY, AND DIRECT POLITICAL ACTION

Despite all the rhetoric about living in voluntary simplicity, respect for the environment, animal liberation, deep ecology, and global harmony, the neo-Gnostic narrative tends to freeze at the levels of self-absorption and global abstractions, and is essentially apolitical, even reactionary, in its understanding of what it will take to bring about social and cultural reform at the macro levels. Stephan Bodian (1991) has edited a very popular neo-Gnostic text, *Timeless Visions, Healing Voices: Conversations with Men & Women of the Spirit*. Not surprisingly, 13 of the 16 contributors speak mainly of the need for people to work on *self*-transformation, and the other 3 contributors are primarily interested in linking the "planetary crisis of our time" to the need for a *personal* orientation that "honors the sacred" and "encourages spiritual expression" (n.p.).

It soon becomes apparent to the reader of Bodian's (1991) work that even though many of the interviews in the text are meritorious and inspiring, the one social cause worth mentioning repeatedly appears to be the ecological crisis, the only social activists worth including in the volume are environmentalists, and the only solution to the world crisis is for people to undergo a "paradigm shift" to a Jungian-Christian-Eastern understanding of our "interconnectedness." In a nutshell, according to Steven M. Tipton (1984), the neo-Gnostic approach to political change, in the Bodian (1991) volume and elsewhere, is predicated "on the monistic assumption that the society is one interdependent whole and that social change, so far as it is possible, begins with self-transformation and spreads harmoniously" (p. 166). From this ecological perspective, the Earth is sacred, the "feminine principle" must awaken, high-tech civilization is lethal, and only nature can save us.

Neo-Gnostic politics is a million miles away from the revolutionary tactics and bombastic rhetoric of the 1960s student radicals, although many neo-Gnostics graduated from the various resistance movements of that era. Neither is neo-Gnostic politics concerned with the organized coalition-building of groups like the Protestant fundamentalists, who have actively sought to influence national political policy in this country during the last three decades. And unlike the prophetic orientation, neo-Gnostic politics has heretofore shown little direct interest in promoting social justice agendas. In contrast to these macropolitical orientations, the neo-Gnostic approach to social change is to decentralize bureaucracies, seek consensus, live the inner life genuinely, let reality be, defend the integrity of the "whole Earth" by taking on a "small-is-beautiful," personal lifestyle, seek a mystical merging of the self with the cosmos, and treat all living things with compassion and respect—all worthy and noble goals, indeed. But there are problems, nevertheless.

In the 1970s, Peter Marin (1975) feared that neo-Gnostics had "deified the isolated self," and in so doing had contributed to the breakdown of community in America, along with the "smothering of social conscience" (p. 75). Marin worried over the fixation on personal growth and spiritual transformation he saw in the schools and colleges, and he warned that organizations like the CIA, the KKK, and IBM would have no objection at all to the entire American population's being "blissed out." Blissed-out people are more pliable; they tend to consume more; they shut off their critical intellects; they become apolitical. Marin wondered what would happen to a generation of young people who were being taught to become more aware, more in "touch with themselves," in the schools and colleges. While Marin inaccurately tended to collapse the whole of what I am calling the neo-Gnostic movement into the human potential movement (what he termed the "awareness trap"), his concerns are nonetheless serious, with obvious ramifications for educators more than two decades later. (Even more recently, Marin [1996] has issued similar types of caveats for those who rush to embrace religious myths and illusions because they cannot live with "freedom's terrors.")

It is a commonplace by now that America has become a self-absorbed society as we prepare to enter the 21st century. Self-esteem education is ubiquitous in the elementary and middle grades. Apart from the efforts of a highly vocal but small group of students in colleges and universities to promote social justice, multiculturalism, and human rights, most college students in the United States today generally give more epistemological weight to the subjective over the objective dimensions of their lives, and most prefer their own personal development over direct political activity (Loeb, 1994; Willimon & Naylor, 1995). Whenever adults are troubled about the ontological or axiological quality of their lives, they tend to seek the interventions of psychotherapists instead of educators, political scientists, priests, moral philosophers, or even friends. Prozac and other antidepressants are the drugs of choice for the millions who find it increasingly difficult to cope with the ups and downs of human finitude (Kramer, 1994). And some people, as we have seen, find consolation in the religious certainties of fundamentalism and in the spiritual soothing of alternative religions. What all of the above have in common, however, is *the temptation to turn inward* for answers, to center and work on the self, to bypass the social world. And those with a contemplative, neo-Gnostic bent try to find, in Trungpa's (1973) words, something that is "independent of the body and life's circumstances . . . found in the depths of being . . . something universal, limitless, continuous" (p. 12).

Ironically, many neo-Gnostics in my classes completely miss the obvious social and political implications of several of the writings they love to cite. For example, while it is true that Mahayana Buddhism and its Zen sect does tend toward a type of monasticism that results in a withdrawal from the political world, Hinayana Buddhism is more worldly. The monastery is seen as a social institution whereby compassion must express itself in action directed toward various social agencies such as the family and the state. The Bodhisattva has virtually attained complete enlightenment, but refuses to enter into Nirvana as long as other sentient beings are still suffering (Johnson, 1997; Sharma, 1993). Also, there is a noticeable activistic tendency in such contemporary Zen representatives as Krishnamurti (1974), who states that "right education should be a danger to sovereign governments" (p. 106). Haridas Chaudhuri (1974), a disciple of Aurobindo, advocates a form of "integral yoga" whose ultimate aim is a political one, "the collective liberation of all the world's people through a unique world order ruled by spiritual values" (p. 51).

Furthermore, social leaders like Mahatma Gandhi and Thich Nhat Hanh, a leader of the Vietnamese Buddhist antiwar movement, saw themselves as political activists. And even though Taoistic thought sings the praises of spontaneity, naturalness, and stillness, Confucianism stresses social responsibility (Sharma, 1993). And while the Native American Church, best known for its use of peyote in worship, is the most influential new religion among today's American Indians, other Native American religions have been more overtly political. In the 18th century, Handsome

Lake's religion consciously addressed America's changing political and economic culture and provided a divine sanction for new ways of adapting to capitalism. *Mutatis mutandis,* the 19th-century Shawnee prophet Tenskwatawa preached that his followers must actively oppose Euroamerican, Christian intrusions by reverting to the religious lifestyle of previous generations of Indians (James R. Lewis in T. Miller, 1995).

Even though, as I have argued in an earlier chapter, the prophetic narrative errs by overstressing the political, thereby conflating religion with politics, it does remind us of an important truth: If religious accounts freeze at the level of self-improvement only, they will accomplish little more politically than what Joel Kovel (1976) calls the "palliation of a few ounces of alcohol" (p. 154). While I acknowledge that it is important to help students to develop a mystical standpoint toward their everyday experiences, this does not mean getting them merely to look *through* things to see their ultimate unity; it also means helping students to look *at* things, to see their particular differentiations and all the discrete implications these carry for political action. To offer but one small example at the university level, much of what upsets James Carse (1994) about the *rigor mortis* of educational policymaking at New York University might be more directly addressed by his planning concrete kinds of political action at a number of bureaucratic levels, in order to bring about the specific curricular changes he favors. Carse might start the reform process by becoming an active member of his departmental curriculum committee and university faculty senate, if he isn't a member already. A viable theory of neo-Gnostic social reform will somehow have to hold in dynamic tension such polarities as reflection, affirmation, renunciation, specific local action, and wider sociopolitical reform. The careers of Gandhi and King indicate that this is an achievable ideal, albeit an extraordinarily difficult one.

As yet, however, the neo-Gnostics are still searching for the most effective ways to adequately combine their apparently incommensurable concerns for self-transformation *and* global transformation. For example, today much of the commune movement in this country reflects a trajectory from 1960s social activism, to communalism, to individual and spiritual self-fulfillment, to environmentalism, to micro-capitalist business ventures in order to achieve some degree of economic solvency. Meanwhile, the average age of the communalist in America reaches 40, with the majority of members today more than content to "work on themselves" or to "hide out" from the world, according to one expert observer (Pinchbeck, 1997).

Closer to home in my seminars, among the neo-Gnostics the *self-*transformers far outnumber the *global* transformers, despite the widely heralded environmental politics of both groups. Regardless of their different transformative emphases, though, both groups appear naive to me when it comes to social reform, because neither has a comprehensive or systematic political program. For the most part, their politics are symbolic, content mainly to make a personal statement via individual lifestyle about what the good society might look like if all people just shared the neo-Gnostic moral vision.

I, for one, find it difficult to understand how Tipton's (1984) "eco-millennial unification of society" is going to happen by isolated individual acts of recycling, using windmills and compost toilets, and growing organic gardens. I am less sanguine than Tipton (1984) about the ability of neo-Gnostics to change society in the utopian terms they so often use. I am unconvinced that individual acts of daily meditation, or of eating a strict vegetarian diet, or of practicing herbal medicine, are going to save the rainforest, deliver Central American peasants from political oppression, result in nuclear disarmament, develop the Third World economically, and produce world peace (all desired objectives mentioned by neo-Gnostic interviewees in the aforementioned S. Bodian's *Timeless Visions, Healing Voices*, 1991). To my skeptical mind, isolated environmental acts based on a neo-Gnostic spirituality, often done in an ostentatious or boastful manner and absent a motivation to organize people outside the in-group for concrete political action, will succeed only in making individual adherents feel better about themselves. But for those of us who remain sincere agnostics on the cause of environmentalism, or are just plain unwilling to drastically change our lifestyles until credible scientific evidence is available, we will continue to raise critical questions, to challenge political orthodoxy, and to construct our own ecological *modi vivendi*.

I must respectfully disagree with Wade Clark Roof's (1993) assertion that neo-Gnostic baby boomers tend to subscribe to an "ethic of commitment" more than did previous generations. Roof believes that today, neo-Gnostic boomers are less "obsessed" with inner needs, and more genuinely concerned with the "well-being of society" (p. 246). I have noticed just the opposite: I find neo-Gnostic boomers in my courses even *more* concerned about themselves than others before them, in spite of their Johnny-come-lately interests in volunteerism, community service, and concern for the environment. Presently, neo-Gnostic social interest appears to me to be more self-calculating than in the past, rooted in the operative boomer assumption that, indeed, everything might be possible after all, and if it is not, then the 3 M's—"mortgage, menopause, and mortality"—take priority, as one respondent admitted candidly to Roof (1993, p. 248). Or as one of my own students declared in class: "When push comes to shove, when my social causes get in the way of my personal life, then the social stuff gets filed in favor of what is in my, and my family's, best interest." *Contra* Roof's research, Robert N. Bellah et al.'s (1985/1996) classic study, *Habits of the Heart*, drives home one vital point about the boomer generation: Libertarian aspiration and a heightened concern for the self are central boomer values deeply entrenched in American culture.

More important, though, the self-righteousness and certainty of some neo-Gnostic environmentalists, like the other kinds of religious self-righteousness and absolute certainties I have criticized throughout this book, invite nonbelievers to be skeptics, if not outright cynics (Carter, 1993). Harold Bloom (1993) has observed that "a religion of the self is not likely to be a religion of peace, since the American self tends to define itself through its war against otherness" (p. 265). What Bloom is getting at is that no matter how edifying and right, a religious cause *starting with the self* automatically pits a believer who has achieved personal salvation against a nonbeliever or a disbeliever, who are seen to exist in a kind of nonsalvific limbo. And in the event that one or the other party fails to come around, the result is likely to be combat against an alien otherness. Bloom's ultimate prediction is grim: " . . . the twenty-first century will mark a full-scale return to the wars of religion" (p. 265).

DILUTION, COMMERCIALIZATION, AND EXPLOITATION

During the 1970s heyday of the neo-Gnostic movement in America, Robert Bly (1976) warned that too many alternative spiritualities adherents were behaving like "soft fascists." Bly spoke of the need for gullible Americans to ground themselves first in their own religious traditions before accepting neo-Gnostic teachings and disciplines. He lamented the presence in the United States of too many celebrity meditation "masters" whose followers were like lost sheep in their presence. For Bly, these masters were self-promoting, sexist, and self-indulgent. But what concerned Bly the most in the 1970s was the ability of the media, colleges, public schools, business, and government to coopt the neo-Gnostic influence in order to pacify the population, smuggle psychotherapy under another name into the schools, and make money.

In contrast, Carl Jung (in Suzuki, 1973) was more realistic: He predicted that Westerners would ultimately reject Eastern thought systems because, as natural skeptics, they would refuse to place "implicit trust in a superior master"; they would not sacrifice the many years it took to pursue and achieve enlightenment; and they would reject the heterodoxy of Eastern satori experiences because they lacked the authoritarian quality of orthodox Western religions (pp. 9–29). Despite their differences, though, both Jung and Bly (1976) were deeply concerned about the excessiveness of neo-Gnostic spiritual claims, especially on the topics of personal enlightenment and global transformation. Both also cautioned against the multiplication of "cultic" heroes and the use of Western merchandising techniques to sell the neo-Gnostic product. And closer to the present, James R. Lewis (in Miller, 1995) is critical of what he calls "cultural imperialism" regarding the current affection for Native American spirituality among educators and psychotherapists; for Lewis, "whereas the older Euroamerican invaders stole the land, the new [neo-Gnostic] invaders are trying to steal the religions of native peoples" (p. 384).

During my lengthy involvement with schools and colleges, I have counted more than 150 so-called major "innovations" that educational authorities have mandated for schools and colleges: from behavioral objectives, to various kinds of accountability formulae, to career education, to citizenship training, to mastery learning, to whole language reading, to mainstreaming, to diversity/multicultural awareness, to cooperative learning, to background knowledge. Some of these innovations have rightfully endured, but, gratefully, most have long since departed from the current scene. I have often said that possibly the best professional preparation a teacher can ever receive is to cultivate a healthy skepticism toward "change agents." Teachers need to know how to resist all the high-gloss educational palliatives that "experts" will hawk in the name of innovation, probably until the end of recorded time. Such has it always been in the business of religion; so too will it always be in education. Because there is so much in the neo-Gnostic orientation that is merchandisable for educators and for religionists, I believe there has also been much cheap reproduction, extravagance, and overstatement. In my opinion, Jung and Bly were right to be worried.

For example, in the 1970s and 1980s, advocates of Transcendental Meditation (TM), the Science of Creative Intelligence, offered hundreds of courses for credit in high schools and colleges throughout the country. The popularity of TM reached its zenith in Illinois when the House of Representatives passed a mandate in 1972 that "all educational institutions in the State of Illinois . . . offer courses in Transcendental Meditation and the Science of Creative Intelligence . . . " (quoted in H. Bloomfield, 1975, p. 235). According to Maharishi Mahesh Yogi himself, TM will accomplish all of the following for educators: "develop the full potential of the individual; improve governmental achievements; realize the highest ideal of education; solve the problems of crime . . . ; maximize the intelligent use of the environment; bring economic fulfillment to individuals; and achieve the spiritual goals of mankind in this generation" (quoted in H. Bloomfield, 1975, p. 245). Even today the TM craze lingers on in several schools and corporations in my own state.

On another note, holistic health programs seem to be omnipresent in the culture—in schools, colleges, corporations, churches, the media, even in the military. Neo-Gnostics enjoin us to treat each person as a holistic, living organism, rather than as a broken machine in need of repair, and they believe that healing must originate from *within* the person before it can happen *outside* from medicine or surgery. And now, because self-healing is said to be everyone's personal responsibility, holistic advocates proclaim the benefits of alternative medicines and therapies over conventional medical models. Presently, several cable television networks (e.g., ESPN 2) give over entire morning schedules (sometimes in the form of "infomercials") to exercise shows, health food dieting, body sculpting, alternative healing regimens, and mind-body integrations.

In the schools, the neo-Gnostic influence has been gaining through the years, so much so that Christian fundamentalists have targeted what they call the "New Age Conspiracy" as the greatest threat to Christianity in America today (Hunt, 1983). Some of these allegedly "dangerous" New Age practices are: centering exercises, visualization, death education, deep-breathing exercises, dream journaling, guided fantasies, imaging, intuition activities, left/right brain work, meditation techniques, relaxation exercises, and whole brain learning, *inter alia*. I know personally of at least two state departments of education in the Northeast whose unofficial policy is to hire trained professionals to give district-mandated workshops in these practices to teachers several times each school year.

Donna Steichen (1991) documents a number of neo-Gnostic practices she claims are widespread throughout the Catholic Church in America. Among the practices she observed in the churches and at religious conferences during her 12 years as an investigative reporter were: yoga, tai chi, meditation, circle dances, widdershins, voodoo, witchcraft, channeling, spirit guides, vision quests, sweat lodges, and goddess-worship ceremonies.

I readily acknowledge that many of the above neo-Gnostic practices, taken separately, practiced in an appropriate time and place, and studied diligently, can be of great potential value to some people, depending on their individual temperament, level of intelligence, personal need, and ability to give fully informed consent to "leaders" who presume to teach these techniques. But to lump these practices all together in an apparently indiscriminate way (as many schools, colleges, churches, and business corporations do), and then to make exorbitant claims in behalf of their putative spiritual (and health) benefits, produces a neo-Gnostic smorgasbord that, I think, dilutes their fundamental worth. It also invites unfriendly critics to impose their own religious/political/educational agendas on neo-Gnostic spirituality, and even to ridicule it, without taking the time to examine each spiritual practice separately, carefully, and in depth, *on its own terms* (see the aforementioned Doonesbury cartoons).

From my perspective with regard to the holistic health movement, and with no particular religious axe to grind, I reject the silly assumption (see the *Mozert* case in Bates, 1994) that there is a "New Age Conspiracy" to undermine Christianity, or any other belief system for that matter. I believe the claims made in behalf of the reputed health benefits of such approaches as homeopathy, acupuncture, biofeedback, meditation, psychic healing, root medicine, aerobic exercise, the martial arts, deep breathing, and tai chi have been extravagant, to say the least. Maharishi Mahesh Yogi, for one, would have us believe that TM can cure cancer and AIDS, stop crime, clean up the environment, and end sickness, poverty, and hunger everywhere. I remain a skeptic—but without laughing—as should all educators. We should demand rigorous scientific documentation of all the reputed health benefits of these experiences; and we must not be put off by those intransigent neo-Gnostic believers who accuse us of being in thrall to the medical model or to the scientific method (Bodian, 1991) merely because we raise honest questions concerning the objective validation of self-reported health outcomes that are, at the very least, questionable.

These types of excessive claims and commercializations of neo-Gnostic practices, whatever their adherents' motives, raise an important anthropological question regarding the degree to which the United States is able to assimilate a neo-Gnostic perspective without radically altering its unique philosophical-religious basis. (Or, in the non-anthropological language I have been using throughout this book, how can we in America adapt a religious narrative of outsiders to the dominant religious narratives of insiders, without diluting or trivializing any of the religious stories?) Acculturation happens when a group of individuals having a different culture comes into continuous firsthand contact with another culture, with subsequent changes in the original cultural patterns of either the host and/or the visitors.

Acculturation, according to the anthropologist Robert Redfield (1936), is usually successful when contact between groups is direct, prolonged, and cumulative. And total cultural assimilation occurs only when ideational systems change concurrently with material changes, that is, when the internal structures of beliefs, values, and attitudes of a culture change along with the material circumstances of life. Anthropological research has shown how early training habits, certain economic, educational, and political practices, and basic intellectual and religious assumptions are most difficult to change; while certain techniques to achieve specific goals in technology, elements of taste and self-expression, and low-status positions in the workplace undergo change with relative rapidity (Keesing, 1971).

Thus, I believe one reason why the neo-Gnostic worldview lends itself to easy cooptation and exploitation in this country is that its deeper Eastern roots have been in relatively brief, indirect, and sporadic contact with America. Furthermore, because this culture's ideational system is grounded so profoundly in the values of profit-making, individualism, self-realization, scientific progress, and pragmatism—the modernist agenda—it follows that, at least initially, new ideas will be collapsed into, and serve, the entrenched modernist values. Consequently, change will occur primarily at the most superficial levels of taste and self-expression. For these reasons, I hold that *significant* educational, political, or religious change in this country through contact with neo-Gnostic teachings is highly unlikely. Innovation will remain largely superficial.

One religious critic, Harold Bloom (1993), believes that New Age religion is actually a bastardization of authentic Gnostic beliefs derived from the East; and, as he charges, Gnosticism in this country is the result of a poor cultural adaptation in the sense that personal freedom, rather than mystical insight and salvation, becomes the main goal of "California Orphics" like Shirley MacLaine and Oprah Winfrey. (In a recent book, *Omens of Millennium: The Gnosis of Angels, Dreams, and Resurrection*, 1996, Bloom surprisingly confesses his own conversion to Gnosticism, a long way indeed from what he earlier contended was the California corruption of this unique spiritual perspective.)

If Maharishi (in Bloomfield, 1975) believes that simple meditation without a complete overhaul of an individual's, and a culture's, worldview and narrative will bring about "global qualitative improvement in all aspects of individual life with a parallel improvement in all aspects of the social environment" (p. 214), then, I contend, he is being naive, stupid, or deliberately deceptive. His hope that TM will be "internal therapy for America" and will automatically transform the industrial worldview smacks ominously of Charles Reich's *The Greening of America*, written in the counterculture spirit of 1970. So, too, I fail to see how all the dedicated environmentalists, holistic health advocates, and one-world peaceniks are going to transform American industry, media, government, business, and education without a concomitant transformation in people's worldviews and personal narratives. A society that produces for public emulation Clint Eastwood, General Motors, IBM, the Dallas Cowboys, and *Seinfeld* will find it extremely easy either to coopt, ignore, or ridicule the integral yoga of a Patanjali (1938), the Satyagraha of a Gandhi, the compost pile of an earnest environmentalist, and the macrobiotic diet of a diligent yuppie trying to live a healthy life.

I may sound skeptical about neo-Gnostic change prospects in this culture, and to some extent I am, but I am neither cynical nor defeatist. At its core, I believe the neo-Gnostic vision is a highly praiseworthy one. I especially applaud its postmodern spirit, its respect for difference and heterodoxy, its resistance to the hegemony of science, its basic instinct to challenge religious orthodoxies and authoritarianisms of all kinds, and its natural inclination to approach social change from the inside out. I lose my ardor for this narrative, however, whenever it becomes simple-minded, exploitative, and authoritarian in its own right. Thus, I maintain that the central question for educators ought to be this one: What is authentic and what is bogus in this story?

The answer to this question will necessitate teachers' reading widely, deeply, and critically in the neo-Gnostic literature. For starters, they will have to immerse themselves in the grandeur of the Upanishads, the poetry of the *Bhagavad Gita*, the soaring power of the *Ramayana*, and the simple wisdom of the *Tao Te Ching*. (See A. Harvey's *The Essential Mystics: Selections from the World's Great Wisdom Traditions*, 1997.) They must practice firsthand, for themselves over a long period of time, the neo-Gnostic spiritual disciplines. They must consider seriously what in the neo-Gnostic orientation is transferable to their own lives and what is not. They must be able to determine which human problems are "micro-structural" (e.g., loneliness, anxiety, depression, metaphysical angst, joylessness) and which are "macro-structural" (e.g., political corruption, crime, poverty, and welfare abuse). The former, I contend, lend themselves more easily to neo-Gnostic interventions, while the latter require Western understandings of science, technology, economics, and politics, and the pragmatic strategies that accompany them.

CONCLUSIONS

And so the pivotal question remains for the alternative spiritualities orientation: *Is the neo-Gnostic narrative a credible narrative for the late 20th century and beyond?* Does it give religious truth-seekers a satisfying account of where they come from, why they are here, and where they might be going? Does it hold up a set of worthy and achievable moral ideals, provide a legitimate basis of authority, and, most of all, offer an inspiring sense of purpose? Does the narrative touch our lives, hold together, edify us? Does it help us all to see the "real world" in a more imaginative way?

From the fundamentalist perspective, the neo-Gnostic narrative is a dangerous and irreligious one, because it is part of the great conspiracy of secular humanism to de-Christianize America. Neo-Gnostics are said to represent the anti-Christ, and they are responsible for everything that is bad in the world, including world-government initiatives, Satanism, abortion and divorce, the epidemic of suicides and drug use, AIDS, abortion, homosexuality, and atheism (Michaelsen, 1989). For fundamentalists like Charles Colson or Pat Robertson, the neo-Gnostic narrative contains a set of characters who are areligious and subversive, who plot to overthrow Christian civilization. The climax to the story, according to fundamentalists, has already taken place in America: Secular values have replaced Christian norms everywhere, especially in the media and in the schools. At the present time, we find ourselves in the throes of a tragic narrative denouement wherein the "dark ages" are already upon us. Sadly, only a few will ever discover the light of Jesus and His eternal salvation, while the rest will be condemned to the darkness forever.

From the prophetic point of view, the neo-Gnostic story is an irresponsible and apolitical account of what is no more than a social fantasy. From a prophetic angle, neo-Gnostics appear to spend a third of their time devising vague, pseudo-utopian cosmic manifestos, another third wallowing in their own inner states of consciousness, and a third promoting their *haut monde* spiritual practices and collecting high fees from credulous middle-class students and professionals. Meanwhile, or so the prophetic reading goes, social justice issues in the United States continue to clamor for attention, and political energy gets siphoned off in a frenzy of narcissistic religious activity. The neo-Gnostic story ends, according to the prophetic interpretation, with a few mystics finding enlightenment (and wealth), while much of the rest of the world continues to suffer from unbelievable poverty and political oppression.

In contrast to the fundamentalist and prophetic twists, most of my students like the neo-Gnostic story. It is true that some see it as an unrealistic tale, particularly in its wishful predictions that global transformation is imminent. And others poke fun at its more esoteric, otherworldly preoccupations, preferring to "read" the story simply as an escapist dream for the gullible. But generally, students in my classes see a genuine need for a serious alternative to the mainline religions in a postmodern world. Tired of the older religious stories and ready to consider the benefits of a no-fault spiritual orientation that starts with the self and emanates outward, many of my students try on the neo-Gnostic worldview, if only at the margins. Some attend neo-Gnostic workshops and conventions sponsored by their school systems, many peruse the literature in the voluminous self-help sections of their region's largest bookstores, and some try to contribute directly to social reform through active involvement in holistic health, environmental, and Native American movements.

From my more skeptical students' perspective, the neo-Gnostic story is relatively harmless on a micro level where isolated individuals might be involved, and is probably even useful to them in some ways. In actuality, while most would demur from spending time in a monastery or an ashram practicing the more rigorous meditative disciplines, or in seeking their "higher selves" through fasting, hallucinogens, or hynotic trances, or even in contemplating the spiritual dimension of Gaia, more than a few would enthusiastically attend a stress reduction clinic to learn some appropriate Gnostic technologies in order to relax their overly busy minds and bodies. Some would stipulate, however, that any semblance of spiritual proselytizing be conspicuously absent from the instruction they might receive. Most of my students, no matter how sympathetic or critical, prefer their religious stories to be open-ended, non-cultlike, and anti-authoritarian.

It is now time to move to the fourth and final worldview I teach, the post-theist. This religious narrative is the newest to arrive on the American scene, circa 1980, and its eclectic, philosophical roots are deep in hermeneutics, existentialism, postmodernism, post-structuralism, neo-pragmatism, and critical theory. I have coined the designation *post-theism* to include a variety of postmodern and theistic perspectives; but, most particularly, I have tried to identify those thinkers whose work attempts to find some kind of common ground between what appears to be two radically opposed narratives—theism and postmodernism—hence the appellation *post-theism*.

CHAPTER 8

The Post-Theist Narrative

The *post-theist* (L., after God) orientation is the "religious" position that my students who identify themselves as thoroughly *postmodern* in outlook are most likely to hold, especially those who still remain involved, however hesitatingly and marginally, with the mainline religions of their youth. These students, a small group but growing in number each semester in my classes, frequently come out of an academic background in the humanities or social sciences where they have learned the languages of critical theory and post-structuralism; they often teach in high schools and colleges; and they tend to approach conversations about religion with a hermeneutic of frustration, suspicion, and general incredulity. Although they are not quite ready to jettison their earlier religious beliefs and practices entirely, they do find themselves growing more and more skeptical regarding the truth claims made by religious authorities in their own faith traditions, as well as by the fundamentalists, prophetics, and neo-Gnostics we have examined in previous chapters.

POSTMODERNISM AND POST-THEISM IN THE CLASSROOM

At least somewhat fluent in the postmodern languages of post-structuralism, critical pedagogy, and philosophical hermeneutics, these skeptical students openly wonder if it will ever be possible to accommodate the older theological languages to the more current postmodern vocabularies they are learning to speak so well. Some of these students are more than willing, even proud, to identify themselves as postmodern agnostics (in my language, *post-theists*) on an open-minded mission to find newer, more challenging ways to express their deepest religious inclinations, while a few are close to foreclosing altogether on the promises of religion in favor of a kind of jaded atheism. These latter students often talk about how tired they are of the intellectual and emotional compromises they feel they must make in order to continue calling themselves religious believers.

Many in this group have at least a passing acquaintance with postmodern authors like Jacques Derrida, Michel Foucault, Martin Heidegger, Thomas S. Kuhn, Jean-François Lyotard, and Friedrich Nietzsche, and they are quick to use the language of existential finitude, social construction of knowledge, emergent paradigms, indeterminacy, hermeneutics, and deconstruction to debunk those religious dogmas and rituals they view as "totalitarian" and "oppressive." A few who are more politically inclined take special delight in deflating the colonialist and imperialist aspirations of organized religion throughout the course of human history. For them, the Christian religion is largely the invention of a white male European elite class whose purpose it has been through the centuries to dominate and exploit others.

In teaching the four narratives, I find the student response to the post-theist perspective to be the most guarded, and the least volatile, during actual class conversations. In contrast, as I have pointed out in earlier chapters, students generally react loudly and scornfully to the fundamentalist story. Their stereotypes of this orientation have long been in place, and their initial contempt is palpable, particularly when we begin our unit on fundamentalism. Moreover, few viewpoints ever change by the end of our study of this perspective. There is always something in my unit on fundamentalism to elicit a strong response from even the most phlegmatic student.

While the prophetic narrative generally receives a more gracious reaction, those students who are skeptics still tend to question energetically why a religious rationale is necessary to further the cause of social justice. Whatever their individual ideological views, however, almost everyone expresses a deeply felt opinion regarding the political and religious ramifications of this orientation. Most students, though, especially those with a liberal religio-political agenda, enthusiastically approve of the world-transforming mission of the prophetic agenda, in spite of its potential political excesses.

The alternative spiritualities narrative has both its vocal detractors and its ardent supporters, and I can usually count on each group to move the conversation along with verve and passion. The practicing neo-Gnostics in class, while more laid-back than proponents of the two previous narratives, are no less excited about the spiritual efficacy of their orientation, and they rarely miss an opportunity to promote their views. I find that the lines get most clearly drawn in discussions between those who sympathize with this story and those who do not, and the resultant interchange is always spirited. I also detect more of a willingness on the part of critics in my class to find a possible truth in this account than in the other perspectives, probably because this religious narrative is itself so individually malleable.

In contrast, the *post-theist* story, at least at the outset, seems to be the most puzzling, albeit intriguing, to the majority of those students who come to my classes with no background at all in postmodern theory. Their initial reaction to post-theism is at once judiciously respectful, somewhat fearful of the ultimate religious implications of this view, and noticeably intimidated by the daunting technical vocabulary. For these reasons, I usually start my unit on the post-theist orientation with the following nonthreatening questions: What is the story that *postmodernism* tries to tell the world, and how successful has it been in displacing the dominant modernist story? And is post-theism an effective postmodern response to all the grand (religious) narratives that currently circulate in our secular pluralist society? Where is it strong and where is it weak in its own narrative appeal?

WHAT IS THE POSTMODERN STORY?

Obviously, there is an enormous literature on postmodernism, and I do not intend to deal with even a tiny percentage of it here. Likewise, I realize that postmodernism itself is a huge portmanteau term that covers a wide range of assumptions and accommodates a large amount of pluralism, contradiction, and disagreement, some of it at times unruly. Nevertheless, I hold that postmodernists actually do agree on some things (although even this is a debatable proposition for some postmodern scholars), and in the next section, I summarize the basic assumptions I think many share in common. When teaching this narrative, I am interested mainly in texts that touch on the topic of religion and postmodernism, particularly those works that attempt to forge some kind of a postmodernism-religion synthesis, no matter how critical, cautious, preliminary, or thin. Because of space and focus constraints in this chapter, I will only be able to suggest a few key postmodern commentaries, in addition to some pivotal primary sources. (In the next chapter, I will suggest some texts that are critical both of postmodernism and also of what I am calling post-theism.)

For excellent, balanced commentaries on postmodernism, I always recommend that students sample the work of Richard J. Bernstein (1992), Shaun Gallagher (1992), John McGowan (1991), Richard Rorty (1979, 1989), and Barbara Herrnstein Smith (1997). For challenging primary source material, I urge them to read Jacques Derrida (1976), Stanley Fish (1989), Michel Foucault (1992), Hans-Georg Gadamer (1993), Jean-François Lyotard (1984), Friedrich Nietzsche (1885/1954b, 1886/1966a, 1895/1954a), Paul Ricoeur (1981), and Gianni Vattimo (1991). I continually remind my students, however, that postmodern thinkers speak in highly specialized, complex languages, and while they might be in general agreement as to what they should *oppose* in the modern world, they are in little accord as to what they ought to advocate as constituting the good life.

Postmodern thinkers, by definition, tend to be stronger on critique and analysis and far weaker on prescription and advocacy. They spend much of their time deconstructing classical "texts," deflating the pretensions of the powerful, unmasking the rhetorical tactics of writers, disassembling "totalizing" political structures, and exposing racism, sexism, and heterosexism in social institutions—all the while advancing the causes of "oppressed" minorities. For these reasons, the above sources are often difficult to understand, hypercritical in tone, and more than a little depressing in their profound suspicion of a "metaphysics of presence"—the age-old dream that somewhere there is a universal or transcendental standpoint that explains, consolidates, and gives meaning to all the confounding complexities of life.

In my courses in recent years, I have been assigning Stanley J. Grenz's *A Primer on Postmodernism* (1996) because he introduces the topic of postmodernism to neophytes in a succinct and sympathetic manner, without either patronizing or overwhelming them. In one compact volume, Grenz manages to cover both the "broader intellectual and cultural ethos" (p. x) of postmodernism as well as the various intellectual forces and figures that have challenged modernity during the last two centuries. And his brief analysis of the work of three major postmodern thinkers—Michel Foucault, Jacques Derrida, and Richard Rorty—is masterful; the teachers in my course, in particular, always appreciate the clarity of his approach and the basic tools he provides for helping them to make some sense of these thinkers' highly technical (and upsetting) ideas for their own lives. Furthermore, to my advantage in offering a religiously oriented course to teachers, Grenz is both an educator—a professor of theology—and a theist—an evangelical who believes that Christians and Jews everywhere must address the challenge of postmodernism as a "needed corrective to modernity" (p. xi).

Grenz believes, as do I, that postmodernism marks the end of what Jean-François Lyotard (1984) calls the *meta-narrative* (an all-encompassing, legitimizing myth, without empirical proof, that supports a particular community's notion of truth). My introduction to postmodernism in class, for students who usually know little or nothing about the subject, emphasizes the critique of meta-narratives that postmodern thinkers make. To accomplish this, I carefully examine the work of Lyotard, which, for my purposes here, I will attempt to summarize in the next few paragraphs.

Lyotard (1984) asserts that postmodernism is "incredulity toward meta-narratives" (p. xxiv), and because I make this assertion the linchpin for my examination of postmodernism, I look at postmodernism and its theological counterpart, post-theism, as a type of counter-narrative to fundamentalists, prophetics, and neo-Gnostics who strive to make their stories normative religious narratives for all the rest of us. For the postmodernist, *modernism* as a legitimizing story has failed in the late 20th century because, in truth, the promise of Enlightenment reason leading us to a utopia of scientific progress and equality for all has become a myth without crediblity. So too the story of metaphysics (both philosophical and theological) has lost its power, as has the medieval conception of the university and church that relied on it for its sustaining energy and purpose. For Lyotard (1984), what has replaced the universal meta-narratives of the Middle Ages, the Enlightenment, and the major world religions have been "clouds of narrative language elements" (p. xxiv), local languages that each of us speaks as we try to give shape and texture to our jobs, our education, our families, and our personal histories.

In the postmodern world, then, according to Lyotard (1984), each of us is left to engage in a number of incompatible "language games," geared to specific locales and purposes, and bereft of a universal "meta-language" (one all-embracing prescriptive language into which all other languages can be translated). Linguistic pluralism becomes a fact of life everywhere—in the schools and universities, in the churches and government offices, in the courts and businesses, and in the homes and recreational centers. Objective truths and absolute values disappear in a swirl of context-specific languages; and a heterogenity of competing lifestyles and values, now defined as subjective preferences, vie for display and survival in the public square. Religions become only "useful" or "evasive" fictions, without any divine warrant, mere social constructions to help us cope with life's vagaries. No human act is ever independent of culture, class, race, or gender interests. And truth is mainly a matter of interpretive perspective, local stories, or, in Nietzsche's words, a "mobile army of metaphors, metonyms, and anthropomorphisms" (quoted in Grenz, 1996, p. 91), waiting to be deconstructed by individual hermeneutes whenever self-interests come into conflict and paradigms undergo a shift.

In summary, Lyotard's (1984) "incredulity toward metanarratives" results in a world where one story competes with another, endlessly, and where the likelihood is nonexistent that players of language games will ever reach a meta-consensus on which narrative ought to carry the day. In Grenz's (1996) perceptive words:

> Lyotard welcomes a world in which multiple incompatible language games flourish alongside one another. He rejoices that we are no longer ruled by

the modern concern that all discussion lead toward consensus. He pointedly concedes that he has given up the quest to reconcile the differing language games. (p. 48)

"BUT WHAT'S LEFT? IS THIS ALL THERE IS?"

At this point, my students' questions flood the room. "How can we live without 'meta-narratives'?" "Do you mean to say there is no capital-T Truth, that everything is actually a myth, that it's all 'socially constructed'?" "Isn't this relativism?" "Doesn't this postmodern 'story' play into the nihilism and skepticism of the world we experience today?" "What can we ever tell our own students when they ask us for reasons why they, and we, their teachers, should take their lives seriously?" "Is this the kind of world we want to live in, a world where we only play 'language games'?" "Are postmoderns content simply with expressing 'incredulity,' with 'critiquing' and 'delegitimizing' 'meta-narratives'?" "Doesn't this appear to be taking a hermeneutic of suspicion and skepticism to the nth degree?" "How exactly is this story a plausible substitute for all the other religious stories we have examined this semester?" "What's left to live for? Is this *it*?"

It is at this point, as a technique for responding to these questions, that I introduce some key elements of the postmodern narrative (a conception, by the way, most postmoderns would strenuously resist, and about which I will say more in the next chapter). What immediately follows, then, is a brief explication of several background principles in the postmodern hermeneutic, with an emphasis on their implications for religious belief/nonbelief. I will examine the post-theist corollary to postmodernism in greater depth in the next section, particularly as it gets expressed in the works of Don Cupitt (1997), a postmodern Anglican priest and theologian whom I think of as a highly enthusiastic "convert" to postmodernism. Cupitt believes he has gone "beyond God" with his theologically radical movement, the Sea of Faith Network.

Secular Pluralism, Incommensurability, and Shifting Paradigms

Postmodern thinkers hold that because Western societies are secular and pluralistic, and not theocratic, they are irreversibly (and gloriously) fragmented. No single philosophical, ethical, religious, or political viewpoint will ever again be able to carry the day in an age where postmodern critics (e.g., Derrida, 1976; Nietzsche, 1887/1966b; Rorty, 1979) have denounced, and banished forever, the old metaphysical and moral certainties. Classical, Judeo-Christian, Enlightenment, and modernist-secular syntheses have been replaced by a polytheism of worldviews, a cacophony of competing narratives, especially in the religious realm. In some senses, we are all religious strangers to each other, because our variegated supernatural beliefs, both individually and communally, separate and divide us, resulting in permanent strife and conflict. The postmodern religious predicament is how to create a world where people can remain unavoidably "polytheistic" (believe in many gods, visions, ideals, and meaning systems) without resorting to invasive proselytism or violence to satisfy the overwhelming need to convert nonbelievers to a predetermined, theological point of view. In this formulation, capital-T religious Truths become dangerously dictatorial when carried to their logical extreme, which, for a "postmodern theist" like H. Tristram Engelhardt Jr. (1996), is, sadly, where most tend to end up.

For the postmodernist, the presence of religious incommensurability is a condition we must learn to understand, accept, and even revere in a postmodern world. There is simply no common basis, no contextually independent standard, anywhere for comparing or measuring the "truth" of competing religious claims. In a secular pluralist society, we will always disagree with each other on matters of morality, religion, and politics. For example, fundamentalists are locked within their own community of memory and meaning, with their peculiar religious language, as are the prophetics and the neo-Gnostics with theirs. How can they ever agree collectively on what is right or wrong, truth or error? If it is a commonplace that terms such as *multiplicity, pluralism, plasticity, changing paradigms,* and *otherness* accurately describe the secular pluralist world we live in today, then it becomes increasingly difficult, if not impossible, to rationally compare and validate one religious claim over another, one language or one narrative over another.

Thomas Kuhn (1970), in his landmark work *The Structure of Scientific Revolutions,* posits that any scientist's effort to convert others to a particular way of perceiving science is doomed to fail (except in some extreme cases), because like each of us, scientists are invariably trapped in the framework of their own worldviews. These worldviews (or *paradigms*) are a product of their intellectual training, cultural backgrounds, expectations, aspirations, and especially their languages. These disparate scientific paradigms thus become mostly incommensurable, in the sense that it takes what Kuhn calls a drastic "gestalt switch" or a total "conversion" (in the fundamentalist sense of *metanoia*) for someone to drop an old scientific paradigm in favor of a new one. For Kuhn, these radical paradigm shifts are few and far between in science, in spite of all the fashionable talk today in the academy about the need to get students to make extreme intellectual fluctuations in the ways they understand the natural sciences, social sciences, and humanities.

By implication, religious commensurability, like the scientific, is even more difficult to achieve. Religious frameworks such as the fundamentalist, the prophetic, and the neo-Gnostic present the postmodernist with a number of stubbornly contrasting narratives, languages, worldviews, traditions, and truth claims. These frameworks are especially resistant to "gestalt switches" because believers hold to them as supernaturally designed master narratives, whose primary purpose is to universalize and absolutize a set of particular religious claims in order to win converts.

The major problem with each of the transcendental narratives, from the Kuhnian point of view, is that as yet, none has bothered to help unbelievers or nonbelievers to discover commensurability (commonality and criss-cross) between and among the rival (mostly alien) religious paradigms. None is genuinely (disinterestedly) ecumenical. At least for one postmodern philosopher (Bernstein, 1992), a way to live peacefully and productively with these rival narratives in a secular pluralist democracy, beyond simply expressing a watery "tolerance" for difference, is what a rancorous, religiously divided world requires at this time. Bernstein's (1992) greatest fear is that mere toleration of the "Other" too frequently results in the violent need to make the "Other" the "Same" (p. 74). Tragically, as I have suggested throughout this book, this has become the all-too-familiar, much-rehearsed religious narrative of past and present times. For most postmodern thinkers, transcendental accounts of one kind or another can never become the "final [peaceful] solutions" to the problem of radical difference in democracies unless they are first willing to acknowledge the weaknesses of their own frameworks of understanding as well as the strengths of opposing paradigms of meaning. The prospect of this ever happening, as we have seen in previous chapters, is highly unlikely.

Anti-Essentialism, Anti-Realism, Anti-Foundationalism

Postmodernists tend to be epistemological skeptics who challenge those religious thinkers who believe that absolute knowledge can be grounded in a conception of an essential human or divine nature; that there is, in fact, a "real" world out there, created by a real God, that the human mind can mirror and discover, and to which all religious truth claims must correspond; and that it is possible to ground religious truth claims in some kind of objective, metaphysical reality. Postmodernists argue that a belief in transcendence can never rest on a fixed, indubitable foundation, because every sense of what constitutes an unimpeachable foundation is only a specific kind of interpretation, local rather than universal, and contingent rather than absolute. All conceptions of an essential human nature or of a fundamental religious truth, for example, are but particular constructions made by particular people living in particular communities at particular times.

In fact, one could say that religious beliefs, like religious conventions, are no more than arbitrary contrivances, important social "fictions" meant to certify certain types of culturally approved behaviors. For the postmodernist, nothing definitive can ever be said about the nature of human beings or their belief systems other than the assertion that language and culture are all that matter; moreover, the claim that there exists somewhere an irrefutable core of immutable values (religious *or* secular) fails to confront the pluralism and difference that typify so much of contemporary life in complex postindustrial societies. For the postmodernist, there can never be an essential religious or moral language that is accessible, applicable, and credible to everybody, one that is independent of membership in particular cultures or subcultures.

Terry Eagleton (1996), usually a staunch critic of the postmodern repudiation of essentialism, foundationalism, and realism, nevertheless has this to say in support of the postmodern assault on essentialist certitudes:

> Postmodern anti-essentialism has a point. There are indeed reductive, falsely eternalizing, brutally homogenizing uses of the concept of essence, and they have wreaked especial havoc in the fields of gender and ethnicity. Essentialism there means something like "reifying to an immutable nature or type," and has been a potent weapon in the arsenal of the patriarchs, racists, and imperialists . . .

From the postmodern perspective, religionists have had a bad habit throughout history of "eternalizing" and "homogenizing" their supernatural claims, and in so doing they have wreaked "especial havoc" everywhere, in the name of an always-elusive, culture-free Transcendent Truth.

Perspectivism and Fallibilism

For Nietzsche (1911/1968), there are only interpretations—perspectives—and nothing else. In *The Will to Power*, he asserts: "In so far as the word knowledge has any meaning, the world is knowable; but it is interpretable otherwise, it has no meaning behind it, but countless meanings.—Perspectivism" (p. 481). Nietzsche, the leading forerunner of postmodernism, believes that because we can know only from a particular perspective, there can be no such thing as "pure reason," or a "will-less . . . timeless knowing subject" (p. 481). If it is true, as Nietzsche contends, that all knowers, without exception, are driven by needs and passions (what he calls a "will to power"), how much more true, then, is the assumption that the intellects of religious believers are conditioned by their will to power, a power that finds ultimate expression in a need for a self-validating Transcendent Truth or Power Source. Religious believers, by Nietzsche's definition, can never be genuinely disinterested. They will always have, in his words, their "Fors and Againsts." Thus, what fundamentalists, prophetics, and neo-Gnostics have in common is that their religious knowledge, when presented as invariant, impartial, or universal, is nothing more or less than a "will to power," a matter of self-regarding interpretation, entirely devoid of objectivity and universal validity (Hunt, 1993).

Today, as strenuously as the fundamentalists warn against any act of individual interpretation when reading the Bible, postmodernists, *a fortiori*, propose that because interpretation is unavoidable, we must spend our time unmasking the interpretive biases of those who pretend to know the Truth for everyone. We need to encounter all self-proclaimed religious truthtellers as people with distinct theological perspectives who are not above pigeonholing the Other in behalf of prior political interests. In the words of Anthony C. Thiselton (1995), a critic of postmodernism, "interpretation is often [understood by postmoderns to be] a manipulative disguise to legitimate power-claims by another group" (p. 12). Postmodern thinkers today, like Nietzsche earlier, are adamant that our presuppositions and prejudices, both conscious and unconscious, irremediably color our interpretations of texts. Thus, fundamentalists, prophetics, and neo-Gnostics, in order to advance their own interests, actually predefine those religious truths they would like to absolutize and universalize for all of us.

If postmodernists are right, what then will be the outcome for the postmodern world if we give up the need for metaphysical absolutes? What will happen if we agree that in a secular pluralist society, religious truth is simply a matter of personal perspective, and that opposing paradigms and irreconcilable moral and religious incommensurabilities have more or less equal worth? Do my students have a case when they charge postmodernists with a depressing relativism, leading only to a corrosive cynicism (and a nihilism) that often accompanies any movement that does little more than critique and debunk? Have postmodernists lost all sense of purpose and direction? What *is* left to believe in, after all?

In my opinion, one postmodern thinker, Richard J. Bernstein (1992), offers us a plausible way out of what I call the "postmodern cul-de-sac": the assumption that all roads lead necessarily to extreme subjectivism, cynicism, and eventual despair, because in the end there is nothing we can ever take for granted as objectively true. In speaking of the early American pragmatists, Bernstein (1992) declares:

> Their alternative to foundationalism was to elaborate a thoroughgoing fallibi-
> lism where we realize that although we must begin any inquiry with prejudg-
> ments and can never call everything into question at once, nevertheless there
> is no belief or thesis—no matter how fundamental—that is not open to further
> interpretation and criticism. [Charles] Peirce advocated that we displace the
> "foundation" metaphor with the metaphor of a "cable." (p. 327)

Bernstein (1992) goes on to explain that in the world we live in today, we ought to appreciate the richness and variety of dissimilar truth claims rather than look only to the conclusiveness of any single one. For him, there can be profound joy and purpose in coming to terms with difference, in learning how to live with people who have complex, contrasting per-spectives on the world. He quotes Charles Peirce on the cable metaphor:

> Reasoning should not form a chain which is no stronger than its weakest
> link, but a cable whose fibers may be ever so slender, provided they are
> sufficiently numerous and intimately connected. (p. 327)

Bernstein argues that a commitment to *fallibilism* (the perspective that no truth claim is ever self-evident, intuitively obvious, or inerrantly true; at best, claims are probable and not certain) helps us to realize that truth claims of all types are forever interpretable, tentative, and open to dispute and correction. This, he suggests, ought not to imply an epistemological pessimism or despair however. For Bernstein (1992), like the scientist or philosopher we must submit all of our truth hypotheses, religious or otherwise, to "public critical discussion" if we want them to be adopted by others. He says, "It is only by the serious encounter with what is other, different, and alien that we can hope to determine what is idiosyncratic, limited, and partial" (p. 328).

Where Bernstein (1992) ends up is to advocate an "engaged fallibilistic pluralism" (p. 336) as the best way to live peacefully and productively with others in diverse, democratic communities. This is a response to conflict that is "dialogical" and desirous of a "mutual reciprocal under-standing" between and among people with different views. By implica-tion, Bernstein would likely frown upon religiously authoritarian commu-nities—whether fundamentalist, prophetic, or self-absorbed—who see themselves only as adversaries, and who care little about reaching a mutual understanding (or even a "defensive pluralism") with those who might believe differently. For Bernstein, unless there is a "play, a *to-and-*

fro movement in dialogical encounters" committed to finding common ground with others, then disagreement and conflict will continue to plague our social practices.

Bernstein's desirable community is ultimately one where people wish to break down ideological boundaries, where they are willing to explore their similarities and differences in conversations marked by mutual respect and responsiveness, with an understanding that at the very least, people must be willing to agree to disagree about their differences. Although this is an admittedly "thin" construction of civic life in a secular pluralist democracy, Bernstein wants, nevertheless, to bond people together in dialogue rather than divide them in contentious argument. For postmodernists like Bernstein, the tragedy of all the transcendental perspectives is that in the absence of an "engaged fallibilistic pluralism," they serve mainly to rupture, rather than to foster, harmonious human relationships.

THE POST-THEIST AS RADICAL
RELIGIOUS TRANSFORMER

At this time, it has been mainly Christian theologians who are trying to come to terms with the intellectual challenges of postmodernism, perhaps because Christian scholars in particular have made it their special mission throughout history to try to accommodate or assimilate opposing philosophical views in the hope of reaching some kind of grand intellectual synthesis (Johnson, 1976). The results have not always been satisfactory, however. Some contemporary theologians (e.g., Hebblethwaite, 1988; John Paul II, 1993; Thiselton, 1995; Ward, 1997) prefer to pass on this latest endeavor, and instead become what I would call ardent "restorationists," eager to restore and reaffirm the truth of traditional religious doctrines in the face of the postmodern assault on absolute truth. They are the *holdouts* against postmodernism.

Others (e.g., Allen, 1989; Grenz, 1996; Griffin, 1989; Peters, 1992; Tracy, 1994) become reluctant "accommodationists," earnestly seeking some kind of noninjurious rapprochement between two essentially irreconcilable belief systems. They are the *peacemakers* between postmodernism and liberal religion. And still others (e.g., Cupitt, 1980, 1984, 1989, 1994, 1997; Freeman, 1993; Hart, 1993) become enthusiastic "converts" to postmodernism, and in the process they expose traditional supernaturalist illusions, create entirely new religious vocabularies, and recast religion as merely an alternative linguistic theory. They are the *transformers*, the post-theists, who attempt to radically redefine religion to confront the challenges of a postmodern age where, they believe, God has come and gone—for good.

Whenever I finish with my introduction to postmodernism, and begin to make the transition to post-theism, my students raise additional questions. "But how can a theist be a *post*-theist? How can somebody claim to be a believer, yet advocate the demise of traditional religious views?" "Why doesn't a 'post-theist' just admit to being an atheist or an agnostic without having to use the trendy *post* prefix?" "If two mutually incompatible perspectives do in fact exist—theism and atheism—then how in the world can post-theists reconcile them, especially when their own postmodern premises tend to be atheistic? How can they have their cake and eat it, too?" "Isn't post-theism actually a denial of hope and optimism in the future? If it is the theological offshoot of a critical, deconstructive postmodernism, how can it avoid collapsing into despair, endless conflict, cynicism, and eventual violence?" "How can we ever present the post-theist story to our students in public schools and colleges without running the risk of relativizing all their own religious truth claims, and without inviting their accusation that religion appears to be nothing more than a manipulative tool used by power groups to secure some social or political advantage?" "Actually, how is post-theism a religion at all? Isn't it simply a negation of religion, a kind of anti-religion?"

DON CUPITT: "ATHEIST PRIEST" AND "HERETIC'S HERETIC"

One scholar who takes questions like the above very seriously is Don Cupitt, perhaps the leading post-theist thinker in the world today. Cupitt is an ordained Anglican priest, theologian, author of over 20 books from 1976 to 1997 on the future of religion in a postmodern world, and former Dean of Emmanuel College, Cambridge University. In order to summarize Cupitt's post-theist views in this section, I will concentrate on his latest work, *After God: The Future of Religion* (1997), probably his most accessible (and most controversial) redefinition of what he calls a "religion without God." Through the years, Cupitt has provoked the enmity of dozens of Christian critics; *After God* is his attempt to set the record straight, in a quasi-personal writing style that even nontheologians can readily understand.

On the two occasions I have used *After God* (1997) in my courses, students are initially at a complete loss as to how to respond coherently. Most simply do not have the background to challenge a priest-theologian-atheist who has made a career formulating postmodern animadversions against organized religion and theism. A few students, although in general agreement with the basic content of his attack, wonder openly about the bleakness of Cupitt's views, the all-or-nothing rejection of any God-centered religious faith. They are just not as willing to go as far as he.

One day, in response to my question—"What on earth does Cupitt (1997) mean when he says that 'I actually think that I love God more now that I know God is voluntary. Perhaps God had to die to purify our love for him' (p. 85)"—the class sat in stunned, bewildered silence for minutes before mustering a reaction. Finally, one student ventured:

> Cupitt's obviously a postmodernist who takes postmodernism to the extreme, and, after Nietzsche, he announces God's death, for the second time. This is where postmodernism leads for those who once believed in a God—*right back to the self*. We construct our Gods, we freely give our consent to believing in them, and we can kill them anytime we want. They depend on us, we don't depend on them. And when our Gods get old, we have to find new ways of talking about them, if we are to love them all over again. At least, I think this is what Cupitt means. Have I got it, or am I way off base here?

Yes, even with the embellishment, I believe this student "got" the core of Cupitt's post-theist story. In general, Cupitt's (1997) narrative takes the following shape: The old mythologies developed after 7500 B.C. when farming and fixed settlements originated. These early gods were functional fictions created to embody the authority that the early city-states would require. First came this socially constructed divine authority, later to be followed by various forms of public authority. Cupitt concludes that for over six millennia religion's major task has been to convert homeless wanderers into hunters, gatherers, and stay-at-homes, and then into state citizens.

Correspondingly, our earliest ancestors created "narrative explanations" in order to give life meaning. This quest for "universal" meaning systems leads to Plato's world of Forms, later to the church's belief in metaphysical absolutes, and finally to Kant's universal conceptual categories. For Cupitt (1997), this entire process is actually a "mythical representation of the world of language" (p. 16). This world of language, according to Cupitt, actually presages the postmodernist (and post-theist) turn to language today that has had such a huge influence on religious thinking. Early beliefs in God had little to do with metaphysical issues regarding God's existence, and much more to do with how people could "become themselves and live well" (p. 28).

For Cupitt, God was first a proper name meant to identify people with a divinely ordered scheme of things; then God was a way for people to commit themselves to a particular political order; then God became a way to "make human selfhood cosmic" (p. 31), to connect human beings to universals. At each historical interval, God as a name was an "imaginary personification" who was "loved, praised, thanked, grumbled about, argued with, and questioned" (p. 34). Cupitt has little use for the Greek notion of God as a timeless Form, or for Kant's notion of God as a rational concept. For him, God is just a word, not an absolute rationale for law and order, or a divine justification for rigid churchly doctrine, or a cosmic support for a particular political ideology. There is no "real" God out there, only a word, "God," in here, that is emphatically a human creation. And according to Cupitt, it all began with the human biological need to evolve a world of rich and complex symbolic meanings to give life some purpose.

Cupitt is firm in his belief as a "non-realist" that an antecedently existing world of Ideas out there is actually a translation of our inner needs and drives into language that we project onto the physical world. Gods, religious leaders, and believers are all interdependent language users "whose utterances are words of power" (p. 47). A belief in transcendence and supernaturalism actually comes down to the mistaken principle that some key religious words are absolutes, objective truths, dogmas to be obeyed. Cupitt contends that we rule our own lives, and the lives of others as well, by the use of a prescriptive religious language that we alone certify as official. Thus, religious language becomes both a tool for social control and a means for eternal salvation. Cupitt's post-theist project for more than a quarter of a century has been to unmask "realistic" conceptions of God perpetrated by religious authorities in order to consolidate power, and to show how God is nothing more than a name that people can use to make themselves and others happy. Cupitt will settle for nothing less than the "end of [a] dogmatic metaphysics" that postulates a "divine creation objectively finished and complete" (p. 68).

Cupitt argues that because our religious linguistic meanings will never be "steady," we will never, ever have a religious linguistic standpoint that is absolute or fixed. Therefore, we will always be caught between a nihilism, a neopragmatism, a nonrealism, and a postmodernism. But for Cupitt, this is no reason to fret. We should rejoice, because we live now in a "time of the angels," a world "after the gods," where religions multiply exponentially, and we can know for sure that every new religious movement promising final deliverance will eventually turn out to be a fad. Finally, mercifully, God cannot be saved because God is dead forever, a mere passing fancy.

What we are left with, according to Cupitt and his Sea of Faith network (a European group of religious radicals and revisionists), is a "nonrealist faith in God" resulting in a "'God's-eye' view of oneself and of our life, *after* the death of God" (p. 82). In Cupitt's (1997) memorable, shockingly honest words:

> A Christian nonrealist like me may often find himself dropping back into the old type of God consciousness, praying or worshiping because he wants to or because it helps. And why not? I actually think I love God more now that I know God is voluntary. I still pray and love God, even though I fully acknowledge that no God actually exists. (p. 85)

In response to those critics who would accuse him of leaving individuals with no transcendent purpose to give their lives meaning, Cupitt claims to have rescued the true meaning of religion from the harmful "legacy of the old" oppressive meanings. Now, according to Cupitt, we can be free to preserve and cultivate a belief in the word "God" only insofar as the word heightens our consciousness of ourselves, "as if we were to look at ourselves *through the eye of God*" (p. 85). Moreover, says Cupitt, in the metaphysical void where "nothing any longer has any assured and objective value, basis, or foundation" (p. 88), we can learn how to meditate, Buddhist-style, upon the emptiness and nothingness, if we wish. We can put our lives into perspective, see the natural flux of all life and how we actually participate in this universal process; we can experience what Cupitt calls the "*blissful void.*" And, finally, as the ultimate makers of meaning and value in a world free of patriarchal gods, we can undertake a kind of "*solar living,*" wherein we keep moving, continually recreating our selves, "pouring ourselves out and passing on" (p. 90), living as "solarity," in a sense dying all the time. For Cupitt, religion is best understood and experienced as a "toolkit" for living well and not as an immutable system of reassuring transcendental dogmas.

Cupitt has evolved over a 25-year period into the quintessential postmodern theist, as someone who believes he has renounced forever the old religious tribalisms and ethno-nationalisms that have produced the nightmares in Northern Ireland, Bosnia, and Israel/Palestine. For him, the venerable God of the fatherland must die immediately. This "God" is the God that stirs up all the old ethnocentric passions, the God that divides people into killing machines and creates "heretics, apostates, heathens, infidels, enemies, and dirty foreigners" (p. 98). Listen to Cupitt on why people need to develop a postmodern identity:

> We no longer actually need roots, identity, stability, or a provenance. We can do without all these things. Me, I don't want them anymore. I prefer to

be without identity. I'd like to belong to no ethnic group, and to have no Other. They call me a nihilist: but I'm beginning to feel at ease, at *home* in nihilism. (p. 99)

Most of my students come to empathize, at least to some degree, with the postmodern truth in Cupitt's passion to purge religion of fixed orders and objective truths, hierarchies and heresies, and popes and mullahs, even though they might reject his overall theme that in the end, there is only us, and nobody else. Actually, declares Cupitt, all we possess is our language, the selves we have created through our use of language, and the conceptions we have constructed to identify the Gods we think we need (and deserve) at strategic intervals throughout our history. The old grand religious narratives have collapsed, never to be resurrected. What is left, however, for Cupitt is something for us all to celebrate rather than to mourn. This is *our* world, not the property of some inaccessible supernatural creature, and we form it with our language, bestow meaning on it with our feelings, and understand it with our theories.

And even though God has disappeared forever, according to Cupitt (1997) and other post-theists like him, we can live God-like lives ourselves by trying to exemplify those qualities we genuinely admired in the older, atavistic images of the Gods. Furthermore, we can learn to be comfortable with the possibility of nihilism by finding our own place within it—not by despairing over life's ultimate purposelessness, but by embracing what it is we have and what it is we can still contrive both alone and together. And, finally, we can live our lives intensely, holding nothing back, "burning without being afraid of burnout" (p. 104). Life in this overall formulation becomes even more precious than before, because now it cannot be pinned down: It is elusive, contingent, always in flux, its languages infinitely multipliable, and its meanings endlessly interpretable. For post-theists, our human prospects are limitless.

CONCLUSIONS

What the post-theist Cupitt and other like-minded authors have in common is the postmodern insight that what constitutes religious reality is actually a state of mind; religious reality is a function of perception, a product of endless and multiple interpretations, a complex series of mental constructions made by an observer embedded in a particular culture and time. No longer is there an objective, supernatural world "out there" waiting for a naive subject to perceive and to make sense of, on *its* own terms. Henceforth, there are to be no more fixed metaphysical centers of meaning, no absolute core religious structures independent of subjective understandings, historical contexts, or sociopolitical interests. This postmodern consciousness, this recognition that reality is subjectively constructed and language-defined, is where the work of such thinkers as Marx, Nietzsche, Heidegger, Freud, Wittgenstein, Kuhn, Derrida, and Foucault has taken us as we transition into the 21st century.

Cupitt and other postmoderns are telling us that there can be no turning back to the simple-minded medieval certitudes of a universe where "God is in His Heaven, and all's right with the world." Neither, they inform us, can we ever return to the supremely confident Enlightenment view that a world committed to the values of autonomy, reason, science, and progress will result in a political and economic utopia for everyone, whereby equality, fraternity, and liberty will flourish beyond our wildest dreams. In Tarnas's (1991) troubling words,

> Under the cloak of Western values, too many sins have been committed ... the West's long history of ruthless expansion and exploitation—the rapacity of its elites from ancient times to modern, its systematic thriving at the expense of others, its colonialism and imperialism, its slavery and genocide, its anti-Semitism, its oppression of women, people of color, minorities, homosexuals, the working classes, the poor, its destruction of indigenous societies throughout the world, its arrogant insensitivity to other cultural traditions and values, its cruel abuse of other forms of life, its blind ravaging of virtually the entire planet. (p. 400)

Today, postmodernists take nothing for granted. Neither do posttheists. Their hermeneutic is one of disenchantment, skepticism, critical consciousness, and, particularly in the post-theist case, an informed, this-worldly optimism and hope. All is in flux; paradigms are constantly shifting; we are "locked" into our own unique interpretive frameworks; truth at best is radically ambiguous; and all knowledge is contingent and parochial. As a major consequence of this postmodern turn in our nation's colleges and universities, canonical texts are everywhere being "deconstructed," the hubristic insensitivities of white male European elites are being exposed, and the unmasking of power relationships, exploitation, and oppression in every social institution is becoming the order of the day. More and more frequently this kind of deconstruction is taking place in our nation's public schools as well, in the name of multicultural education (Banks, 1997).

A postmodern theologian like Cupitt concludes that there can be no metaphysical standpoint from which to judge whether one religion is any more valid than another *vis-à-vis* its supernatural claims. For him, there is simply no unassailable, transcendent source to ratify *a* truth as *The*

Truth; there are only contestable local "fictions," peculiar to their own times, places, and conditions. The fundamentalist and prophetic world-views, far from being divinely ordained, otherworldly narratives, take shape instead out of particular historical situations in order to meet partic-ular human needs. Thus they are always flawed, self-interested, and, at least in theory, capable of great political treachery.

Cupitt would agree that the alternative spiritualities story, as we have seen in previous chapters, is a typically postmodern phenomenon, a pastiche of Western and Eastern spiritual elements combining both secular and religious sensibilities, and finding expression in movements ranging from the human potential movement to New Age spirituality and Eastern mysticism. As long as this type of religious expression remains pluralistic, open, and experimental, then I think Cupitt would say it represents a revitalized, postmodern, spiritual vision; but whenever it becomes compulsively triumphalistic, dogmatic, and Gnostic, he would accuse it of being self-deceptive and alienating. It confuses a comforting set of spiritual practices with a set of esoteric truths alleged to ground, and validate, those practices as normative for all.

It might not be surprising to know that very few of my students are ever eager to accept the sum total of Cupitt's (1997) completely postmod-ern religious iconoclasm. Particularly toward the end of our unit on the post-theist narrative, when students start to feel more comfortable with the technical language and concepts, passages like the following usually precipitate much personal soul-searching, as well as discerningly critical class discussions:

> [The truth about religion is] that *we made it all up*. We evolved the entire syllabus. We have slowly evolved our own languages, our values, our systems of knowledge, our religions, and our world views. . . . In which case, surely, one should be happy to see the three thousand or so New Religious Move-ments, the thousand or so New Age groups, and the hundreds of sects of the various major faiths that are all flourishing, teeming in Western countries today. If their beliefs work out well for them, then their beliefs are true for them; and since there is no independent Truth out there, and all of us are entirely free to build our worlds in the ways that seem best to us, we have no basis for calling other people's worlds irrational. Let a hundred flowers bloom! (pp. 123, 126)

Finally, for those students who find Cupitt's Zen-based, anarchistic repudiation of theism far too radical, John Shelby Spong's (1998) brand of post-theism comes across as considerably less threatening. In my own estimation, I find Spong's approach to post-theism just about right for those students who refuse to abandon the reality of God even though they have irrevocably abandoned the Christian construction of God. Spong is outspoken in his belief that all institutional definitions of a theistic God—as one who is "external, supernatural, and invasive"—have more than outlived their usefulness and have rendered the traditional concept of God vapid and "contentless." The fact is that the theistic God of the West has "no more work to do" (p. 54). What is needed at the present time, according to Spong, is for us to create new God images, to get beyond theism, to become "Christians without being theists" (p. 56). Spong's highly controversial new work, *Why Christianity Must Change or Die: A Bishop Speaks to Believers in Exile* (1998), is less concerned than Cupitt's with questioning God's existence and arguing for a free-floating Zen Buddhism than it is in showing that "the death of the God we worshiped yesterday is [not] the same thing as the death of God" (p. 41). Thus, for Spong, God may very well exist, but the old constructions, the "contentless concepts," must give way to constructions that are more reliable and credible to those postmodernists who think for themselves but who reject outright the enticements of anarchism and atheism.

In the next chapter, I intend to develop the types of criticisms that students usually make of the post-theist orientation, often in reaction to highly polemical passages like Cupitt's above. And while I strongly agree that the post-theist narrative has much to offer a postmodern society unsure of its metaphysical moorings and skeptical about absolute appeals to religious truth, in defense of the principle of religious indeterminacy, I do not want post-theists to have the *final*, uncontested word on religion in this book. And so, in examining the failure of the post-theist viewpoint in the next chapter, and by way of summarizing a number of views I have already presented in this book, I will incorporate what I think some of the dissenting voices we have heard throughout the study might say about this perspective. I will also include some reactions to post-theism by those I have labeled the restorationists and the accommodationists—the holdouts and the peacemakers.

CHAPTER 9

The Failure of the
Post-Theist Narrative

Ironically, Alan Wolfe (1997), a secular, liberal academician with some postmodern tendencies, is one of a growing number of educators who is calling for a revival of religious study in American colleges—in order to confront the moral skepticism of postmodern/post-theist thinkers like Don Cupitt (1997). Wolfe regrets the dominance of postmodern thinking in the academy, particularly where religion is concerned. For him, postmodernism does not constitute some narrative-free philosophical perspective whose lofty function is to make critical pronouncements on the worth of more conventional religious stories. Rather, Wolfe suggests that postmodernism is itself a story, a meta-narrative like all the others, and should be treated as such.

Thus, Wolfe reasons, if there are postmodern ways of knowing, why are there not religious ways of knowing equally as valid? If there is a postmodern narrative worth studying in the academy, why is there not a conventional religious narrative worth telling as well? And if we are willing to critically assess religious stories by using postmodern criteria, why not assess the postmodern narrative by using more traditional religious criteria? Wolfe would not allow post-theists like Don Cupitt (1997), discussed in the previous chapter, to have the final, uncontested word on perspectivism, cultural relativism, incommensurability, secular pluralism, and non-foundationalism. Instead, Wolfe (1997) believes "those [postmodernists] who have triumphed so thoroughly in the modern university could be a bit more generous in welcoming critics of [their] own bedrock assumptions" (p. B5).

As I hope I have made clear throughout this book, I sympathize greatly with Wolfe's (1997) attempt to revive the study of religion in the academy. And even though I find my own religious leanings closer to the post-theist view than to the other perspectives I have earlier examined, I share Wolfe's concern that in the last several years, a kind of postmodern skepticism has held the upper hand in secular educational institutions whenever the topic of religion comes up. For this reason, in these final pages I intend to look closely at what I believe are some key weaknesses, as well as some potential strengths, in the post-theist worldview. Generally, I find post-theism to be vulnerable to the following interrelated charges, the first leading logically to the second charge, and both culminating in the third challenge:

1. The post-theist story fails to adequately address the contradictions inherent in its thoroughgoing relativism.
2. The post-theist story lacks an inspiring *raison d'être*, one that includes a tragic sense of life, a predilection for mystery, and a compelling set of moral maxims (Wolfe, 1997).
3. The post-theist narrative will be unable to transcend, and ultimately repair, the more damaging religious rifts in the larger society unless it positions itself at the reconciling center of religious discourse, rather than at the disputatious margins.

THE CONTRADICTIONS OF A
THOROUGHGOING RELATIVISM

What restorationist critics (whom I am calling the "holdouts" against post-theism) find especially distressing about post-theist relativism comes through vividly in a totally unrelated article by Kay Haugaard (1997), "Suspending Moral Judgment: Students Who Refuse to Condemn the Unthinkable." Although the essay is only indirectly related to religion, when I first assigned it in class, it stirred up considerable controversy among my students, who immediately saw its relevance to the post-theist perspective. Haugaard (1997), an instructor of creative writing, writes ruefully about her experiences with students who absolutely refuse to make moral judgments about such events as the Holocaust, Vietnamese and American atrocities during the Vietnam War, South African apartheid, prostitution, drug abuse, and even human sacrifice. Haugaard laments the fact that her students have always been willing, too willing, it seems to her, to look nonjudgmentally at the other side for possible explanations for even the most horrible acts of inhumanity.

In one of her classes, after a reading of James Frazer's *The Golden Bough*, not a single student was willing to go out on a limb to take a position against human sacrifice. Haugaard (1997) quotes one of her students: "Well, I teach a course for our hospital personnel in multicultural understanding, and if it is part of a person's culture, we are taught not to judge if it has worked for them" (p. B5). This article disturbed the majority of my students because it depicted for them, in a striking way, the extent to which a stance of postmodern nonjudgmentalism has permeated the subcultures of most human service professionals, as well as the culture at large. In contrast, one of my more traditional religious believers, a quasi-fundamentalist Christian, had no compunctions at all about declaring that for her, human sacrifice must always and everywhere be wrong, even when it occurs in the Bible, because she felt it was "against God's law." And she emphatically added: "No all-loving God is going to require the murder of any of His creatures to satisfy some Divine Ego Need!"

During that same class, an articulate post-theist (sounding ironically like the Islamic Iranian, Mojtaba, from Chapter 2) quickly responded to the fundamentalist by leaping to Haugaard's students' defense. One series of comments, in particular, aptly conveyed her prevailing sentiment regarding the issue of relativism:

> If we decide we have the right to impose our standards of morality on *other* cultures, we must be willing to receive their moral judgments on *our* practices as well. While war atrocities, apartheid, and human sacrifice do, indeed, sound thoroughly evil to *us*, how morally ugly must our country's incredible corporate greed, runaway divorce and abortion rates, vicious acts of racial and homophobic bigotry, and widespread sexual assault sound to *them*? Why should *our* moral standards always be superior to *theirs*? Whose judgments hold the ultimate trump card? The truth is that because there are no unimpeachable moral ultimates, on what grounds can we, or they, ever decide which vices are more repugnant and which are merely the lesser of two evils and, thus, permissible, in some circumstances?
>
> Isn't morality a crapshoot after all, and doesn't it really depend on where you were born and what language you learned to speak about right and wrong when you were growing up? I, for one, don't happen to believe in the existence of your "all-loving" God. In fact, I stand with Cupitt (1997); I'm *beyond* God, at least beyond the God *you* espouse. Moreover, because there is no global, consensually validated, *religious* language to give me that unwavering sense of moral certainty, what is left? In a Godless world, all we can really do is lobby hard against violations of human rights by trying to be as morally persuasive as we can about the principles *we* believe in. If we fail to get our way around the world, then, short of going to war, we must step back, admit we live in a fallible world, try to improve our own moral languages, and get on with our efforts to build a more just and humane society. This,

I'm sad to say, is all there is. Let's face it: We're inescapably alone in an amoral universe, and there *can* never be, *will* never be, a divine court of appeals on moral matters.

This student's Cupitt-like fulminations against theism, foundationalism, universal morality, commensurability, and objective knowledge are remindful of the Sophists, Critias and Protagoras, who lived in the latter part of the 5th century B.C.E. Like my relativist student, these thinkers rejected any notion of objective truth or absolute deities in favor of subjective judgments and personal beliefs. For the Sophists, religious truth was always a matter of convention, and could only be judged by its practical utility in everyday affairs. According to the Sophists, what philosophers and priests claimed represented divine reality was actually nothing more than the creation of clever allegorists. Moreover, the Sophists delighted in challenging those rationalists who believed that human reason alone was capable of understanding the nature of the cosmos or of arriving at absolute truth. But even though it is true that the Sophists succeeded in freeing individuals to think on their own regarding metaphysical, moral, religious, and political matters, the cost was great: They also encouraged a radical skepticism and atheism in citizens that eroded the securities found in the older Hellenic philosophies and cosmologies. Tarnas (1991) has recounted how the Sophist spirit in Ancient Greece both reflected and encouraged an "amoral opportunism" among the people, a weakened and compromised democracy, and "cruel exploitation of women, slaves, and foreigners" (p. 30).

Closer to home, Brian Hebblethwaite (1988) and Anthony C. Thiselton (1995) are two of the more prominent "restorationist" theologians who consider Don Cupitt a kind of latter-day theological Sophist, and they have taken him (and, by implication, my student above) to task over the issue of relativism. I believe their concerns are worth exploring, if post-theists like myself are to fully understand the relativistic flaws in our own "bedrock [anti-foundationalist] assumptions." If Lyotard (1984) is right (as I think, in general, he is) in his contention that any religious truth is nothing more than a local version of a particular language-game—neither inherently superior nor inferior to other local religious language-games—then we post-theists must logically conclude that the search for grand religious narratives is largely a waste of time. In fact, according to this account, it might not even be worth our while to engage in conversations of any type with others about our own local religious languages, because the effort to find consensus or common ground among them violates their heterogeneity, their "otherness."

Religious dialogue, for Lyotard, is merely another test of people's capacity to "tolerate the incommensurable" (p. xxv). Religious tolerance, insofar as it can be said to exist at all, must always start with an acceptance of Nietzsche's dictum that truth is fiction. And as everyone knows, what counts as "good" or "bad" fiction is mostly a matter of subjective taste. Thus, religion is nothing more than somebody's good or bad story, something that tickles (or tortures) a person's particular metaphysical fancy. In Cupitt's (1997) words, religion is "merely those illusions without which we cannot live . . . we made [them] all up. . . . We evolved the entire syllabus" (p. 126).

Contra the Sophists, Nietzsche, and Cupitt, however, I often ask my students to consider a series of anti-relativism questions—How is it actually possible for "religious" believers to live this way? For that matter, how can postmoderns or post-theists be totally free of their own "illusions"? How can anyone? How can Cupitt, my student, or even myself stand up courageously (whenever this is required), or even persuasively, for the strength of our convictions, while simultaneously holding that our own story is nothing more than a tenuous, self-constructed language-game, a contingent local narrative, whose truth is never more than a moment away from being controverted—depending on the attractiveness of an opposing language-game, or the cogency of one or another local narrative? Do we, in our everyday existence, actually go about living our lives as if they were fictions? How is it possible to sustain this thoroughgoing skepticism, this willingness to surrender our religious convictions at the first sight of a better religious fiction?

Are Nietzsche, Lyotard, and Cupitt correct when they say there is no way we can ever really get outside of our own individual skins—outside our unique languages and our "situatedness"—to find a meta-story we can live, and die, by? How do they, and we, know for sure that there is no external moral law, no commonsense, objective experience, no mind-independent scientific or religious reality? Is it true that the post-theist turn to the subject is inexorable? Is Cupitt (1997) right when he claims he has moved beyond an "imperfect" relativism, even though he proudly, and at times disdainfully, rejects a belief in metaphysical and moral realism? Do his "Eye of God" (to live "as if" under the eye of God and to assess one's life "as if" from the standpoint of eternity), his "Blissful Void" (to live "as if" there is only universal emptiness and nothingness so that one can better understand the flux in all of life), and his "Solar Living" (to live "as if" one is the only maker of meaning, and, like the sun, one is dying all the time) provide enough of a foundation for "the development of a new world faith" (pp. 87–90)?

A British neo-Marxist, Terry Eagleton (1996), contends that postmodernists (and, by implication, post-theists) deceive themselves if they genuinely believe they have eschewed any and all belief in absolutism, universalism, and meta-narratives. At the very least, according to Eagleton, postmodernists are philosophically inconsistent; at worst, they are intentionally disingenuous. For one, they have constructed a narrative announcing the death of the meta-narrative that is every bit as grand and as absolute as any narrative they wish to destroy. Moreover, for Eagleton, postmodernists are not anti-ideological, as they sometimes boast: They are actually libertarians, even though for them there is not much of a subject left to be liberated. With their enthusiasm for an account of the world (a story) that stresses the values of pluralism, provisionality, antifoundationalism, freedom, and difference, postmodernists begin to look more and more like dogmatic Millsian libertarians in anarchist clothing.

Postmodernists absolutize the values of otherness, contingency, and liberty while relativizing religious foundations, essentialist notions of human nature, and moral absolutes. They want to be left alone to pursue their particular projects. They want their individual freedom, autonomy, happiness, and political equality without the necessity of having to elevate any of these particulars into universal or absolute metaphysical propositions. They are anti-elitist and anti-universal, even though the goods they seek to fulfill in their own lives depend on some universal agreement that individuals have a political and moral right to pursue these goods in their own best ways. Or as the neo-Gnostic environmentalists from a previous chapter would contend, it is an incontrovertible, indeed, a categorical moral truth that because all of us inhabit the same Earth, therefore, without a joint global effort across our local differences to preserve our world, the postmodern political and moral goods would simply have no viable future.

In a sense, postmodernist goods constitute a kind of American essence, a universal abstraction that really does go "all the way down" in defining the American character. Americans do have many things in common; moreover, it is not wholly untenable even for postmodernists to propose that individuals from other cultures may have many things in common with us. As Eagleton (1996) asserts:

> If cultures are internally self-validating, then it would be sheer imperial arrogance for our own culture to seek to pass judgment on any other.... Postmodern "anti-ethnocentrism" thus leaves our own culture conveniently insulated from anyone else's critique. All those anti-Western bleatings from the so-called third world may safely be ignored, since they are interpreting our conduct in terms quite irrelevant to us.

Eagleton is warning us that too much postmodern nonjudgment-alism, skepticism, localism, and relativism could very well result in a tolerance for human rights abuses abroad, and a fascism at home. After all, if what happens in cultures outside our borders lies beyond moral critique, and if respect for the "otherness" of individuals and groups in our own culture is always to be given top moral priority, and if there are no noncontingent moral or political foundations that can be taken for granted, then our political future is hopeless. For Eagleton, it is unlikely that postmodernists will be interested in taking the necessary steps to forge a theory of collective political agency, and to provide the collective political resources, that might be able to withstand fascist takeovers either from within or from without. Eagleton (1996) worries that politically, "postmodernism is . . . part of the problem rather than of the solution" (p. 135).

In fact, Anthony C. Thiselton (1995), a British theologian and staunch restorationist takes Cupitt and other post-theists to task because of where he believes the post-theist political agenda is likely to end up. Echoing Eagleton, Thiselton contends that post-theists like Cupitt speak with "forked rhetoric" (p. 111) whenever they proclaim the virtues of political and religious pluralism. With all the emphasis on difference, competing truth claims, and local narratives, post-theism has potentially destructive social consequences. In the world that Cupitt wants so enthusiastically to inhabit, there is an alarming loss of stability, identity, and moral certainty. People soon get defensive, anxious, and, according to Thiselton (1995), become preoccupied with self-interest, control, and exercises of power. They "assume a stance of readiness for conflict" (p. 131). For Thiselton, the collapse of objective norms and truths and the concomitant reversion to relativism and subjectivism lead inevitably to empire-building, to power interests, even to sexism, racism, and economic domination. Thus, the post-theist is left to seek in vain an ephemeral security and self-protection (p. 159).

From a different theological angle, Brian Hebblethwaite (1988), a foundationalist theologian, challenges Cupitt and other post-theists to stop being so skeptical regarding the existence of objective human and supernatural knowledge. Hebblethwaite believes there is obvious rational order in the universe; moreover, that there exist intelligent, self-transcend-ing human beings who profess the values of beauty, goodness, and love. And since the beginning of recorded time, people have experienced a widespread sense of God. For Hebblethwaite, aside from any appeal to divine revelation or church teachings, it is intuitively obvious to most human beings that they are born into an objective, preexisting, determinate world, a world that possesses physical qualities (animal, vegetable, and mineral) that are mind-independent, a world out there waiting to be discovered and not created. So, too, is there an objective, mind-independent Creator God waiting to be discovered via a natural theology. According to Hebblethwaite (1988), it is the very contingency of the universe and all life in it that "makes us seek the cause, in the metaphysical sense, of its being in being" (p. 89). The system itself can never explain the existence of the system; thus, it is necessary to go outside the system in order to understand how life and mind come into existence in the first place.

Hebblethwaite renounces the multiple-universes/paradigms, infinite regresses, and anarchy-chaos theories of the post-theists as, in principle, more unverifiable, indeed more extravagant, than theism itself. Hebblethwaite goes on to conjecture that Cupitt's (1997) post-theism, on its own terms, utterly fails to account for the presence of goods in life, including human freedom, self-transcendence, creativity, and ethical and moral behavior. It makes more sense to Hebblethwaite to postulate the existence of an objective, transcendent being who is "ground, designer, and source of value" (p. 97) than it does to leave the whole thing to chance; or in Cupitt's case, to a "functional" need to create an anthropomorphic deity, via language, in order to prepare people to be citizens of modern state societies.

In brief, for Hebblethwaite (1988), the argument from objective truth to an objective God is predicated on the assumption that an objective world existed before we were born, and that it is our project to discover, rather than invent, those things in the world that make our lives possible and meaningful, including language and love, stars and planets, education and worship, and thinking and knowing persons as well (p. 112). Therefore, for Hebblethwaite, it is simply good common sense to believe that if an objective world does in fact exist, and it is good, then it must be God-given and God-preserved. Only God—not the postmodern constructivist, or the post-theist "symbolic expressivist" (Cupitt, 1997)—is the "creator and guarantor" of all those things that possess enduring value, truth, and love. And it is our responsibility to discover God's divine law, the universal and objective norm of morality, without which ethics and morals would be little more than matters of subjective whim.

In summary, restorationist writers (e.g., Ward, 1997) reject the thoroughgoing relativism of post-theists on the grounds of its inconsistencies, its inner contradictions, its political accommodations, and its metaphysical arbitrariness. Post-theists claim to have done away with grand narratives, only to replace them with the grandest narrative of them all—the narrative that says definitively that *there is no grand narrative*. Post-theists repudiate absolute religious values, but then they proceed, without a second thought, to absolutize their own values, including plurality, transgression, anti-foundationalism, perspectivism, and, yes, cultural relativism.

Post-theists argue vehemently in favor of political and religious difference, but, ironically, this "universalist" celebration of individual and group difference for its own sake too easily lends itself to social and economic exploitation by others. As we are reminded time and time again by oppressed minorities in America and elsewhere, not all individuals and groups operate on a level playing field. To be sure, postmodern celebrations of cultural difference are good; but active political initiatives to redress the existence of soul-crushing socioeconomic and educational inequalities based solely on cultural difference would be better. As Eagleton points out, "Not everyone, as yet, enjoys freedom, happiness, and justice" (p. 118). Remarkably, and revealingly, post-theists like Cupitt (1997), Freeman (1993), and Hart (1993) say nothing at all about the collective political activity that will be necessary to sustain and strengthen the basic religious (and political) freedoms they claim to cherish for themselves and others.

And, finally, in proclaiming the need for religion without God, for moral commitment without objective foundations, and for hope without a sustaining truth, post-theists offer us little more than a message of despair, the subject of the next section. In Hebblethwaite's (1988) words: "A supremely good and beautiful ultimate reality behind all finite forms of existence *alone* explains the values we perceive on earth in such partial, temporary and fragile ways" (p. 147).

THE LOSS OF AN INSPIRING REASON FOR BEING

Perhaps the most haunting (and troubling) memory I have of a student, whose religious will seemed to have been broken in one of my courses, involved a former Christian fundamentalist whom I will call Paul, an elementary school principal. Raised in a strict, Bible-based, middle-class home, Paul, the grandson of a Baptist minister, began to seriously question his religious beliefs during the semester he took a religion and education course with me. I remember all too well the disillusioned, often alarmed look in his eyes as the course unfolded, the anxiety and disappointment in his voice, and the sadness in his writing as we covered each of the religious worldviews during the semester. Embarrassed by the anti-intellectualism and overzealousness of our fundamentalist guests, put off by all the prophetic stridency expressed in class in behalf of social justice for the poor and oppressed, and frankly skeptical of a neo-Gnostic self-centeredness that appeared to leave God completely out of the equation,

Paul was an easy mark for the post-theist worldview when the time came to study it toward the end of the semester. I do not recall if he ever said one public word in class regarding this narrative, but I do remember clearly three questions Paul uttered to me *sub rosa* on the last day of class: "Why do I feel so totally empty?" "What's the sense of trying to lead a good life, if, in the end, it's all a matter of personal taste?" and "Is it possible I've just made the whole 'God-thing' up—out of a pathetic bit of wishful thinking?"

While I believe Paul's crisis of faith must have been a long time coming (even before he took my course), and while I deeply regret his religious anguish—particularly if I did anything professionally unethical or educationally injudicious to provoke it—I think he accurately identified what bothers most of my students about the post-theist perspective: *It fails to respond with any degree of satisfaction to the deeply disquieting existential questions of a Tolstoy or a Pascal.* "Is there any meaning in my life that will not be destroyed by my inevitably approaching death?" asks Tolstoy. "Who put me here? By whose command and act were this time and place allotted to me?" asks Pascal. Or, as the Basque philosopher Don Miguel de Unamuno (1921/1954) asks in the *Tragic Sense of Life*, "Whence do I come and whence comes the world in which and by which I live? Whither do I go and whither goes everything that environs me? What does it all mean?" (p. 32).

It is one thing for a seasoned philosopher and Cambridge University theologian like Cupitt (1997) to disavow any need he has for a stable ethnic identity or religious provenance, and, in the process, celebrate his embrace of nihilism as an attractive and spiritually fulfilling way of life both for himself and for others. Cupitt, the scholar and disenchanted ex-Anglican cleric, can boast about becoming "postmodernized," and be pleased that he has finally found a religion "without God." And he can then challenge the rest of us to construct a new religious vocabulary, and to experience religion more as a "tool kit" for spiritual survival than as a set of desiccated church doctrines that kill the soul. But the ordinary "Pauls" who sign up for my courses each semester, and the "Pauls" who sit in classrooms at all levels of schooling throughout the United States, are looking for something more than Cupitt's "blissful void" of Zen Buddhism.

For them, Cupitt's religious insouciance begins to look elitist: His post-theism appears esoteric and remote, and his redefinition of religion as nothing but an expressive linguistic theory, without any objective truth value whatsoever, seems vapid in the extreme. Indeed, most of my students, after reading post-theists like Cupitt (1997), Freeman (1993), and Hart (1993), are left to ask, like Paul: "What does it all mean?" "When all is said and done, are all religious stories lies?" "Is Cupitt right when he says we only made the whole thing up?"

Accommodationist theologians like Diogenes Allen (1989), Stanley Grenz (1996), David Ray Griffin (1989), Ted Peters (1992), and David Tracy (1994) attempt to go halfway to meet the challenges of post-theism. They are the peacemakers, who believe they can augment a hermeneutic of suspicion with a hermeneutic of religious belief; in Peters's (1992) words, "We must understand in order to believe, but we must believe in order to understand" (p. 28). Accommodationists tend to ask a hermeneutical question: In what ways can the ancient symbols, rituals, and content of religious faith speak to the postmodern mind today with its plurality of moral perspectives, its shifting philosophical/scientific paradigms, and its abiding skepticism toward meta-narratives, absolutes, and universals?

Some accommodationists (Griffin, 1989) settle for a kind of process theology, wherein a "naturalistic theism" is meant to revise the concept of a premodern, all-powerful, outside-of-nature God advanced by the fundamentalists. In this Whiteheadian, process interpretation, a flawed but evolving God is said to work bilaterally with a postmodern generation to improve the world by resisting imperialism, war, and, especially, nuclear armaments (pp. 127–145). God and his creatures thus become co-dependents (and co-creators) in the process of worldmaking. And while some accommodationists (Grenz, 1996; Tracy, 1994) side with the post-theists in repudiating the certainties of Enlightenment epistemology—for example, the supremacy of reason and autonomy—and in recognizing the (historicist) inevitability of multiple perspectives on the truth, they still hold on to the validity of religious grand narratives. For them, there is a transcendent and unifying center that explains and redeems all things. Thus, the Christian Grenz (1996) can assert:

> Therefore, we agree that in this world we will witness the struggle among conflicting narratives and interpretations of reality. . . . [but] we simply cannot allow Christianity to be relegated to the status of one more faith among others. . . . We believe not only that the biblical narrative makes sense for *us* but is also good news for *all*. (p. 165)

I must acknowledge, though, that I do not believe the accommodationists are ultimately successful in their conciliatory ambitions. In spite of their efforts to retrieve something valuable from post-theism—and as I listen overall to how my students respond to their peacemaking attempts—I find that the accommodationists fall into the same trap as do the post-theist converts: *Because their religious narrative is watered down, it is uninspiring and compromised; it lacks a true sense of the tragic, an element of mystery and awe, a nobility of purpose, and a set of beliefs worth living and dying for.* They do not convincingly answer the most penetrating questions about post-theism: If we cannot appeal to a common humanity, or to an essential human nature, or to some irreducible core of morality, how can we ever agree on how we should live individually and collectively? Why on earth must we try to abolish pain and suffering in the world if there is no unimpeachable source that affirms this task to be morally praiseworthy? Why should a Mother Teresa, the "secular saint" whose work with lepers and the poor in Calcutta earned her a Nobel Peace Prize, and great international honor at her death in 1997, spend her entire adult life serving the needs of those the Bible considers the "least" among us? Why should she care about lepers if the "entire supernatural world of religion is [nothing but] a mythical representation of the world of language" (Cupitt, 1997, p. xv), including such religious qualities as *service, love, faith, hope, humility, sacrifice,* and, yes, *God?*

Post-theists would consider the existential questions I ask earlier to be symptomatic of the never-ending but futile search for some quasi-divinity, or a "final language," that has eluded hapless God-seekers for centuries. They would judge these kinds of questions to be pretentious, ill-advised attempts to discover an ultimate knowledge or authority. In contrast, and even though I identify strongly with the post-theist project of deconstructing any notion of a final language, I do not think Pascal's, Tolstoy's, or Unamuno's questions are without merit. These questions try to place human actions into a larger existential context by provoking us to think about issues of permanence, purpose, meaning, faith, hope, and morality. Sometimes these questions lead us to theism; sometimes to politics; sometimes to philosophy; and sometimes they can lead people like me to a cautious and, I hope, open-minded post-theism.

At least in one case, they led Socrates to philosophy, an activity he believed was the best preparation for living a moral life, and for dying a noble death. Tolstoy, Pascal, and Unamuno are discerning enough to distinguish a tragic sense to life: a sense that at times reason springs more from the heart than from the head, and thus may be more reliable; a sense that human beings can behave in ways that are at once unspeakably wicked and indescribably good; and a sense that the less a person believes in ultimate truths, the more likely that person will exaggerate the worth of transitory things. I think John Updike (1997) beautifully captures the tragic sense when he describes his own Christian (Kierkegaardian) vision:

[We are] in a state of fear and trembling, separated from God, haunted by dread, twisted by the conflicting demands of [our] animal biology and [our]

human intelligence, of the social contract and the inner imperatives, condemned as if by otherworldly origins to perpetual restlessness . . . (p. 9)

Where do what I am calling the "disquieting existential questions"
lead fundamentalists, prophetics, and neo-Gnostics, as opposed to the
post-theists? The first three groups, in their own way and at their best,
embrace a form of love. Each recognizes that we live our lives every day
in the shadow of the *eschaton* (Gr., last things), in the realization that life
is ephemeral and that the daily reminders of our finitude mock all of our
worldly accomplishments, our hopes and expectations. Thus, for fundamentalists, the questions lead to a love of biblical teachings, inerrant
supernatural truth, and personal metanoia; for prophetics, the questions
lead to a love for social justice, the poor, and the establishment of an
egalitarian utopia in this world; and for neo-Gnostics, the questions lead
to a love of self-knowledge, Gaia (Mother Earth), and global peace. But
for post-theists, where do the questions lead? They lead mainly to a
disheartening skepticism: an awareness that the questions themselves
are erroneous, because they conceal theistic biases that are self-serving,
atavistic, and linguistically untenable.

My own post-theist response to the "disquieting existential questions" I am asking in this section leans more toward Reinhold Niebuhr's
(1941/1964a; 1943/1964b) Christian realism (*minus* the divine and doctrinal pieces of the Christian story) that I mentioned in Chapter 5 than
toward Cupitt's "polytheistic" nihilism. Niebuhr, a Protestant theologian
who held a hermeneutical view of life long before the designations *postmodern* and *post-theist* were fashionable, possessed a tragic sense of life I
believe to be extraordinarily insightful and still timely, especially today.
Niebuhr knew the world to be forever "full of grace and grief." For all
his doubts about the efficacy of human efforts without a sustaining belief
in God, Niebuhr knew that human beings were always called to create
their own history—in full awareness of the pride and foolishness that
would continually plague their efforts. Like me, Niebuhr was put off by
easy belief, angered by cost-free piety. Niebuhr's lifelong task was to weld
together the tragic sense of life and the pursuit of justice, while pointing
out the "viciousness of self-idolatry."

For Niebuhr (1941/1964a), self-idolatry "encourages wrongly ordered loves or a failure to recognize and meet our obligations" (pp.
175–176). The important truth for me in Niebuhr's Christian realism,
and one mostly overlooked by post-theists like Cupitt (1997), is that the
postmodern self (or the group) is much too fragile, ephemeral, and egoistic
ever to be the appropriate focus of our ultimate confidence, fidelity, hope,
and love. I find that too many post-theists have de-divinized "God" only

to end up divinizing the individual self, or the "interpretive community," or the local narrative. Or else they end up expunging these entities altogether and divinizing (and universalizing) *difference, language,* and *history.* Rarely do I hear these writers speak of the treacheries and futilities of an individual or group autonomy (often understood by post-theists to be synonymous with a Nietzschean assertion of self-creation, or even a self-love) that has been pushed to intolerable extremes by some human service professionals—especially some multiculturalists, therapists, and educators—in the United States.

What I think Niebuhr meant by self-idolatry is that when the postmodern self (with its own peculiar set of rigid doctrines and dogmas) is held up as the sole source of meaning in the world, then loving relationships, ordered lives, and proper duties for others fall by the wayside. Sooner or later, an autonomy (or an alterity) without limits comes face to face with the sheer fragility of the human ego. Revealingly, I have never heard a post-theist like Cupitt (1997), reputedly a man of soaring self-confidence, speak of the fragility of the human ego. Thus, his grand faith in a new "world religion," one that is "naturalistic," "nihilistic," "globalized," and "expressivist" (pp. 121–128), comes off merely sounding hollow and shallow.

Contrast Cupitt's pallid descriptions of the "globalized nihilist"—a free-floating Zen Buddhist who lives "after God" in a time of rootlessness and high technology, and who finds religious faith irrelevant—with the existential depth and complexity of John Updike's (1997) "Kierkegaardian [postmodern] man." For Updike, the postmodern individual is someone "caught in a state of fear and trembling, separated from God, haunted by dread, twisted by conflicting demands, and given to perpetual restlessness" (p. 9). For me, Updike's description applies to the struggles of my own students far more accurately than Cupitt's, and according to their firsthand reports, it seems to ring more true for these students as well. And, ironically, as existentially bleak as Updike's depiction of the postmodern individual appears, it seems to carry more *hope* for them.

The stark reality throughout the world is that currently, too many leaders with God-like egos, "twisted by conflicting demands" and thoroughly convinced that their own religious "idolatries" are unimpeachably right, are urging their more-than-eager followers to wage bloody religious and political wars. Thus, any kind of idolatry, whether of the self, the group, or the "sacred" doctrine, threatens to become, in Niebuhr's amazingly prescient (written in 1941) word, "vicious."

Finally, in the absence of any realistic and inspiring reason for being, can there ever be a compelling set of moral maxims in the post-theist story for ordinary people like my student Paul—and, for that matter, students and nonstudents everywhere—to embrace? If in a postmodern world we can never again recover the "absolute" moral truths bequeathed to us by the traditional religions, what will be left to guide human behavior? Indeed, why should any of us even bother making the effort to rid the world of injustice, cruelty, and needless human suffering—a question that post-theists like Cupitt (1997) adroitly sidestep? In another place (Nash, 1997), I have attempted to demonstrate that postmodernism need not be entirely devoid of an uplifting ethic; in fact, I argued that certain virtues (e.g., openness to otherness, respect for plurality, patience, tolerance, empathy, a sense of irony and humor, and a humility in the face of shifting and elusive conceptions of truth) peculiar to the postmodern project could possibly help us in the resolution of those significant moral and religious differences that divide us as a people. But, as my students delight in informing me, my post-theist virtues, while suggestive, are largely cerebral and uninspiring; they fail to raise high hopes or feed grand ideals. And, they always add, it is unlikely that my post-theist virtues would ever encourage the supererogatory moral deeds of a Mother Teresa or a Martin Luther King Jr.

In part, I agree with my students. Post-theists need to help students, and all the rest of us as well, to find morally galvanizing substitutes (or in Richard Rorty's [1989] word, linguistic "redescriptions") for the "absolute" truths that no longer appear defensible or universally cherished in a postmodern world. These truths include the following: All human beings are created equal in that they are endowed by their "Creator" with certain unalienable rights; the spirit of religious tolerance ought to be supported and oppressive fanaticism opposed; freedom is better than despotism; the ontological irreducibility of the worth of the individual is not necessarily incompatible with being a functional member of small communities with their own unique histories and traditions; all human beings have a right to make claims to a minimally decent life as a matter of social justice; and not all human dilemmas are remedied by political means—in reality, some may not even be solvable (Kolakowski, 1986).

In a radical departure from my own post-theist language, I would suggest, in a vocabulary more suited to the first two narratives I have earlier examined, that there will be no moral "salvation" for us as a people until we have some recognition of a *common* good, one that does not crush but enhances the freedom of *individuals* to pursue their own unique goods, including the spiritual and the religious goods. This common good transcends, but does not preclude, the sharing of such "thin" procedural goods as due process protections and liberty rights. This common good ought to be rooted in a set of enduring and vital, moral reference points similar to the ones I mention in the previous paragraph. Also, there will be no salvation without a profound sense that my neighbor is my obliga-tion and that communal life, and the qualities it encourages, necessitates shared ideals and common dreams. In fact, in the long run, these shared ideals and common dreams offer the best protection for individual inter-ests, because the welfare of the individual has always been the pivotal ideal at the center of the American dream.

Furthermore, there will be no salvation until we agree that a radical respect for *postpartum* life forbids the direct killing of the innocent. This radical respect for life preserves the victim, the agent, the ideal of alterity, and, indeed, morality itself. Also, there will be no salvation unless we create a private and public meta-narrative that encourages a respect to-ward *opposing* meta-narratives (especially religious ones), even though we understand that all meta-narratives (especially religious ones) are seriously, and irreversibly, defective in some ways. And, most signifi-cantly, there will be no salvation unless there is something that my stu-dents believe is clearly worth living and dying for (Nash, 1996).

Obviously, a meta-narrative clearly worth living and dying for has grave implications for *how, what*, and *why* we teach, not just in our religious institutions, but also in our nation's secular schools and colleges. In the words of Leszek Kolakowski (1986), a conservative Catholic philosopher I referred to in Chapter 2, without a set of galvanizing moral reference points we are left with a society that:

> reduces politics to the technical rules of success, or that tries to dissolve its existence in a mindless and fanatical devotion of one kind or another, or escapes from life into a variety of self-stunning devices. (p. 36)

POST-THEISM: HYPER-CRITICAL AVANT GARDE OR HEALING PRESENCE?

In Chapter 1, I raised several interrelated educational questions about teaching religion in public schools and colleges. In this section, and in the Conclusions, I intend to speak directly to many of these questions by reshaping the post-theist narrative somewhat. My overall purpose in this section is to respond to those educators who might be looking for fresh ways to think about, and to teach, religion in secular institutions. My primary argument here is that post-theism can be a healing presence in a troubled culture only if it positions itself less at the disputatious *margins* of religious discourse and more at the reconciling *center*. At least in the ideal, I believe post-theism could become a harmonizing presence, because it alone values a diversity of religious voices; also, it privileges no single story—not the agnostic, or the neo-Gnostic, or the religiously orthodox. And because post-theism, in theory, refuses to push a particular religious narrative (including its own) on anyone, it alone has the ability to forge new and more *inclusive* forms of religious community.

But before reconciliation can happen, postmodernists, including post-theists like Cupitt (1997), must resist slipping into the role of the hyper-critical avant-garde, the transgressive outsiders who, on principle, oppose and dismiss *all* meta-narratives. As Steven Connor (1997) accurately points out,

> There is much to be gained from this cooling-down of the self-aggrandizing rhetoric of marginality, outsiderdom, and transgression in postmodern theory, and from the movement beyond the concept-metaphors of center and margin which so insistently reproduce absolute polarities and, more importantly, disguise the complicity of postmodern theory in the construction of the totalizing global systems which it fantasizes about getting "outside" of. (p. 275)

In Bernstein's (1992) metaphor I mentioned in Chapter 8, post-theism must help believers, nonbelievers, and disbelievers to engage in a *"to-and-fro movement in dialogical encounters" with each other*, something I have tried to do in this book in examining the four religious perspectives. The purpose of such encounters is to find *common ground* as well as to identify irreconcilable differences, to bring religious groups together rather than to pit one group against another. Again, using Connor's (1997) language, the question that post-theists must ask is not, "How do you persuade people to agree with you who are already inclined to do so?" but "How do you persuade people to agree with you who do not already do so?" (p. 276).

Or, in my own *to-and-fro* language: How can teachers of the four narratives encourage open, honest, and critical dialogue among believers and nonbelievers in the postmodern classroom, a dialogue that recognizes and respects the irreducible diversity of religious voices throughout the world? How can teachers promote a conversation that will effectively forestall the imposition of a religious uniformity (or a religiously correct blandness) on everyone, along with the mind-numbing, soul-killing repression that usually accompanies such an imposition? How can teachers further a discourse that seeks not so much to persuade students to agree with them as to understand and accept religious differences so that they might live together in some kind of concord?

Is it possible for post-theist teachers to enlarge the "conversational space" about religion in the classroom without asking adherents of the various stories to "bracket" their own strong religious beliefs? How, for example, can fundamentalists or prophetics engage with integrity in a postmodern, pluralistic dialogue that might appear to them to establish one primary rule at the outset: *Religious believers must voluntarily annihilate a significant piece of themselves, and enter the postmodern classroom conversation looking only for what they and others share in common, absent all the sectarian particulars?* At this juncture, the short answer to each of these questions is for us to avoid teaching the stories with the sole purpose of securing students' acceptance of one or another religious story. The main objective in teaching for religious literacy in secular settings should be to help students appreciate what has shaped their own, and others', religious lives, and to get them to read *all* religious "texts" with insight, empathy, and critical discrimination; ideally, as a direct consequence of this activity, each student's religious language and narrative will be significantly deepened, enriched, and enlarged.

Thus, I believe the best way to encourage authentic religious dialogue in a secular classroom is to avoid setting ground rules that intentionally (or unintentionally) favor one or another of the viewpoints. What is required is that teachers and students be honestly open and responsive to the diversity of religious views that are bound to come up. Although this technique is admittedly biased toward a postmodern respect for plurality and tolerance, in the end, according to Stephen Carter (1993), it manifests a real appreciation for "epistemic diversity"—it looks for strengths as well as weaknesses, for truth as well as error, in opposing views, *in an evenhanded way*. Says Carter (1993):

> What is needed, then, is a willingness to listen, not because the speaker has *the right voice* but because the speaker has *the right to speak*. Moreover, the willingness to listen must hold out the possibility that the speaker is saying something worth listening to; to do less is to trivialize the forces that shape the [religious] convictions of millions of Americans. (pp. 230–231)

In the spirit of respect for "epistemic diversity," then, I offer the following set of post-theist speculations to educators as possible starting points for talking about the teaching of religion in our nation's school and college classrooms.

- Although they arrive at their conclusions from different directions, theists and post-theists both challenge and repudiate the utopian, world-building zeal implicit in modernist grand narratives. Both share a natural skepticism regarding the undemonstrated claims of twentieth-century meta-narratives to deliver the good life to everyone. Thus far, all the faith modernists have placed in reason, science, technology, and in one political ideology after another to fashion a heaven on Earth appears to have been grievously mistaken. Especially disappointing have been those political grand narratives that promise deliverance from suffering, poverty, powerlessness, and injustice but, throughout this century, have managed to end up as props for totalitarianism and tyranny. The lesson for all educators, believer and nonbeliever alike, is to cultivate, both in ourselves and in our students, an informed yet humble skepticism toward grand political claims of all kinds, whatever the source, lest someday we, and our students, become unwitting accomplices to despotism and oppression.

- Theists and post-theists, each in different ways, are acutely aware of the validity of Nietzsche's claim that "All that exists consists of interpretations" (1911/1968, p. 481). These interpretations are inevitably colored, and flawed, by our unique situations and by our soothing illusions. Those who yearn to become our saviors, leaders, or teachers, issuing divine edicts for us to obey, can only offer us their own partial and fallible perspectives on the world, nothing more, nothing less. Therefore, it is important for us to be wary of triumphalistic claims to religious, political, or educational truth, because knowledge is always and everywhere incomplete, partisan, and self-interested. At the very least, a religious, political, or educational truth claim must stand up to rigorous scrutiny, suspicion, and robust but respectful challenge. The best thing that teachers can do when talking about religion is to encourage what Bernstein (1992) calls an "engaged fallibilistic pluralism" in the classroom, wherein students realize that there is no religious story, assumption, or rubric that is not open to further interpretation, elaboration, and critique. In the pursuit of genuine religious literacy, there can be no such thing as an airtight (infallible) account of any religious story, because most "airtight" defenses of religious arguments are actually self-slanted, faith-induced interpretations; and, lamentably, they usually wind up making enemies of doubters rather than securing converts. The most that we can ever do in a classroom is to seek a "mutual reciprocal understanding" about our different religious stories and let it go at that.

- Teachers need to realize that despite its serious limitations, the post-theist religious story is probably the most functional religious story for a secular pluralist society because its central truth criterion appears to be pragmatism and not supernaturalism. Post-theism asks: Does the story work, and if it does, why? In a very real sense, the postmodern world is a post-religious and a post-philosophical one. Some people continue to cling to the older fundamentalisms and traditions, of course, because they find it impossible to bear up under the apparent chaos of thousands of religious vocabularies (some transcendent, some immanent, and some agnostic or atheistic), none of which is translatable into a commonly understood and commonly accepted vocabulary by everyone. We have no choice today but to let a hundred (even a million) religions bloom, if this is what some people crave. The stark truth is, it seems to me, that local religious narratives will never again add up to a single grand religious narrative. Instead, the goal that educators ought to pursue is one of peaceful religious coexistence, or, better, the adoption of what might be called a pluralistic perspective on religious belief— the only approach, in my opinion, that is likely to prevent self-appointed leaders from laying down a series of strict religious prescriptions for all of us to heed. In my conception, concerns about *absolute* religious truth should disappear, to be replaced with *aesthetic* interests in the creative and moral uniqueness of a particular religion. Does the religion tell a good story? Does it invite me to add to the story it tells in order to make it more morally compelling, and, therefore, useful, in my own life?

- The most fair-minded (and stimulating) way for educators to keep religious values alive in a postmodern classroom is to advocate, and practice, a pedagogy of religious agnosticism, complete with balanced (to-and-fro) critiques of each of the perspectives. This necessitates an eclectic, secular presentation of what is best and what is worst in *all* the religious stories—transcendent, immanent, or otherwise. Again, this requires an aesthetic/worldview/narrative approach to the study of religion, in contrast to an approach that emphasizes the search for propositional or revelational "truths." A pluralistic, religious agnosticism separates out, privatizes, and secularizes those principles, values, and virtues that do not require the formal apparatus of church doctrine, revelation, or theology to support them. From a pedagogical perspective, secular educators must *respectfully* view all the rest as denominational distractions—highly significant to particular faith communities to be sure—but less central to outsiders and skeptics. In my view, students will only be able to build a common public world together in peace and mutual understanding when they can agree on those demythologized religious qualities (e.g., love, humility, hope, compassion, nonviolence) that all religions share, at least in some vestigial form. In this way, the moral *spirit* of religion will prevail in the classroom, and hopefully in the larger society, while the *letter* and *law* will recede into the educational background.

- Finally, a to-and-fro approach to religious analysis in the classroom does not have to be disrespectful, combative, or polarizing. But it does have to be candid—both spirited and critical—if it is to be engaging. Diana L. Eck (1993), a professor of comparative religion at Harvard University, differentiates between an "exclusivist," an "inclusivist," and a "pluralist" response to the challenge of religious diversity in the modern world. In my opinion, the educational implications of her terms would take the following forms. The *exclusivist* teacher might begin with the assumption that a particular religious narrative (usually the teacher's own) contains the whole truth, and all opposing narratives, while certainly well-meaning and worthy of study, are treated as fatally deficient in some way. Thus, the exclusivist teacher would spend a great deal of class time attempting to expose the weaknesses of competing religious views while emphasizing the strengths of the favored narrative. The *inclusivist* teacher, while more willing to acknowledge the genuine worth of other religious narratives, would aim always to translate, interpret, and ultimately to absorb all these others into the language and belief system of one particular, preferred religious tradition. Consequently, the inclusivist teacher would work hard to show that even though all religious roads may one day lead to the same destination, only one worldview is guaranteed to get the believer there with the least amount of trouble and without fail. The *pluralist* teacher, in contrast, would love the mutual give-and-take of several voices in religious dialogue and would display great faith that through empathic, enthusiastic, and respectful conversation students might be able to reach a more profound understanding of their own and others' religious traditions. For the pluralist teaching I am advocating throughout this book, to-and-fro religious dialogue would, in principle, be life-affirming; religious exclusivism and inclusivism would be life-denying and lead eventually to ignorant stereotyping and senseless violence. In my own view, whenever students can engage in a pluralistic religious dialogue in the classroom that is honest (and compassionate)—one that forthrightly confronts a religious narrative's internal inconsistencies and compromises as well as its strengths and virtues—then the prospect of genuine "meeting, exchange, criticism, reflection, and renewal" (Eck, 1993, pp. 197–198) among believers of different backgrounds and cultures becomes a tangible reality.

CONCLUSIONS

A post-theist approach to teaching about religion will entail what one widely heralded postmodernist teacher, Kenneth A. Bruffee (1995), has called "collaborative learning." By way of definition, Bruffee (1995) says:

> Collaborative learning makes the Kuhnian assumption that knowledge is a consensus: it is something people construct interdependently by talking together.... we can think because we can talk with one another. (pp. 113, 114)

Bruffee urges teachers to create what he calls a "nonfoundational curriculum." A nonfoundational understanding of *religious material*, for example, assumes, à la Cupitt (1997) and Lyotard (1984), that people create religious knowledge out of a variety of languages available to them at any given time and place. Thus, religious knowledge has no universal or absolute foundation *per se*, beyond the situation-specific faith commitments of believers, because it is always local, historically contingent, and constantly changing, given people's propensity to learn new languages throughout their lifetimes. I would add to Bruffee's notion of nonfoundational knowledge that people are always fashioning new (or revised) religious stories for themselves as they face a never-ending succession of life's inevitable challenges and anomalies.

Thus, by extending Bruffee's (1995, pp. 191–205) suggestions for constructing a "nonfoundational curriculum," secular educators can create a religious curriculum and instructional style containing the following components:

1. Students will need to understand that they already belong to a number of knowledge communities before they even get to school, including religious, recreational, ethnic, national, supranational, and several special-interest groups. The primary educational goal in a nonfoundational curriculum is not simply for students to learn how to develop a cultural identity, or to speak a particular religious language more fluently, or even to defend themselves against prejudicial religious or racial attacks by outsiders. Instead, the main goal, in Bruffee's (1995) terms, is to "help students examine their own and their peers' cultural attachments comparatively" (p. 194). This is an important objective, according to Bruffee, because it enables students to understand the unexamined assumptions by which they frame their own experiences and those of students from other cultures. Especially significant here is that students

become aware that *all knowledge, religious or otherwise, is always something constructed in specific cultural and historical settings.*

2. Students need to understand *how they actually go about justifying their religious knowledge.* They must learn the difference between justifiable and unjustifiable knowledge, the criteria they use for justification—narrative, revelational, doctrinal, and/or propositional knowledge—and the extent to which their at-home religious communities make these distinctions, if at all. Students should be encouraged to explore both the content of their justifiable and unjustifiable religious beliefs, and the ways they learned this content in their communities of origin. How exactly did their religious beliefs get justified in their various communities? What rules of logic or verification prevailed? What faith/truth assumptions were taken for granted? The purpose in understanding the nature of religious justification is that students acquire a healthy suspicion of any type of knowledge that is said to be inerrant, divinely revealed, and beyond social construction.

3. Finally, students ought to examine critically the *historical, conversational, and linguistic dimensions of religious belief.* The nonfoundational outcome of this type of learning is that students will slowly come to perceive all beliefs, religious or otherwise, as being largely community-based, historically situated, conversationally shaped and shared, and linguistically conceived in specialized language systems. Thus, those students who are conventional believers will be able to respond more empathically, critically, and nondefensively to Cupitt's (1997) summary dismissal of religion, cited earlier:

> [The truth about religion is] that we made it all up. We evolved the entire syllabus. We have slowly evolved our own languages, our values, our systems of knowledge, our religions, and our worldviews. We evolved even our own subjective consciousness, because the brightness, the consciousness, the conscious experience is a by-product of language. (p. 126)

Because conventionally religious students will be quick to recognize the historical, conversational, and linguistic conventions in Cupitt's own religious story, they will be less likely to take offense at his remarks; these are remarks which, after all, are merely the product of his own anodyne illusions. I contend that when students have arrived at this point, they will have truly achieved a religious literacy most suitable for life in a postmodern world.

References

African-American Devotional Bible. (1997). New York: Zondervan.

Allen, D. (1989). *Christian belief in a postmodern world: The full wealth of conviction.* Louisville, KY: Westminster/John Knox Press.

Altemeyer, B., & Hunsberger, B. (1997). *Amazing conversions: Why some turn to faith and others abandon religion.* New York: Prometheus.

Anzaldua, G. (1987). *Borderlands/la frontera: The new Mestiza.* San Francisco: Spinsters Aunt Lute.

Armstrong, K. (1993). *A history of God: The 4000-year quest of Judaism, Christianity and Islam.* New York: Knopf.

Aurobindo, S. (1973). *On education.* Pondicherry, India: Sri Aurobindo Ashram. (Original work published 1956)

Averill, L. J. (1989). *Religious right, religious wrong: A critique of the fundamentalist phenomenon.* New York: Pilgrim.

Bahnsen, G. (1984). *Theonomy and Christian ethics* (2nd ed.). Phillipsburg, NJ: Presbyterian and Reformed.

Baker, D. (1997, June 22). Bible class plan stirs Fla. debate. *The Boston Sunday Globe,* p. A22.

Baldick, C. (1990). *The concise Oxford dictionary of literary terms.* New York: Oxford University Press.

Banks, J. S. (1997). *Educating citizens in a multicultural society.* New York: Teachers College Press.

Barna, G. (1992). *The Barna report 1992–1993: America renews its search for God.* Ventura, CA: Regal Books.

Bates, S. (1994). *Battleground: One mother's crusade, the religious right, and the struggle for our schools.* New York: Owl.

Baudrillard, J. (1983). *In the shadow of the silent majorities.* New York: Semiotext.

Bawer, B. (1997). *Stealing Jesus: How fundamentalism betrays Christianity.* New York: Crown.

Bellah, R. N., Madsen, R., Sullivan, W. M., Swidler, A., & Tipton, S. M. (1985/1996). *Habits of the heart: Individualism and commitment in American life.* Berkeley: University of California Press.

Benhabib, S. (1992). *Situating the self: Gender, community, and postmodernism in contemporary ethics.* Oxford: Polity.

Benson, H. (1987). *Your maximum mind.* New York: Times.

Berger, P. L. (1970). *A rumor of angels: Modern society and the rediscovery of the supernatural.* New York: Doubleday Anchor.

Berman, M. (1982). *All that is solid melts into air: The experience of modernity.* New York: Simon and Schuster.

Bernstein, R. J. (1992). *The new constellation: The ethical-political horizons of modernity/ postmodernity.* Cambridge, MA: MIT Press.

Blacker, D. J. (1997). *Dying to teach: The educator's search for immortality.* New York: Teachers College Press.

Bloom, H. (1993). *The American religion: The emergence of the post-Christian nation.* New York: Touchstone.

Bloom, H. (1996). *Omens of millennium: The gnosis of angels, dreams, and resurrection.* New York: Riverhead.

Bloomfield, H. H. (1975). *TM: Discovering inner energy and overcoming stress.* New York: Dell.

Bly, R. (1976). On gurus, grounding yourself in the western tradition, and thinking of yourself. *East–West Journal, 6,* 9–16.

Bodian, S. (Ed.). (1991). *Timeless visions, healing voices: Conversations with men & women of the spirit.* Freedom, CA: The Crossing Press.

Bonhoeffer, D. (1967). *Letters and papers from prison.* New York: Macmillan. (Original work published 1944)

Brown, R. M. (1978). *Theology in a new key: Responding to liberation themes.* Philadelphia, PA: Westminster.

Bruffee, K. A. (1995). *Collaborative learning: Higher education, interdependence, and the authority of knowledge.* Baltimore, MD: The Johns Hopkins University Press.

Butler, J. (1990). *Gender trouble: Feminism and the subversion of identity.* New York: Routledge.

Camus, A. (1954). *The rebel* (A. Bower, Trans.). New York: Harper.

Capra, F. (1977). *The Tao of physics.* New York: Simon and Schuster.

Carse, J. P. (1994). *Breakfast at the victory: The mysticism of ordinary experience.* San Francisco: Harper.

Carter, S. L. (1993). *The culture of disbelief: How American law and politics trivializes religious devotion.* New York: Basic.

Chaudhuri, H. (1974). *Integral yoga.* Madras, India: The Theosophical Publishing House.

Citizens Commission on Human Rights International. (1997). *Creating evil—Psychiatry: Destroying religion.* Los Angeles: Author.

Colson, C. (1989). *Against the night: Living in the new dark ages.* Ann Arbor, MI: Servant.

Connor, S. (1997). *Postmodernist culture: An introduction to theories of the contemporary* (2nd ed.). Cambridge, MA: Blackwell.

Cousins, N. (1984). *The healing heart.* New York: Avon.

Cox, H. (1977). *Turning east.* New York: Simon and Schuster.

Cox, H. (1984). *Religion in the secular city: Toward a postmodern theology.* New York: Simon and Schuster.

Cox, H. (1995). *Fire from heaven: The rise of pentecostal spirituality and the reshaping of religion in the twenty-first century.* Reading, MA: Addison-Wesley.

Cragg, K. (1976). *Wisdom of the Sufis.* New York: Harper & Row.

Csikszentmihalyi, M. (Ed.). (1988). *Optimal experience: Psychological studies of flow in consciousness.* Cambridge, UK: Cambridge University Press.

Cupitt, D. (1980). *Taking leave of God.* New York: Crossroad.

Cupitt, D. (1984). *The sea of faith*. London: British Broadcasting Company.

Cupitt, D. (1989). *Radicals and the future of the church*. London: SCM.

Cupitt, D. (1994). *After all: Religion without alienation*. London: SCM.

Cupitt, D. (1997). *After God: The future of religion*. New York: Basic.

Curran, C. E. (1985). *Directions in Catholic social ethics*. Notre Dame, IN: University of Notre Dame Press.

Daly, M. (1973). *Beyond God the father: Towards a philosophy of women's liberation*. Boston: Beacon Press.

Dass, R. (1977). *Grist for the mill*. Santa Cruz, CA: Unity.

Dass, R., & Bush, M. (1992). *Compassion in action: Setting out on the path of service*. New York: Bell Tower.

Dass, R., & Gorman, P. (1985). *How can I help? Stories and reflections on service*. New York: Knopf.

Derrida, J. (1976). *Of grammatology*. Baltimore: Johns Hopkins University Press.

Dewey, J. (1934). *A common faith*. New Haven, CT: Yale University Press.

Dewey, J. (1960). *The quest for certainty: A study of the relation of knowledge and action*. New York: G. P. Putnam's Sons. (Original work published 1929)

Eagleton, T. (1983). *Literary theory: An introduction*. Minneapolis: University of Minnesota Press.

Eagleton, T. (1996). *The illusions of postmodernism*. Cambridge, MA: Blackwell.

Eck, D. L. (1993). *Encountering God: A spiritual journey from Bozeman to Banaras*. Boston: Beacon.

Ellul, J. (1988). *Jesus and Marx: From gospel to ideology*. Grand Rapids, MI: Eerdmans.

Engelhardt, H. T. (1996). *The foundations of bioethics* (2nd ed.). New York: Oxford University Press.

Ferguson, M. (1980). *The aquarian conspiracy: Personal and social transformation in the 1980s*. Los Angeles: J. P. Tarcher.

Fish, S. (1980). *Is there a text in this class? The authority of interpretive communities*. Cambridge, MA: Harvard University Press.

Fish, S. (1989). *Doing what comes naturally*. Oxford: Clarendon Press.

Fish, S. (1994). *There's no such thing as free speech . . . and it's a good thing too*. New York: Oxford University Press.

Flake, C. (1984). *Redemptorama: Culture, politics, and the new evangelicalism*. Garden City, NJ: Anchor.

Foucault, M. (1988). *Madness and civilization: A history of insanity in the age of reason*. New York: Vintage. (Original work published 1965)

Fox, M. (1988). *The coming of the cosmic Christ*. San Francisco: Harper & Row.

Fox, M. (1996). *Confessions: The making of a post-denominational priest*. San Francisco: HarperCollins.

Fox, R. (1985). *Reinhold Niebuhr: A biography*. New York: Pantheon.

Freeman, A. (1993). *God in us: A case for Christian humanism*. London: SCM.

Freire, P. (1971). *Pedagogy of the oppressed*. New York: Herder & Herder.

Freire, P. (1985). *The politics of education: Culture, power, and liberation*. South Hadley, MA: Bergin & Garvey.

Freud, S. (1964). *The future of an illusion*. New York: Doubleday Anchor. (Original work published 1927)

Gadamer, H. G. (1993). *Truth and method*. London: Sheed & Ward.

Gaddy, B. B., Hall, T. W., & Marzano, R. J. (1996). *School wars: Resolving our conflicts over religion & values*. San Francisco: Jossey-Bass.

Gallagher, S. (1992). *Hermeneutics and education*. New York: State University of New York Press.

Giroux, H. A. (1997). *Pedagogy and the politics of hope: Theory, culture, and schooling*. Boulder, CO: Westview.

Gomes, P. J. (1996). *The good book: Reading the Bible with mind and heart*. New York: Morrow.

Graham, R. B. (1997, July 19). Boomers putting their stamp on spirituality. *The Burlington Free Press*, p. 6C.

Greeley, A. M. (1990). *The Catholic myth: The behavior and beliefs of American Catholics*. New York: Charles Scribner's Sons.

Grenz, S. J. (1996). *A primer on postmodernism*. Grand Rapids, MI: Eerdmans.

Griffin, D. R. (1989). *God & religion in the postmodern world: Essays in postmodern theology*. New York: State University of New York Press.

Gutierrez, G. (1983). *A theology of liberation: History, politics, and salvation*. Maryknoll, NY: Orbis. (Original work published 1973)

Habermas, J. (1988). *The philosophical discourse of modernity*. New York: Political Press.

Hamilton, K. (1990). *Earthly good: The churches and the betterment of human existence*. Grand Rapids, MI: Eerdmans.

Hanh, T. N. (1976). *The miracle of mindfulness in everyday life*. New York: Bantam.

Hanh, T. N. (1991). *Peace is every step: The path of mindfulness in everyday life*. New York: Bantam.

Hart, D. A. (1993). *Faith in doubt: Non-realism and Christian belief*. London: Mowbray.

Harvey, A. (Ed.). (1997). *The essential mystics: Selections from the world's great wisdom traditions*. San Francisco: HarperCollins.

Hauerwas, S. (1977). *Truthfulness and tragedy: Further investigations into Christian ethics*. Notre Dame, IN: Univeristy of Notre Dame Press.

Hauerwas, S., & Westerhoff, J. H. (Eds.). (1992). *Schooling Christians: "Holy experiments" in American education*. Grand Rapids, MI: Eerdmans.

Haugaard, K. (1997, June 27). Suspending moral judgment: Students who refuse to condemn the unthinkable. *The Chronicle of Higher Education*, pp. B4–B5.

Haught, J. A. (1990). *Holy horrors*. Buffalo, NY: Prometheus.

Haynes, C. C. (1994). Beyond the culture wars. *Educational Leadership, 51*, 30–34.

Hebblethwaite, B. (1988). *The ocean of truth: A defence of objective theism*. New York: Cambridge University Press.

Heschel, A. J. (1962). *The prophets*. New York: Harper & Row.

Hirsch, E. D., Jr. (1996). *The schools we need: And why we don't have them*. New York: Doubleday.

Hofstadter, R. (1964). *Anti-intellectualism in American life*. New York: Vintage.

Holmes, A. F. (1975). *The idea of a Christian college*. Grand Rapids, MI: Eerdmans.

Hunt, D. (1983). *Peace, prosperity, and the coming holocaust*. Eugene, OR: Harvest.

Hunt, L. H. (1993). *Nietzsche and the origin of virtue*. New York: Routledge.

Jackson, J. (1987). *Straight from the heart*. Philadelphia: Fortress.

Jaspers, K. (1990). *Socrates, Buddha, Confucius, Jesus*. New York: Harcourt Brace & Company. (Original work published 1957)

John Paul II. (1993). *The splendor of truth*. Boston: St. Paul Books & Media.

Johnson, P. (1976). *A history of Christianity*. New York: Atheneum.

Johnson, P. G. (1997). *God and world religions: Basic beliefs and themes*. Shippensburg, PA: Beidel Printing House.

Jung, C. G. (1968). *The archetypes and the collective unconscious*. Princeton, NJ: Princeton University Press.

Kaminer, W. (1992). *I'm dysfunctional, you're dysfunctional: The recovery movement and other self-help fashions*. Reading, MA: Addison-Wesley.

Kaufman, P. S. (1989). *Why you can disagree and remain a faithful Catholic*. Bloomington, IN: Meyer-Stone.

Keating, K. (1988). *Catholicism and fundamentalism: The attack on "Romanism" by "Bible Christians."* San Francisco: Ignatius.

Keesing, R. M. (1971). *New perspectives in cultural anthropology*. New York: Holt, Rinehart and Winston.

Kintz, L. (1997). *Between Jesus and the market: The emotions that matter in right wing America*. Durham, NC: Duke University Press.

Kolakowski, L. (1986). The idolatry of politics. *The New Republic, 16*, 29–36.

Kolakowski, L. (1997). *Modernity on endless trial*. Chicago: University of Chicago Press. (Original work published 1990)

Kopp, S. P. (1976a). *Guru*. New York: Bantam.

Kopp, S. P. (1976b). *If you meet the Buddha on the road, kill him*. New York: Bantam.

Kovel, J. (1976). *A complete guide to therapy*. New York: Pantheon.

Kramer, P. D. (1994). *Listening to Prozac*. New York: Penguin.

Krishnamurti, J. (1974). *On education*. New York: Harper & Row.

Kuhn, T. S. (1970). *The structure of scientific revolutions* (2nd ed.). Chicago: University of Chicago Press.

Kurtz, P. (1986). *The transcendental temptation: A critique of religion and the paranormal*. Buffalo, NY: Prometheus.

Kurtz, P. (1997). *The courage to become: The virtues of humanism*. Westport, CT: Praeger.

Lamb, M. L. (1982). *Solidarity with victims: Toward a theology of social transformation*. New York: Crossroad.

Larson, B. (1982). *Larson's book of cults*. Wheaton, IL: Tyndale House.

Larson, E. J. (1997). *Summer for the gods: The Scopes trial and America's continuing debate over science and religion*. New York: Basic.

Lawrence, B. B. (1989). *Defenders of God: The fundamentalist revolt against the modern age*. San Francisco: Harper & Row.

Lewy, G. (1996). *Why America needs religion: Secular modernity and its discontents*. Grand Rapids, MI: Eerdmans.

Lifton, R. J. (1986). *The Nazi doctors: Medical killing and the psychology of genocide*. New York: Basic.

Locke, J. (1959). *An essay concerning human understanding*. New York: Dover. (Original work published 1690)

Loeb, P. R. (1994). *Generation at the crossroads: Apathy and action on the American campus.* New Brunswick, NJ: Rutgers University Press.

Lyotard, J. F. (1984). *The postmodern condition: A report on knowledge.* Minneapolis: University of Minnesota Press.

MacFarquhar, L. (1997, Aug. 24). Andrew Weil, Shaman, M.D. *The New York Times Magazine,* pp. 28–31.

Macquarrie, J. (1977). *Principles of Christian theology* (2nd ed.). New York: Charles Scribner's Sons.

Marcel, G. (1980). *The philosophy of existentialism.* Secaucus, NJ: Citadel Press. (Original work published 1956)

Marin, P. (1975, October). The new narcissism. *Harper's,* pp. 45–56.

Marin, P. (1996, December). An American yearning: Seeking cures for freedom's terrors. *Harper's,* pp. 35–43.

Marsden, G. M. (1997). *The outrageous idea of Christian scholarship.* New York: Oxford University Press.

Marsden, G. M., & Longfield, B. J. (Eds.). (1992). *The secularization of the academy.* New York: Oxford University Press.

Marty, M. E., & Appleby, S. (Eds.). (1991). *Fundamentalisms observed.* Chicago, IL: The University of Chicago Press.

McBrien, R. P. (Ed.). (1995). *The HarperCollins Encyclopedia of Catholicism.* San Francisco: Harper.

McFague, S. (1987). *Models of God: Theology for an ecological, nuclear age.* Philadelphia: Fortress.

McGowan, J. (1991). *Postmodernism and its critics.* New York: Cornell University Press.

McKim, D. (Ed.). (1986). *A guide to contemporary hermeneutics: Major trends in biblical interpretation.* Grand Rapids: MI: Eerdmans.

Melton, J. G. (1993). *The encyclopedia of American religions* (4th ed.). Detroit, MI: Gale Research.

Michaelsen, J. (1989). *Like lambs to the slaughter.* Eugene, OR: Harvest.

Miller, J. P. (1994). *The contemplative practitioner: Meditation in education and the professions.* Westport, CT: Bergin & Garvey.

Miller, T. (Ed.). (1995). *America's alternative religions.* New York: State University of New York Press.

Moffett, J. (1994). *The universal schoolhouse: Spiritual awakening through education.* San Francisco: Jossey-Bass.

Moran, G. (1989). *Religious education as a second language.* Birmingham, AL: Religious Education Press.

Muesse, M. W. (1997; April 25). Religious studies and "Heaven's Gate": Making the strange familiar and the familiar strange. *The Chronicle of Higher Education,* pp. B6–B7.

Nash, R. J. (1985). *Creating an existential theology of death.* Unpublished master's thesis, Georgetown University, Washington, D.C.

Nash, R. J. (1996). *"Real world" ethics: Frameworks for educators and human service professionals.* New York: Teachers College Press.

Nash, R. J. (1997). *Answering the "virtuecrats": A moral conversation on character education*. New York: Teachers College Press.

Needleman, J. (1970). *The new religions*. New York: Doubleday.

Neuhaus, R. J. (1987). *The Catholic moment: The paradox of the church in the postmodern world*. New York: Harper & Row.

Niebuhr, H. R. (1975). *Christ and culture*. New York: Harper & Row. (Original work published 1951)

Niebuhr, R. (1963). *An interpretation of Christian ethics*. New York: Seabury. (Original work published 1935)

Niebuhr, R. (1964a). *The nature and destiny of man: Volume 1, Human nature*. New York: Charles Scribner's Sons. (Original work published 1941)

Niebuhr, R. (1964b). *The nature and destiny of man: Volume 2, Human destiny*. New York: Charles Scribner's Sons. (Original work published 1943)

Nietzsche, F. (1954a). *The antichrist* (W. Kaufmann, Trans.). New York: Viking. (Original work published 1895)

Nietzsche, F. (1954b). *Thus spoke Zarathustra* (W. Kaufmann, Trans.). New York: Viking. (Original work published 1885)

Nietzsche, F. (1966a). *Beyond good and evil* (W. Kaufmann, Trans.). New York: Vintage. (Original work published 1886)

Nietzsche, F. (1966b). *On the genealogy of morals* (W. Kaufmann, Trans.). New York: Vintage. (Original work published 1887)

Nietzsche, F. (1968). *The will to power* (W. Kaufmann, Trans.). New York: Vintage. (Original work published 1911)

Noddings, N. (1993). *Educating for intelligent belief or unbelief*. New York: Teachers College Press.

Noll, M. A. (1994). *The scandal of the evangelical mind*. Grand Rapids, MI: Eerdmans.

Nord, W. A. (1995). *Religion and American education*. Chapel Hill, NC: University of North Carolina Press.

O'Brien, D. J., & Shannon, T. A. (Eds.). (1977). *Renewing the Earth: Catholic documents on peace, justice and liberation*. New York: Image.

Otto, R. (1923). *The idea of the holy: An inquiry into the non-rational factor in the idea of the divine and its relation to the rational* (J. W. Harvey, Trans.). New York: Oxford.

Pacwa, M. (1992). *Catholics and the new age: How good people are being drawn into Jungian psychology, the enneagram, and the age of aquarius*. Ann Arbor, MI: Servant.

Pagels, E. (1981). *The gnostic gospels*. New York: Vintage.

Pannoch, J., & Barr, D. (1968). *Religion goes to school*. New York: Harper & Row.

Patanjali, B. S. (1938). *Aphorisms of yoga*. London: Faber and Faber.

Peshkin, A. (1988). *God's choice: The total world of a fundamentalist Christian school*. Chicago: University of Chicago Press.

Peters, T. (1991). *The cosmic self: A penetrating look at today's new age movements*. San Francisco: Harper.

Peters, T. (1992). *God—the world's future: Systematic theology for a postmodern era*. Minneapolis, MN: Fortress.

Pinchbeck, D. (1997, August 3). Paradise not quite lost. *The New York Times Magazine*, pp. 26–29.

Policano, J. D. (1998, January 16). Letter from Iran. *Commonweal*, pp. 9–10.

Postman, N. (1996). *The end of education: Redefining the value of school*. New York: Vintage.

Powell, R. (1975). *Zen and reality*. New York: Viking.

Pregeant, R. (1988). *Mystery without magic*. Oak Park, IL: Meyer, Stone, and Company.

Purpel, D. E. (1989). *The moral & spiritual crisis in education: A curriculum for justice & compassion in education*. New York: Bergin & Garvey.

Rahner, K. (1978). *Foundations of Christian faith: An introduction to the idea of Christianity*. New York: Crossroad.

Ratzinger, J. C. (1985). *The Ratzinger report*. San Francisco: Ignatius.

Rauch, J. (1993). *Kindly inquisitors: The new attacks on free thought*. Chicago: The University of Chicago Press.

Redfield, R. (1936). A memorandum on acculturation. *American Anthropologist, 38,* 149–152.

Reed, R. (1996). *Active faith: How Christians are changing the soul of American politics*. New York: Free Press.

Reeves, T. C. (1996). Not so Christian America. *First Things, 66,* 16–21.

Reich, C. (1970). *The greening of America*. New York: Harper & Row.

Ribadeneira, D. (1997, June 15). Teaching the fourth r: Religion. *The Boston Globe Magazine*, pp. 12, 26–31.

Ricoeur, P. (1981). *Hermeneutics and the human sciences*. Cambridge, UK: Cambridge University Press.

Rieff, P. (1987). *The triumph of the therapeutic: Uses of faith after Freud*. Chicago: University of Chicago Press. (Original work published 1966)

Roof, W. C. (1993). *A generation of seekers: The spiritual journeys of the baby boom generation*. San Francisco: Harper.

Rorty, R. (1979). *Philosophy and the mirror of nature*. Princeton, NJ: Princeton University Press.

Rorty, R. (1989). *Contingency, irony, and solidarity*. New York: Cambridge University Press.

Roszak, T. (1975). *Unfinished animal*. New York: Harper and Row.

Ruether, R. R. (1972). *Liberation theology: Human hope confronts Christian history and American power*. New York: Paulist.

Russell, B. (1957). *Why I am not a Christian*. New York: Simon and Schuster.

Russell, L. (1974). *Human liberation in a feminist perspective: A theology*. Philadelphia: Westminster.

Scholes, R. (1985). *Textual power: Literary theory and the teaching of English*. New Haven, CT: Yale University Press.

Scholes, R. (1989). *Protocols of reading*. New Haven, CT: Yale University Press.

Schur, E. (1976). *The awareness trap*. New York: Quadrangle.

Schwartz, R. (1997). *The curse of Cain: The violent legacy of monotheism*. Chicago: University of Chicago Press.

Sears, J. T., & Carper, J. C. (Eds.). (1998). *Curriculum, religion, and public education: Conversations for an enlarging public square.* New York: Teachers College Press.

Segundo, J. L. (1976). *The liberation of theology.* Maryknoll, NY: Orbis.

Seva Foundation. (1996). *The project on the contemplative mind in society.* Williamsburg, VA: Author.

Sharma, A. (Ed.). (1995). *Our religions.* San Francisco: Harper.

Sheehan, T. (1986). *First coming: How the kingdom of God became Christianity.* New York: Random House.

Siegel, B. S. (1989). *Peace, love & healing. Bodymind communication & the path to self-healing: An exploration.* New York: Harper & Row.

Simonds, R. L. (1994). A plea for the children. *Educational Leadership, 51,* 12–15.

Skillen, J. W. (1990). *The scattered voice: Christians at odds in the public square.* Grand Rapids, MI: Zondervan.

Smart, N. (1983). *Worldviews: Crosscultural explorations of human beliefs.* New York: Charles Scribner's Sons.

Smith, B. H. (1997). *Belief & resistance: Dynamics of contemporary intellectual controversy.* Cambridge, MA: Harvard University Press.

Smith, H. (1991). *The world's religions* (Rev. ed.). New York: Harper Collins. (Original work, *The religions of man,* published 1958)

Smith, J. Z. (Ed.). (1995). *The HarperCollins dictionary of religion.* San Francisco: HarperCollins.

Smolin, L. (1997). *The life of the cosmos.* New York: Oxford University Press.

Soelle, D. (1990). *Thinking about God: An introduction to theology.* London: SCM.

Soelle, D. (1995). *Theology for skeptics: Reflections on God.* Minneapolis, MN: Fortress.

Sowell, T. (1995). *The vision of the anointed: Self-congratulation as a basis for social policy.* New York: Basic.

Spong, J. S. (1991). *Rescuing the Bible from fundamentalism.* San Francisco, CA: HarperCollins.

Spong, J. S. (1998). *Why Christianity must change or die: A bishop speaks to believers in exile.* San Francisco, CA: HarperCollins.

Steichen, D. (1991). *Ungodly rage: The hidden face of Catholic feminism.* San Francisco: Ignatius.

Suzuki, D. T. (1973). *An introduction to Zen Buddhism.* New York: Ballantine.

Szasz, T. S. (1974). *The myth of mental illness: Foundations of a theory of personal conduct.* New York: Perennial.

Tarnas, R. (1991). *Passion of the western mind: Understandings that have shaped our world view.* New York: Harmony.

Thiselton, A. C. (1995). *Interpreting God and the postmodern self: On meaning, manipulation and promise.* Grand Rapids, MI: Eerdmans.

Tillich, P. (1952). *The courage to be.* New Haven, CT: Yale University Press.

Tinder, G. (1989). *The political meaning of Christianity: An interpretation.* Baton Rouge: Louisiana State University Press.

Tipton, S. M. (1984). *Getting saved from the sixties: Moral meaning in conversion and cultural change.* Berkeley: University of California Press.

Tracy, D. (1994). *On naming the present: God, hermeneutics, and church.* Maryknoll, NY: Orbis.

Trungpa, C. (1973). *Cutting through spiritual materialism.* Berkeley, CA: Shambhala.

Unamuno, M. D. (1954). *Tragic sense of life* (J. E. Crawford Flitch, Trans.). New York: Dover. (Original work published 1921)

Updike, J. (1997). A disconcerting thing. *America, 177,* 8–9.

Vattimo, G. (1991). *The end of modernity: Nihilism and hermeneutics in postmodern culture.* Cambridge, UK: Polity.

Ward, G. (Ed.). (1997). *The postmodern God: A theological reader.* Boston, MA: Blackwell.

Weil, A. (1973). *The natural mind.* Boston: Houghton Mifflin.

Welch, S. D. (1990). *A feminist ethic of risk.* Minneapolis, MN: Fortress.

Whitehead, A. N. (1978). *Process and reality.* New York: Free Press. (Original work published 1929)

Willimon, W. H., & Naylor, T. H. (1995). *The abandoned generation: Rethinking higher education.* Grand Rapids, MI: Eerdmans.

Wolfe, A. (1997, Sept. 19). A welcome revival of religion in the academy. *The Chronicle of Higher Education,* pp. B4–B5.

Wuthnow, R. (1988). *The restructuring of American religion: Society and faith since World War II.* Princeton, NJ: Princeton University Press.

Wuthnow, R. (1993). *Christianity in the 21st century: Reflections on the challenges ahead.* New York: Oxford University Press.

Index

ABOUT THE AUTHOR

Robert J. Nash is a professor in the College of Education and Social Services, University of Vermont, Burlington, specializing in philosophy of education, applied ethics, moral education, higher education, and religion and education. He holds graduate degrees in English education/literary theory, theological studies, liberal studies/applied ethics, and educational philosophy. He administers the Interdisciplinary Master's Program, and he teaches courses in all of the above specializations. In addition to publishing 110 articles and book chapters, he has authored two previous books for Teachers College Press, *"Real World" Ethics: Frameworks for Educators and Human Service Professionals* (1996), and *Answering the "Virtuecrats": A Moral Conversation on Character Education* (1997).

Please remember that this is a library book,
and that it belongs only temporarily to each
person who uses it. Be considerate. Do
not write in this, or any, library book.

Date Due